A Home of the Humanities

THE COLLECTING AND PATRONAGE
OF MILDRED AND ROBERT WOODS BLISS

DUMBARTON OAKS MUSEUM PUBLICATIONS 1
SERIES EDITOR GUDRUN BÜHL

Mildred and Robert Woods Bliss at A Retrospective
Exhibition of the Work of George Bellows at the
National Gallery of Art, 1957.

Papers of Robert Woods Bliss and Mildred Barnes Bliss,
ca. 1860–1969, HUGFP 76.74, box 10, Harvard University Archives.

A Home of the Humanities

THE COLLECTING AND PATRONAGE
OF MILDRED AND ROBERT WOODS BLISS

JAMES N. CARDER

Editor

DUMBARTON OAKS RESEARCH LIBRARY
AND COLLECTION, WASHINGTON, D.C.

LIBRARY OF CONGRESS CATALOGING-IN-PUBLICATION DATA

A home of the humanities : the collecting and patronage of Mildred and Robert Woods Bliss / James N. Carder, editor.

   p. cm.—(Dumbarton Oaks museum publications ; 1)

Includes bibliographical references and index.

ISBN 978-0-88402-365-4 (hardcover : alk. paper)

1. Bliss, Robert Woods, 1875–1962—Art collections—Congresses. 2. Bliss, Mildred, 1879–1969—Art collections—Congresses. 3. Bliss, Robert Woods, 1875–1962—Art patronage—Congresses. 4. Bliss, Mildred, 1879–1969—Art patronage—Congresses. 5. Art—Collectors and collecting—Washington (D.C.)—Congresses. 6. Art patronage—Washington (D.C.)—Congresses. 7. Dumbarton Oaks—Congresses. I. Carder, James Nelson, 1948– II. Dumbarton Oaks.

N5220.B664H66 2010

709.2'2—dc22

2010007279

MANAGING EDITOR: Sara Taylor

ART DIRECTOR: Kathleen Sparkes

DESIGN AND COMPOSITION: Melissa Tandysh

Proceedings of the symposium "'A Home of the Humanities,' A Symposium on the Collecting and Patronage of Mildred and Robert Woods Bliss," organized by the Dumbarton Oaks Museum, Dumbarton Oaks Research Library and Collection, Washington, D.C., in honor of the completion of the capital building campaign and the reopening of the museum. The symposium was held on Saturday and Sunday, 12 and 13 April 2008.

COVER PHOTOGRAPH: Mildred and Robert Woods Bliss in the Music Room, 1938. Archives, AR.PH.BL.004, Dumbarton Oaks Research Library and Collection.

www.doaks.org/publications

Contents

Illustrations

Foreword

This volume honors Mildred and Robert Woods Bliss by investigating their contributions to Dumbarton Oaks as collectors and patrons. It explores their avocations, not only in Byzantine and Pre-Columbian art but also in garden design and history, architecture, and music. As such it presents a cross section of the larger area that motivated the Blisses as they sought to transform, under the aegis of Harvard University, their personal home into a "home of the Humanities."

As director of Dumbarton Oaks, I feel privileged to have the charge of bringing forward the Blisses' vision into a century that cries out more than ever for the humanities and all the humaneness and human artistry implied in the expression *artes humaniores*. Dumbarton Oaks was a gift imparted on the basis of a perspective and a prospective that can and must still work, mutatis mutandis, in the twenty-first century. From one day to the next, life grows more hectic, retrospection more elusive, and space more crowded (and perhaps also uglier). It becomes ever more difficult to espouse the value of pausing to have ideas, to contemplate the past, to appreciate the beauty of both nature and culture, and even to pursue all three of these aspirations at once. And the places in which to engage in such ambitions are ever fewer: Dumbarton Oaks, of which its museum is part and parcel, can serve as a site for all these endeavors—as a locus of scholarship, learning, teaching, and even spiritual enlightenment. Participating in

these sundry activities is wholesome for individuals and societies alike, since they are all elements of what being human, humane, and humanistic is (or should be) about. None of these observations are earth-shatteringly new, but sometimes old credos deserve to be repeated.

The essays in this book, occasioned by the reinstallation and reopening of the galleries at Dumbarton Oaks, will help us to contemplate at least two big topics, beyond that of the Blisses' vision. One is the very function of the collection. Where do we draw the line between a museum of art and a museum of anthropology? Similarly, should we regard what is displayed as an aesthetic object, a cultural artifact, or both?

Another obvious issue is collecting, which has (among other things) its own history, psychology, and sociology. The history stretches back before the Medicis and even before Maecenas, despite the fact that the earliest English usage of the word *collecting* in its current technical sense is dated only 1706 in the *Oxford English Dictionary*; but more relevant to an appreciation of the Blisses' achievements is the history of twentieth-century collecting.

As for the psychology of collecting, some modern books build the case that many collectors of our days have gravitated toward their passions for collecting as a result of troubled childhoods. The collectors find in their intimacy with the objects they gather a sense of control that brings relief from the helplessness, loneliness, fearfulness, and frustration of the more chaotic human relationships in their early lives. In the process, their impulse to amass may itself become a compulsion, which explains why collecting is sometimes regarded as an obsessive-compulsive disorder in its own right. Does such psychology come into play with either or both of the Blisses? I would think not, but Robert Woods Bliss, in describing his own passions for collecting, formulated a metaphor that hints paradoxically at disease (and at gardening): he wrote that on the day he saw his first piece of Pre-Columbian art "the collector's microbe took root . . . in very fertile soil."

And what about the sociology of collecting? In our own day, the verb *collect* and its derivatives are often encountered in contexts that pertain to financial transactions of many sorts. We talk about collecting accounts, debt collection, collection agencies, collective bargaining, and "collect on delivery" shipments. These types of revenue collecting have in common with true collecting only the crude sense of "gathering." They differ from collecting in our sense as much as a hoard of money does from a numismatic collection. The former is an accumulation of coins and bills, with amount being the overarching goal, while the latter is a zeal for selective acquisition and organization. The first is wealth, which in many societies, including our own, corresponds closely to power. The second may be a particular form of social display intended to demonstrate wealth and power. What has always been rare, and may have become ever rarer, is the meaningful and community-minded collecting that typified the Blisses, one that eschewed the dryness implied by the phrase "collecting dust" and aimed instead at vivid appreciation and remembrance—at recollection. It is to recollecting their collecting that we now turn.

JAN M. ZIOLKOWSKI
Director, Dumbarton Oaks
Research Library and Collection

*From the Bliss Collection
to the Dumbarton Oaks Museum*

On 15 April 2008—one day after the one hundredth wedding anniversary of the founders, Mildred and Robert Woods Bliss, and three years after the various buildings on 32nd Street were vacated to conduct a major architectural overhaul—the Dumbarton Oaks Museum reopened to the public.

The Dumbarton Oaks Museum, like all museums, is a place for people to enjoy and learn. It is a place of research and exhibition development, and it is a place for fellows, staff, and scholars to engage with the cultural histories of the objects in its collection. However, it has never been a "complete museum," as there have never been blockbuster exhibitions, family programs, or cafeterias. The collections have never been a prime tourist destination or an economic engine packed with visitors. This, indeed, will not change. We are happy to skip the current trend of transforming museums into collective shopping-education-recreation centers, and instead we embrace James Cuno's recommendation that "art museums should get back to basics" (*Boston Globe*, 26 October 2000). Going back to basics means having a deeper engagement with, and appreciation of, the objects that are permanently on display. The way of displaying the permanent collection bears a responsibility that has been widely neglected or played down since the museum world discovered the magnetic power of special exhibitions.

No object or artifact has a single meaning. This is especially true of objects that have been manufactured for specific functions—whether spiritual, representational, or imperial. Objects have been handed down as heirlooms, bequeathed as donations to temples, churches, and other valued community entities, and presented as gifts to political allies, neighboring countries, and societies. Objects represent relationships; the challenge for the museum is to understand these relationships and to use their permanent installations to show how no object ever reveals itself completely in any single context or occasion. The concept of the new installations of the permanent collections at Dumbarton Oaks was composed and designed to stimulate new ways to look at our objects, to reflect and wonder about how these artifacts came into their being and how they have been used through the centuries of their lifespan.

The visitor to the Dumbarton Oaks Museum encounters three distinct collections—besides the specialized Byzantine and Pre-Columbian collections, we have a collection of European Western medieval and Renaissance art that has come to be called the House Collection. The visitor experiences each of these collections on a different "stage":

- The House Collection is displayed in the Renaissance-inspired Music Room, whose grandeur and presentation of artworks embody the founders' desire to create an eclectic private "art ambience." It forms the core of the residential art display at Dumbarton Oaks, and is closest to the concept of a "house museum," in that it reflects the collectors' personal taste and desire to surround themselves with museum-quality art.

- The Pre-Columbian Collection is presented in the jewel-box setting of the postmodernist Philip Johnson pavilion. Objects hover in mid-air against both the glass walls of the early-sixties structure and the greenery of the surrounding gardens. This setting isolates and mystifies the artifacts as works of art.

- The Byzantine Collection is displayed in a 1940s treasure hall; the hall—a palatial interior with high ceilings, an ocular window in the manner of an ancient building, and semicircular clerestory windows—is filled with precious gems presented as objets d'art.

These three distinct architectural frames and, consequently, three different display modes reflect the history of the museum, the personal story of the growing collection, and the entire institution of Dumbarton Oaks. It is the story of a well-to-do American couple, who passionately followed two unconventional collecting interests in the beginning of the twentieth century. It is a story of collecting and connoisseurship—of a "lust of the eye," which (coupled with a desire for possession) led to the formation of an astounding collection. This history has never been as thoroughly and exhaustively analyzed as by the authors of the essays in this book.

This volume sheds light on the lives of Mildred and Robert Woods Bliss and their activities in the realms of diplomacy, art collecting, and patronage, beginning with their relationship with influential French intellectuals in Paris in the early 1910s until their formation of a "home of the Humanities" in the 1930s. Through autobiographical sources and the vast correspondence the Blisses exchanged with friends, art dealers, and scholars in America and Europe, we are able to understand the dynamics of their friendship with Royall Tyler and the role he played as a collector, connoisseur, and advisor. We learn plenty of details about their "art hunting" activities. But these sources remain silent on the display concept and the actual installation of the collections at Dumbarton Oaks. And they provide only a few hints about the Blisses' conception of their collection—for example, in a rare statement about the collection, Robert Woods Bliss remarked to the Harvard Club in 1943: "And gradually from our enjoyment of mediaeval art and a strong sense of the value of

continuity, the conception of a small and modest but specialized 'cabinet des médailles' took form; a research collection to illustrate the books—a library to interpret the objects."

So what type of museum is the Dumbarton Oaks Museum? A house museum? A private collector's museum? An art or anthropology museum? A history museum? A study collection? None of these labels give a comprehensive definition; it is not a lame compromise to say that all of the labels together describe the nature and function of the Dumbarton Oaks Museum. It is a perfect hybrid of an art and history museum by virtue of its specialized collections and by the nature of its collected objects.

The Blisses' main interest and mission was a commitment to promoting beauty and qualitative distinction by emphasizing the original aesthetic of an object and the viewer's ability to experience it under optimal conditions. They fell in love with objects of two very distinct worlds when only a few specialists and private collectors were systematically building collections of Byzantine and Pre-Columbian art. Based on these general thoughts, our concept work for the gallery redesign project began with research on the history of display at Dumbarton Oaks. Historic photographs allowed us to draw certain conclusions about the early and original installation of artworks. Fundamental to our plan of rethinking and updating the installations was the fact that, unlike many private collectors, the Blisses did not specify or dictate a single method of displaying artworks in their galleries and commissioned architectural settings. And yet, to be as true and faithful as possible to the founders' vision, passion, and dreams, we felt an obligation to continue the established culture of display. What, then, was the leitmotiv of each collection's installation, and what changed with the reinstallation of 2008?

THE MUSIC ROOM AND THE DISPLAY OF THE HOUSE COLLECTION

The Music Room—Mildred and Robert Woods Bliss's first major addition to Dumbarton Oaks—was built between 1926 and 1928. The architects had been instructed to ensure the character of a music room in a private home, instead of aiming for a look and feel of a concert hall. From the beginning, the Blisses installed a significant portion of their art here. After deciding in the mid-thirties to give their home, gardens, and art collections to Harvard University, they increased the quantity of works of art displayed in the Music Room. With the design and construction of the Byzantine wing in 1940 and the foundation of the research institute, the Music Room became an integral part of the collection's display space. More than any other area in the institution, it embodies the Blisses' legacy and conception of Dumbarton Oaks. The Music Room is a space where landscape, architecture, decor, art, music, scholarly discourse, and friendly conversation commingle in a sophisticated, art-dominated environment.

The Music Room was originally conceived as a grand, residential room, rather than as a museum gallery (see figs. 1.14 and 4.9). Before 1969—the year of Mildred Bliss's death—it existed more or less as its founders had intended. But in the 1970s, its Oriental rugs, upholstered sofas, and easy chairs were removed, and by 1983, its spaces were restricted by velvet ropes and stanchions. The public was allowed only in the center of the room, and could only access it from the west side under the Palladian arch. Moreover, the plant materials were gradually removed from the room in the early 1990s.

The reinstallation of the Music Room was guided by the historical placement of its artworks and by the notion that it was emblematic of the Blisses' vision of Dumbarton Oaks as a "home of the Humanities"—as a room through which the visitor moved freely in the manner of an invited guest to a grand, residential room. For this reason, the visitor does not find written labels next to the artworks. Instead, the objects are described in short explanations on laminated text panels, which can be carried while walking from object to object. No stanchions restrict access; the visitor is encouraged to experience the entire room, and to access it either from the Palladian arch on the west side or from the staircase on the east side—its original and proper entrance. Copies of historic photographs—featuring the Blisses, Igor Stravinsky, and Ignacy Paderewski, among others—are displayed on furniture surfaces, and, on occasion, Byzantine and Pre-Columbian objects are installed to recapture the original nature of the Music Room.

THE DISPLAY OF THE PRE-COLUMBIAN COLLECTION

The Pre-Columbian Collection was first exhibited at the National Gallery of Art until the 1960s (see figs. 3.16 and 3.17), by which time the architect Philip Johnson had designed and built a new space to bring the collection "home." This pavilion was completed in 1963. It is the only place in the museum where the collector's name appears: upon leaving the Pre-Columbian wing, the visitor reads, inscribed in metal letters, "The Robert Woods Bliss Collection of Pre-Columbian Art." The building—a glass structure composed of eight interconnected cylindrical galleries around an open court with a fountain—has won numerous prizes for its innovative architecture (see figs. 3.1 and 3.2). Philip Johnson explained the idea behind his design: "I'd wanted the garden to march right up to the museum displays and become part of them. You see the bushes brush around the glass wall and architecture. Even the splashing of the fountain is all part of it. Further, a series of roofs under which to display the small collection against green walls, the garden." Consequently, the installation emphasized the airy transparency of the building by using Plexiglas cases, mounts, labels, and text panels. This choice seems to have not been specified in Johnson's original design, but was initiated by staff members, who were faced with the extraordinary challenge of installing a collection of small-scale artifacts in a gallery space without solid walls.

The Pre-Columbian Collection is relatively small, but of exceptional quality. It is historically significant that it was one of the first Pre-Columbian collections to be displayed as fine art, on a par with Greek, Roman, and Byzantine antiquities and European old master artworks. From its inception, the collection showcased the artistic accomplishments of the Pre-Columbian peoples and emphasized the "great rarity and aesthetic appeal" of their artifacts. It was organized by culture in a roughly geographical and chronological sequence, and offered minimal information on the cultural, historical, and geographical context of the objects on display.

Following the spirit and concept of the original 1960s display, the redesigned installation of the Pre-Columbian Collection is still divided by broad geographical and cultural areas. But a greater emphasis is placed on providing contextual information about the objects on view—both individually on descriptive labels and collectively on hanging panels that introduce the visitor to the various themes and cultures displayed in each gallery. Maps printed on these translucent, hanging panels orient and guide the visitor through the galleries. General information about the Pre-Columbian world is provided in the hallway leading to the pavilion. The redesigned Plexiglas cases are still reminiscent of the design language of the 1960s, but their streamlined and standardized shape aims to minimize the "white noise" of the installation "equipment." Sophisticated mounts allow the objects to freely float and hover in mid-air.

THE DISPLAY OF THE BYZANTINE COLLECTION

When the Byzantine Collection was opened to the public in 1940, only a few visitors were expected and the field of museum studies had not been born. Although there was already some debate about museum matters, the thoughts and concept that guided its original installation have not been documented.

The gallery, a rectangular hall measuring 1,150 square feet, was the first collection-specific extension to the Main House to display the Byzantine Collection. It was accessed by a loggia (now the Textile Gallery), which connected it to the entrance hall. Photographs of the first installation show the objects in wooden cases that employed antique rococo boiserie panels (see fig. 1.17). Antique marble and bronze sculptures were placed on long wooden tables or shelves. The works were arranged in a mixed-media approach, which seems to have been based on a balance of shape and size. The presentation emphasized that the works formed a private collection of objets d'art, which were to be admired as precious, aesthetically pleasing, and, in some cases, historically significant.

The collection reflected Byzantine and medieval culture, but chronology, iconography, and function were not primary considerations in the installation. Both the setting of the collection within a purpose-built wing of Dumbarton Oaks and the presentation of the objects were meant to be understood as reflections of the collecting passions, tastes, and sensibilities of the Blisses.

The reinstallation of the Byzantine Collection in the mid-1960s—after the opening of the Pre-Columbian pavilion—moved the works from their rococo cases and wooden tables to cases with travertine bases and Plexiglas vitrines, which allowed them to be seen from multiple viewpoints. Additional travertine cases with bronze and glass doors were hung along the south wall. These new cases allowed more

objects to be put on view. Furthermore, the use of travertine provided a precious environment, which reflected the objet d'art sensibility and appreciably enhanced the value of the works. Although items were generally arranged in their cases to emphasize their uniqueness, there were some attempts to place them in chronological order. Labeling was kept to a minimum in order to further present the works as objets d'art. The works were meant to speak for themselves—although a comprehensive handbook, whose catalogue numbers were coordinated with object numbers, was published and made available to visitors in 1967. Cyril Mango's reflections in *Apollo* in 1984 represent a renewed interest in questions about how to display the Byzantine Collection: "Even though the Dumbarton Oaks Collection is not a representative cross-section of Early Christian and Byzantine art, it is sufficiently extensive to raise certain questions in the mind of the informed visitor. The nature of these questions will naturally depend on the visitor's viewpoint and knowledge. He may be motivated by purely aesthetic considerations as Mrs. Bliss probably was herself. No justification is needed for aesthetic enjoyment; . . . But if the visitor wishes to understand as well as to enjoy, he will have a harder task unless he is content to fall back on accepted verdicts. . . . But how is one to classify Byzantine art? By date? By place? By school?"

In 1987–89, the open courtyard to the south of the Byzantine gallery was covered, enclosed, and converted into an additional exhibition space. The French doors leading from the Byzantine gallery into the open courtyard were closed. Four large display cases, in addition to small hanging vitrines, were organized as themed units according to geographical attribution or medium. The courtyard was considered the introduction to the Byzantine gallery, as it displayed artworks that were chronologically earlier than the late Roman and Byzantine periods. It also featured objects from the edges of the Byzantine Empire, such as those from Coptic Egypt.

At the same time, the museum took the opportunity to provide visitors with more information on the collection in this new courtyard gallery, as was expected by 1989. The cases were designed with interior labels, which provided further historical and art historical information about the objects. The Byzantine gallery was rearranged, but not redesigned nor relabeled, and its presentation, though more consistent, remained laconic. The emphasis on the objects' materials from case to case was a major conceptual line, however one not followed coherently.

The successive presentations of the Byzantine Collection have lacked a pathway through the space, which might have given the visitor a sense of the history of the collection and the periods covered by it. It was not such a noticeable drawback when the number of objects on display was relatively small, but as it grew, the intimacy of the "private collection" gradually became diluted.

The 2008 installation emphasizes a somewhat different approach: it encourages the visitor to consider what the objects can tell us about Byzantine culture and society, its political and religious values, and its material resources. To achieve a better connection and relationship between the Byzantine courtyard gallery and the main gallery, the French doors in the southern and northern walls of the courtyard were reopened and four double-sided cases were installed; this change recreated the original architectural rhythm, increased the display space, and allowed the objects to be viewed from at least two sides by enshrining them behind almost invisible sheets of glass to minimize the appearance of being closed away. The reinstatement of the original architectural openings in the courtyard gallery enhances the visual relationship with the corridor that leads from the entrance hall to the Byzantine gallery, providing this corridor space with better light conditions.

The new installation not only increased the display space, but allowed for a clearer spatial structure and grouping of objects by topics as well as their original function and meaning. The freestanding, double-sided display cases in the Byzantine gallery are placed perpendicular to the north and south walls—similar to the original 1940 case placement. The short walls in the west and east are based on a different type of display disposition, bringing together objects and media under two topics. The west wall showcases silver liturgical vessels of the sixth century in an arrangement that recalls the interior of a Byzantine church, while on the east wall, a wide range of funerary artworks—including a Roman wall painting, a Coptic limestone sculpture, a lead sarcophagus, and a mummy portrait—are grouped around the famous Barberini Collection sarcophagus. These objects from different places, times, and cultural backgrounds convey the diversity of funeral rites.

These examples highlight aspects of the 2008 reinstallation concept, which was based on the understanding that objects in any museum represent only one layer (or one cross section) of a much larger past, time, culture, or era. The objects have been collected by the choice and taste of collectors and museum curators; they are disconnected from their original settings and functions. Museum displays are based on these fundamental facts, and by juxtaposing, regrouping, and creating new relationships the objects become recharged and meaningful.

It is a tribute to the Blisses' vision that we carefully "touched-up" and refreshed the galleries at Dumbarton Oaks. Our intention was not to break or alter the artistic tradition, but to continue the founders' mission of connecting the past and present and to perpetuate the spirit of their highly specialized private collection, which began in the first half of the twentieth century and continued into the twenty-first century "to clarify an everchanging present and to inform the future with its wisdom."

The reopening of the Dumbarton Oaks Museum was an exciting moment, and I would like to express my deepest thanks to the museum staff for the tremendous job they have accomplished. The new installation is the result of a team effort with everyone bringing to the project exceptional thoughts and good humor. Those who were part of the redesign project felt like the luckiest people in the world: we were privileged to work with the best possible objects and were surrounded by a great supportive atmosphere. I would like to thank the former director, Ned Keenan, who greatly supported the development of the museum and the redesign of the Byzantine galleries. My sincerest gratitude goes to the current director, Jan Ziolkowski, for making it possible to add to the project at a late stage the redesign of the Pre-Columbian display cases. His support during the decisive final phase of the reinstallation made us succeed in the ambitious goal to present a "new" museum.

GUDRUN BÜHL
Curator and Museum Director,
Dumbarton Oaks
Research Library and Collection

Abbreviations

Archives	Archives, Dumbarton Oaks Research Library and Collection, Washington, D.C.
Byzantine Collection	Dumbarton Oaks Museum, Byzantine Collection, Dumbarton Oaks Research Library and Collection, Washington, D.C.
House Collection	Dumbarton Oaks Museum, House Collection, Dumbarton Oaks Research Library and Collection, Washington, D.C.
HUA	Harvard University Archives, Cambridge, Mass.
NYHS	New-York Historical Society, New York, N.Y.
Pre-Columbian Collection	Dumbarton Oaks Museum, Pre-Columbian Collection, Dumbarton Oaks Research Library and Collection, Washington, D.C.
Rare Book Collection	Dumbarton Oaks Library, Rare Book Collection, Dumbarton Oaks Research Library and Collection, Washington, D.C.

JAMES N. CARDER

1

Mildred and Robert Woods Bliss
A Brief Biography

Although Mildred and Robert Woods Bliss (fig. 1.1) were resolutely private people, they left behind a considerable amount of correspondence and other documents that reveal much about their lives.[1] Nevertheless, certain key elements of their biographical record are difficult to uncover. For example, the Blisses often engaged in philanthropy, but their desire for anonymity has clouded their support of artists, musicians, and educational and arts organizations. Mildred Bliss—to cite one example—funded a scholarship for a student from the New York School of Applied Design for Women between 1904 and 1914.[2] However, as her name was never used in connection with this annual award, she remained an unknown benefactor to its recipients. Similarly, the Blisses often went to great lengths to avoid publicity and its attendant notoriety. In one instance, Mildred Bliss unsuccessfully attempted to remove her name from a 1928 publication of Marcel Proust's correspondence, despite the fact that the content was in no way damaging. She suggested the abbreviation, "Mme B., une américaine," but as the volume was already in press, she appears as "Mme Bliss."[3]

There is, however, one important exception to the Blisses' pervasive record of privacy and anonymity. And this exception is tied to what undeniably was the Blisses' greatest love—Dumbarton Oaks (fig. 1.2).[4] In a very public manner, the Blisses left their indelible mark on this estate, and ultimately established what Mildred Bliss would call their "home of the Humanities."[5] In creating Dumbarton Oaks, the Blisses redesigned its

buildings and their interiors, added over fifty acres of planned gardens as well as significant architectural additions and outbuildings, hosted important musical evenings and intellectual discussions in their Music Room, and acquired a world-class art collection and library. All of this garnered international acclaim when they gave Dumbarton Oaks to Harvard University in 1940. For it was their final resolve to recreate Dumbarton Oaks as a research center and museum in their own lifetimes, in order to be able to witness the beginnings of what would be their enduring public legacy.

Robert Woods Bliss (fig. 1.3) was born on 5 August 1875, in Saint Louis, Missouri, where his father, William Henry Bliss (1844–1932), was a U.S. district attorney. He prepared for college at J.P. Hopkinson's Private School in Boston in 1894–95, and enrolled at Harvard College in the class of 1900. An average student, he received his only "A" in military science, and by the year of his graduation had not yet traveled abroad.[6] Immediately after his graduation, Robert Bliss clerked in the office of the U.S. secretary of Puerto Rico, and between 1901 and 1903 served as private secretary to the governor of Puerto Rico, William H. Hunt. In 1903, he joined the State Department as a Foreign Service officer and received his first post as U.S. consul general in Venice. Between 1904 and 1907, he served as second secretary of the U.S. Embassy in Saint Petersburg, where he was presented to Czar Nicholas II and Czarina Alexandra Romanoff in 1905 (fig. 1.4). His diaries from those years—in

addition to detailing current events, such as the Russo-Japanese War—chronicle his impressions of the Saint Petersburg cultural world and describe the opera productions and other musical events that he attended.[7] In 1907, he was appointed secretary of the U.S. Legation in Brussels, where he was chosen as the U.S. delegate to an international conference on the revision of arms and ammunition regulations in 1908.[8]

It was also in 1908 that Robert Bliss returned to New York City to marry Mildred Barnes, his stepsister (fig. 1.5). He had first met her sometime before 1894, when his widowed father wed Mildred Barnes's mother, Anna Dorinda Blaksley Barnes (1851–1935), formerly of Saint Louis, Missouri.[9] Immediately after their marriage, Mildred and Robert Bliss went to Brussels, where he returned to his post as secretary of the Legation. In Brussels, Mildred Bliss spent much of her time, as she would throughout her life, visiting museums and libraries. Early in 1909, for example, she visited the Bibliothèque Royale to examine its collection of illuminated manuscripts. Afterward she mused in her diary whether it was "the emotional religion of the latins" or "the intellectual religion of the Flemish" that best suited

FIG. 1.4.

Czar Nicholas II and
Czarina Alexandra
Romanoff, an unidentified
U.S. Embassy employee,
and Robert Woods Bliss,
Saint Petersburg, 1905.

Archives, AR.PH.BL.055,
Dumbarton Oaks Research
Library and Collection.

pictorial expression. She noted her admiration for the late medieval images that she had viewed and lamented the loss of their charm with the advent of the more "realistic" Renaissance style. She concluded her entry by writing: "There is in the Bibliothèque, a livre d'Heures more pure in its conceptions and colours than anything I know. Fra Angelico alone excepted."[10]

In 1909, Robert Bliss was appointed secretary of the U.S. Legation in Buenos Aires (fig. 1.6). The Blisses undertook an overland crossing of the Isthmus of Panama and traveled down the west coast of South America, visiting Lima and Santiago and crossing the Andes on muleback.[11] Although such an arduous journey was virtually unheard of at the turn of the century

for people of the Blisses' social class, it was almost second nature to Mildred Bliss, who was both an accomplished equestrian and the owner of a working farm, which she had overseen before her marriage.

Mildred Barnes Bliss (fig. 1.7) was born in New York City in 1879. She was the daughter of Demas Barnes (1827–88), who had served as a U.S. Congressman from the Brooklyn District in 1867–69. Demas Barnes had invested in a number of proprietary medicine companies and patent medicines, including Fletcher's Castoria, whose phenomenal success made him a wealthy man.[12] When he died in 1888, his real estate holdings and other investments passed to his wife, but his interest in the Centaur Company,

FIG. 1.5.

Mildred Barnes Bliss
in her wedding dress,
Paris, 1908.

Papers of Robert Woods
Bliss and Mildred Barnes Bliss,
ca. 1860–1969, HUGFP 76.74p,
box 18, Harvard University
Archives.

FIG. 1.6.

Mildred and Robert
Woods Bliss and their
dog, Sue, Buenos Aires,
ca. 1910–12.

Papers of Robert Woods Bliss
and Mildred Barnes Bliss,
ca. 1860–1969, HUGFP 76.74,
box 6, Harvard University
Archives.

the manufacturer of Fletcher's Castoria, went to Cora Barnes (1858–1911), the only child of his first marriage. By later agreement, the dividends of the company's stock were divided between Cora and her stepmother, Anna Barnes Bliss, until the then nine-year-old Mildred came of age, at which point the dividends were split among the three. On 29 September 1911, Cora committed suicide.[13] Her will named Mildred Bliss as her primary beneficiary, and bequeathed to her stocks and bonds valued at $4,608,371 and jewelry valued at $8,400.[14] This inheritance was managed by William Bliss until his death in 1932; the relatively conservative nature of his investments insured that her wealth survived the stock market crash of 1929 virtually intact.

From an early age, Mildred Barnes took violin, piano, and French lessons, becoming highly proficient in all three. She attended Miss Porter's School in Farmington, Connecticut, where she was "finished" according to the traditions of her time and class. She traveled frequently in Europe, particularly in England and France, and obtained firsthand a thorough knowledge of both historic and contemporary art and music. She also began collecting. Walter Muir Whitehill has written that, as a teenager, she acquired an *Opus Anglicanum* textile fragment "at a time when such medieval embroideries were little studied or known."[15] She assembled an exceptional collection of etchings and engravings, as she was particularly astute in obtaining quality impressions and states.[16] She also collected rare books from an early age,[17] and acquired a Stradivarius viola.[18]

After reaching the age of eighteen, Mildred Barnes purchased a working farm in Sharon, Connecticut, in 1898 (fig. 1.8). She improved the house on the property, and built a double tenant house and a stable for her horses in 1905. When she advertised a long-term lease for the tenant

house at the time of her marriage to Robert Bliss, she described the property as having approximately sixty-five acres of tillable land, acres of woodland for pasturing purposes, vegetable gardens, orchards, flower gardens, lawns, and a tennis court. In addition to the main house, there was a greenhouse, cold frames, guesthouse, garage, doghouse and kennels, stable, tenant house, cow barn and silo, ice house, barn, machine and tool barn, hen house, and pig sty.[19] After marrying Robert Bliss, she sold the property in 1909.[20]

In 1912, Robert Bliss was appointed secretary (and later counselor) of the U.S. Embassy in Paris. The Blisses would remain in Paris through 1919. The time they spent there would have a profound influence on their lives, both then and in the future. They rented an apartment at 4, rue Henri Moissan (Quai d'Orsay), which would be maintained for twenty-one years and which would serve as a place of periodic respite for Mildred Bliss. With the help of Geoffrey Dodge, a young American designer in Paris who had worked at the U.S. Legation in Buenos Aires during Robert Bliss's tenure, the Blisses redesigned the apartment and filled it with period paneling, textile wall coverings, antiques, and artworks (fig. 1.9). They also became reacquainted with Mildred Bliss's childhood friend, Royall Tyler, and his wife, Elisina (see fig. 2.1). The Tylers and the Blisses would socialize

with the writer Edith Wharton[21] and the artist Walter Gay and his wife, Matilda, who lived in the remarkable eighteenth-century Château du Bréau, near the Fontainebleau Forest.[22] They, in turn, introduced the Blisses to their friends, such as the art connoisseur Bernard Berenson, the writer Henry James, and the lawyer and diplomat Walter Berry. This group of expatriates remained close friends throughout their lives.

Royall Tyler[23] also introduced the Blisses to important Parisian art dealers, and, most importantly, shared with them his enthusiasm for art—in particular, Byzantine art—and nurtured their growing interest in collecting art that lay somewhat outside the mainstream of what others collected at the time.[24] Robert Bliss famously recounted this influence when he wrote:

FIG. 1.7.
Mildred Barnes Bliss, ca. 1927.
Papers of Robert Woods Bliss and Mildred Barnes Bliss, ca. 1860–1969, HUGFP 76.74p, box 18, Harvard University Archives.

FIG. 1.8.
Mildred Barnes at her home in Sharon, Conn., ca. 1905–7.
Papers of Robert Woods Bliss and Mildred Barnes Bliss, ca. 1860–1969, HUGFP 76.74, box 1, Harvard University Archives.

FIG. 1.9.
Salon, Bliss apartment,
Paris, ca. 1914.

Papers of Robert Woods Bliss
and Mildred Barnes Bliss,
ca. 1860–1969, HUGFP 76.74,
box 4, Harvard University
Archives.

"Soon after reaching Paris in the spring of 1912, my friend Royall Tyler took me to a small shop in the Boulevard Raspail to see a group of pre-Columbian objects from Peru . . . I had never seen anything like these objects . . . [And] that day the collector's microbe took root in . . . very fertile soil. Thus in 1912, were sown the seeds of an incurable malady!"[25]

Royall Tyler had both great knowledge and exceptional taste, and his influence on the Blisses' collecting was profound. Almost immediately, he began to write them frequently about artworks that he had uncovered, describing their attractions and urging the Blisses to acquire them. For example, in 1912—the year Robert Bliss acknowledged as the beginning of his incurable malady—Tyler wrote them compellingly about a Gothic

Madonna and Child from the Île-de-France, exclaiming: "I have seen the little statue, and you and Mildred must not on any account omit to look at it. There is nothing so fine in the Louvre; and the Keeper of Sculpture at South Kensington, whom I took to see it, says it is finer even than Mr. Morgan's famous and rather similar one."[26] Captivated by such descriptions, the Blisses acquired this as well as other Tyler discoveries, steadily building their collection (see fig. 2.7).

The Blisses frequently hosted musical evenings at their Parisian apartment, as on 6 August 1913, when they dined with the pianist Ignacy Paderewski and his wife. Mildred Bliss noted in her dinner book: "Paddy played."[27] It was at this time that Mildred Bliss began her lifelong patronage of composers and musicians. For example, after attending a concert given by the composer and pianist Enrique Granados, she became his influential friend and patroness. She introduced his "Tonadillas," or songs based on the paintings of Francisco Goya, in her apartment in 1914. The composer was at the piano at this private premiere.[28] The Blisses later worked through diplomatic channels to help Granados return safely to Barcelona in 1916, and urged their mutual friend, the composer Ernest Schelling, to convince the Metropolitan Opera to give Granados's opera *Goyescas* its world premiere after it failed to occur in Paris due to the war.[29]

Indeed, the First World War was undoubtedly the event of the Blisses' years in Paris that had the most profound influence on them. Witnessing the war firsthand, they would be affected by the destruction and hardship that it brought for the rest of their lives. From the war's onset, Mildred Bliss offered financial and personal assistance where she could. For example, in 1914, she and Robert Bliss anonymously funded the purchase of an entire fleet of twenty-six ambulances for the American Field Service, an organization she helped to found. (Plaques on each ambulance identified the anonymous donors as "Aux Soldats de France, Deux Américains Reconnaissants" or "Offert aux défenseurs de la France par Deux Reconnaissants.")[30] She headed the "Service de Distribution Américaine," which provided supplies to hospitals throughout France.[31] By the end of 1916, the service had delivered nearly five million medical supplies to over eleven thousand French towns.[32] She also served as the executive board chairman of the American Red Cross's "Woman's War Relief Corps in France" and the vice president of the "Comité Franco-Américain pour la Protection des Enfants de la Frontier," begun in August 1914, which established over twenty-five homes and a tuberculosis sanatorium to care for some fifteen hundred displaced or orphaned French, Belgian, and Alsatian children.[33] The French government would later acknowledge her work by inducting her into the Legion of Honor.

However, despite both the war and their work responsibilities, the Blisses continued to collect. Even at the height of the Hindenburg offensive, they paid a record price to acquire *The Song Rehearsal* (fig. 1.10) at the famous 1918 sale of Edgar Degas's estate.[34] Their close friend Walter Gay bid on their behalf to protect their anonymity. Indeed, the Parisian press erroneously reported that the Metropolitan Museum of Art had acquired the painting, but later stated that an American heiress had sold her pearls to get the work, exactly the kind of notoriety that the Blisses assiduously attempted to avoid.[35]

In 1919, the Blisses returned to the United States, to Washington, D.C., where early the next year Robert Bliss was assigned to the State Department as chief of the Division of Western European Affairs and later as third assistant secretary of state. The Blisses began house hunting; they found and purchased "The Oaks" (fig. 1.11), as Dumbarton Oaks was then known, in October 1920, thereby fulfilling what Robert Bliss later called "a dream during twenty years of professional nomad-ism of having a country house in the city."[36] The Blisses immediately set about transforming the Victorian house into a Georgian revival mansion and creating garden rooms and vistas from the surrounding undulating farmland. With Mildred Bliss's active input, the gardens were designed by Edith Wharton's niece, the landscape architect Beatrix Farrand.[37] While work was underway on the house, the Blisses resided in the McCormack Apartments at 1785 Massachusetts Avenue, where they were neighbors and friends of the collector Andrew Mellon.[38] They also rented a duplex apartment on Park Avenue in New York City. And yet, despite this activity and their absence from the European art market, they continued to collect artworks, including Rembrandt's *St. Bartholomew* (ca. 1633; now in the Worcester Museum of Art) in 1920.

In 1922, the Blisses engaged the historian J. C. Fitzpatrick, of the Library of Congress, to research the history of "The Oaks."[39] From him, they learned that the original eighteenth-century land grant to the property had been patented as

the Rock of Dumbarton. They considered renaming the property Dumbarton House, but by 1925, they referred to it simply as "Dumbarton," and by 1933, they decided on the name "Dumbarton Oaks." This name was first used on their letterhead and bookplates in that year. The Blisses periodically continued their research, and in 1959, they engaged two historians from the National Archives to provide a draft text on the history of the property.[40] In 1964, this draft was given to Walter Muir Whitehill, who used it as the basis for his book, *Dumbarton Oaks: The History of a Georgetown House and Garden, 1800–1966*.

Although it was nearing completion, the renovation of Dumbarton Oaks was still unfinished in 1923, when Robert Bliss was appointed minister to Sweden or "Envoy Extraordinary and Minister Plenipotentiary," as his full title read.

When the Blisses arrived in Stockholm in June, the city newspapers quickly took note of the elegant couple (fig. 1.12). One article declared: "Mr. Bliss gives one an extraordinarily sympathetic impression, and his wife will be something for the Stockholmites of both sexes to admire and look at." Another stated: "As soon as Mrs. Bliss stepped upon the Stockholm platform she caused some attention owing to her distinguished elegance and noble type.... Her little finely chiseled face and the red blond hair might well come from the Island of Albion, from Gainsborough's and Reynolds's paintings.... Mrs. Bliss ... is curious and interested about everything Swedish, and wants to learn about Swedish customs and usages and she has absolutely decided to learn the difficult Swedish language, and will soon begin lessons."[41]

Continuing to find themselves somewhat removed from the European art market, the Blisses increasingly relied on Royall Tyler in Paris to inform them of important pieces that were available. In 1924, he alerted them to the extraordinary Riha paten (fig. 1.13),[42] "a most snorting, magnificent object," as he described it, which was from the same hoard as a chalice that he had acquired in 1913 (see fig. 2.12).[43] He wrote to them, saying: "to me [it] is perhaps the most moving thing—possibly excepting my chalice—I've ever seen for sale.... If you do get it, live with it for a good long time. It will teach you a great deal about the age when Santa Sophia and the great churches of Ravenna were built, when the most perfect Byzantine enamels were made and the throne of Maximian was carved."[44] The Blisses acquired the paten; in 1955, Elisina Tyler and her son, William Royall Tyler, who would later serve as the second director of Dumbarton Oaks, gave the chalice to the Byzantine Collection in memory of Royall Tyler.

Being absent from Dumbarton Oaks except for brief and infrequent visits, the Blisses had to rely heavily on long-distance advice from Beatrix Farrand and their architect, Lawrence Grant White of the architectural firm of McKim, Mead, and White. Nevertheless, they remained intimately involved in the planning of additions to the gardens and house, and especially with the design for their new Music Room (fig. 1.14). Descriptions, blueprints, architectural "mock-ups," and seemingly endless discussions of revisions were sent back and forth between Washington, D.C., and Stockholm (and later Buenos Aires). Robert Bliss alluded to this when he wrote to White: "We know that it is a darned nuisance to have to deal with clients at a distance, especially those who go into details as we do, and we are therefore very glad that you like our suggestions as we do yours. It is bearing fruit."[45] Indeed, the proof of the necessity of this long-distance collaboration was the ultimate success of the gardens and the house.

The Blisses joined the Friends of the Fogg Art Museum in 1926, and Robert Bliss became reacquainted with his former Harvard classmate Paul Sachs, who served as its associate director from 1924 to 1944. The Blisses offered regular support to the Fogg, enabling, for example, the museum to acquire a collection of old master drawings. They also contributed to Fogg interests, such as Aurial Stein's 1929 expedition to acquire Buddhist sculptures in Asia.[46] They later offered similar support to the Peabody Museum of Archaeology and Ethnology, where Robert Bliss became reacquainted with two other classmates, Donald Scott (director, 1932–48) and Alfred Tozzer (chairman of the Division of Anthropology at Harvard University, 1919–48). Both institutions regularly assisted the Blisses in the vetting and conservation of artworks that they acquired.[47]

In 1927, Robert Bliss was appointed U.S. ambassador to Argentina, a position he held until his retirement from the Foreign Service in 1933. His diplomatic agenda included two somewhat interrelated, high-priority items: the heightening of the United States's visibility in Argentina, and the acquisition of a suitable building for the embassy residence. He attained these goals by convincing President-elect Herbert Hoover to

FIG. 1.12.

Mildred and Robert Woods Bliss, Stockholm, ca. 1923–27.

Papers of Robert Woods Bliss and Mildred Barnes Bliss, ca. 1860–1969, HUGFP 76.74, box 6, Harvard University Archives.

visit and tour the country in 1928—the first U.S. president to do so—and by acquiring a Beaux-Arts mansion, the Bosch Palace, as the new ambassadorial residence in 1929 (fig. 1.15).[48] The Blisses used their own funds to purchase French antique furnishings for the residence, and donated them to the State Department.[49] And, again, despite their isolation in South America, the Blisses continued to oversee the projects underway at Dumbarton Oaks and to acquire art. Through Lawrence White, they entered into negotiations with the Paris designer Armand Albert Rateau to create a Renaissance-style beamed ceiling and parquet floor for their Music Room.[50] And in 1927, they purchased the *Bacino di San Marco* (ca. 1780–90; now in the Stiftung Sammlung E. G., Bührle, Zurich) by Francesco Guardi. Characteristically, Robert Bliss requested that the dealer not disclose the fact that they had made this purchase,

saying: "It is embarrassing and very distasteful to us to have such matters the subject of the gossip which they usually create."[51] In Paris, Royall Tyler continued to serve as a scout and advisor. Throughout 1928, he wrote them about various objects—including a sixteenth-century carpet, an important Byzantine ivory from the collection of Walter Burns, and Coptic jewelry found in 1910 in the Piazza della Consolazione, Rome—that were presently with Parisian dealers.

With these recommendations in hand, Mildred Bliss returned briefly to Paris in November 1928 and saw the ivory and jewelry, which Tyler then acquired for the Blisses after negotiating reduced prices.[52] According to Mildred Bliss's appointment diary, she also saw and entertained their friends—particularly the Tylers, the Gays, Edith Wharton, and Geoffrey Dodge—and hosted musical evenings, including one with the composer,

pianist, and pedagogue Nadia Boulanger.[53] Mildred Bliss visited with art dealers, including Joseph Brummer, and met with Rateau, who had just completed and shipped the ceiling and floor of the Music Room to Washington, D.C. She then returned to Dumbarton Oaks for the first time in five years in order to see the ceiling installed, having informed White that it would be a great help to them in working out the furnishing of the Music Room if the ceiling and floor were in place when they arrived.[54] At Dumbarton Oaks, she met again with Rateau, who also had come to see the ceiling, and during two days of discussions, she set in motion plans for Rateau to redesign the Dumbarton Oaks living room and oval salon and to submit ideas for hardscape elements in the gardens. When Rateau returned to France early in 1929, Mildred Bliss wrote to Lawrence White, saying: "The man is a treasure, isn't he?"[55]

Back in Buenos Aires, the Blisses again relied on Royall Tyler to acquire on their behalf some of the best artworks on the market. They astutely recognized, as Mildred Bliss would later articulate, that Tyler's knowledge of art was uncommonly thorough, that he followed closely all of the sales of interest, and that his unusual familiarity with the museums and most of the private collections of Europe gave him a connoisseur's standard of measurement.[56] Indeed, Royall Tyler continued to find museum-quality artworks for the Blisses, although, unlike the Rembrandts and Guardis that they found on their own, his finds frequently lay somewhat outside the realm of the mainstream. In 1929, he wrote them about a Coptic gold and lapis lazuli necklace with a representation of Venus (see fig. 2.14), telling them that it was a marvel and that he loved it.[57] At the 1930 sale of Albert Figdor's estate in Vienna, he

acquired Bernhard Strigel's *Portrait of Mary of Burgundy* (fig. 1.16) for the Blisses. In agreeing to the latter purchase, however, Mildred Bliss cautioned Tyler: "Our bank account is low. Although we've come through the crash unscathed there is a temporary shrinkage. We're not worried, but we don't feel like drawing on capital."[58]

In 1931, Royall Tyler was a principal organizer of the Exposition internationale d'art byzantin at the Musée des Arts Décoratifs in Paris, one of the first exhibitions of Byzantine artworks to be shown to the public.[59] The Blisses were important lenders to this exhibition, although circumstances prevented them from attending. Mildred Bliss wrote to Geoffrey Dodge, saying: "I shall be eager to hear your detailed impressions of the Byzantine show. As I have the catalogue you can mention objects by number. It must have been a unique opportunity for comparative study, and we very keenly regret, and always shall, not to have been there to profit by it."[60] In the following year, Tyler and Hayford Peirce published the first volume of their seminal study on Byzantine art.[61]

In 1932, when the Blisses returned briefly to the United States, they somewhat surprisingly took the first steps to leave Dumbarton Oaks to Harvard University and to create a research center and fellowship program. They met with Edward Forbes and Paul Sachs, directors of the Fogg Art Museum, in Cambridge and Washington, D.C., and then presented a plan to Harvard University president Lawrence Lowell on 10 March. Sachs wrote enthusiastically that the Blisses' idea should be carried out, as it was perfectly clear that an older generation of scholars would benefit immensely if they could be set free to finish a book or to carry on a further investigation under the "sheltering arm of the Bliss Institute."[62] He stressed that the Blisses had already begun to acquire a critical component of this plan: a scholarly library.

Robert Bliss retired from the Foreign Service in 1933, becoming the first officer to retire with the rank of ambassador and to receive a pension. The Blisses returned to Washington, D.C., and to Dumbarton Oaks, where, for the first time since they acquired the property thirteen years before, they would take up permanent residency. In early 1935, Robert Bliss made a long-anticipated, two-month trip to Central America, where, in the company of Frederic Walcott, a member of the board of trustees at the Carnegie Institution of Washington, he visited many important Pre-Columbian sites and excavations.[63] Also in early 1935, Mildred Bliss's mother died at Casa Dorinda, her home in Montecito, California. Mildred Bliss became the principal beneficiary of her mother's estate, which was valued at $12,386,000.[64] Perhaps because of this increase in capital, on 4 November 1936 and against the advice of their lawyers, the Blisses drew up new legal documents to convey Dumbarton Oaks to Harvard University during their lifetimes rather than at the time of their deaths. The lawyers estimated that the amount specified for the endowment fund represented slightly less than half of what was Mildred Bliss's current wealth.[65] The next year, the Blisses would also make a million dollar gift to the Fogg Art Museum, apparently in order to help alleviate its "burden" in taking on "these important new obligations."[66]

Having resolved to establish Dumbarton Oaks as a research library and museum during their

FIG. 1.15.

Bosch Palace (U.S. Ambassador's Residence), Buenos Aires, ca. 1930.

Archives, AR.DP.BL.009, Dumbarton Oaks Research Library and Collection. Photograph courtesy of Elisa Figueroa Bosch de Gainza, Buenos Aires.

FIG. 1.16.

Bernhard Strigel, *Portrait of Mary of Burgundy*, German Renaissance, ca. 1520, oil on pine panel.

House Collection, HC.P.1930.04.(O), Dumbarton Oaks Research Library and Collection.

lifetimes, the Blisses began to increase the pace of their collecting, which considerably accelerated in 1936–37 and reached its peak in 1938–40. Edward Forbes counseled them to "stick more or less to Byzantine art and great European paintings and sculptures," and this is essentially what the Blisses did.[67] Royall Tyler, who not surprisingly was an enthusiastic supporter of their plan, expressed alarm over their acquisition of a number of non-Byzantine artworks, including an El Greco painting, a Tilman Riemenschneider sculpture (see fig. 2.8), an ancient Chinese bronze, and Edgar Degas, Édouard Vuillard, and Georges Rouault paintings.[68] But he nevertheless successfully steered the Blisses to superb Byzantine acquisitions in this period. And despite his alarm over their non-Byzantine purchases, he also continued, as he always had and would, to flame their passion for masterworks of artists that he favored. For example, he wrote to describe an upcoming sale of El Greco paintings from the king of Romania's collection, saying: "There are some holy snorters among them. Of course this is a bad, bad business, and my love for Byzantine very nearly (but not quite) prevents me from communicating these horrible tidings to you."[69]

In early 1937, Mildred Bliss happily told Geoffrey Dodge that Robert Bliss was enjoying the kind of activity that now filled his life, namely "the collecting end of the Dumbarton Oaks plan."[70] However, later that year, the ominous prospect of war in Europe and possibly even in America affected their plans to transfer Dumbarton Oaks to Harvard University. Robert Bliss wrote to Tyler: "Goodness knows what may happen to us at the end of twelve months and it is just as well that we should acquire now, while we can, all these objects," and "We are very low in our minds over the situation in Europe and see little hope for a peaceful outcome. It is monstrous."[71] In 1938, the Blisses decided to advance the transfer date of Dumbarton Oaks to Harvard University, and hired the Washington, D.C., architect Thomas T. Waterman to design gallery and library additions for the new institution (fig. 1.17). As always, the Blisses were intimately involved in the details of these additions, as indicated by the construction blueprints issued by Waterman's office, which cite Robert and Mildred Bliss as the designers.

To further facilitate the new research institution, in 1938 the Blisses acquired a second copy of Charles Morey's *Princeton Index of Christian Art*, funded a *Census of Early Christian and Byzantine Art* and its photographic documentation that was to become the Byzantine Photograph Archives, and laid the groundwork for publishing a series of *Dumbarton Oaks Papers*, inviting Royall Tyler and Adolph Goldschmidt to contribute to the first volume. However, perhaps the most significant event of 1938 was the Blisses' celebration of their thirtieth wedding anniversary, for which Mildred Bliss had commissioned Igor Stravinsky to compose a concerto loosely based on Bach's Brandenburg Concertos.[72] Nadia Boulanger suggested and facilitated this commission, and, because of the composer's indisposition from tuberculosis, prepared and conducted the premiere performance in the Music Room. When Royall Tyler made his second visit to Dumbarton Oaks in 1938, he enthusiastically wrote to his friends: "It was a great joy to find the Oaks so settled . . . and so nobly enriched with the things we care for. I've again and again had the conviction come over me that I never would have had such a thrill of happiness from them had they come to rest in any other place. And there's something mysterious but powerful in the feeling that one has been associated in an enterprise meant to continue long beyond one's own span of days."[73]

As part of the planning for the new institution, the Blisses acquired and installed mosaics obtained from the Antioch excavations that they had financially supported.[74] The prominent installation of a large mosaic on the museum foyer floor prompted Royall Tyler to write: "It delights me to think of *Apólausis*, represented as a lady smelling a flower, welcoming visitors to Dumbarton Oaks. For what but *Delectation* is the object of art?"[75] Mildred Bliss wrote back enthusiastically of the eight thousand volumes in the library and the new exhibition cases to be made from antique French boiserie after a design sent by Rateau (fig. 1.17, left side of image). She told him: "I know that what Dumbarton Oaks has to give—the work that it can do—can never be done in a big center—it must be small and quiet and unemphatic: a place for meditation and recueillement. . . . It is such a far-reaching dream—so enthralling and so useful—if only we can see it through!"[76]

In a letter addressed to the president and fellows of Harvard University and dated 2 July 1940, the Blisses formally established the Dumbarton Oaks Research Library and Collection and its initial endowment. The letter offered the university the gift of Dumbarton Oaks, with its grounds, buildings, library, art collections, and other contents, and underscored the Blisses' expectation that the gift "be used for study and research in the Humanities and Fine Arts, with especial emphasis upon Byzantine art and the history and culture of the Eastern Empire in all its aspects." It further expressed their hope that Dumbarton Oaks itself would become a center of research and a place of residence for scholars, students, and artists.[77]

The official inauguration of the Dumbarton Oaks Research Library and Collection occurred on 1 November 1940, and was attended by Harvard administrators, scholars, and friends.[78] In 1945, Robert Bliss reminisced about the event, saying: "As the depression increased and Nazism gained control of Germany we knew war was a certainty and that inevitably this country would be sucked into the cataclysm. So we faced the future squarely and decided to transfer Dumbarton Oaks to the University in 1940. To ease the wrench, we assured each other that freedom of choice is a privilege not often granted by Fate and that to give up our home at our own time to assure the long range realization of our plan was the way of wisdom."[79] By the end of the year,

John Thacher began his twenty-nine-year tenure as the first director of Dumbarton Oaks. Paul Sachs was named chairman of the Administrative Committee and co-director (with Edward Forbes) of the Dumbarton Oaks Museum.[80] Art historian Henri Foçillon became the first research fellow in residence.[81] On the last Sunday of the first official month of business, Dumbarton Oaks hosted an inaugural concert by the Musical Art Quartet in the Music Room for both the scholarly and social world of Washington, D.C.

As the war escalated, the Blisses, fearing a German invasion and occupation, had the museum closed and the collections moved to outside storage facilities. Robert Bliss resumed work at the State Department as consultant to the Division of Cultural Relations in 1942 and special assistant to the secretary of state in 1944. Beginning in 1942, part of Dumbarton Oaks was taken over by the National Defense Research Committee.[82] Although this development pleased him, Robert Bliss observed: "Dumbarton Oaks now presents a strange juxtaposition. One half of the building is devoted to evolving means to kill human beings

FIG. 1.17.
Thomas T. Waterman, Byzantine Collection gallery, as installed ca. 1947.

Archives, AR.PH.MW.BZ.013, Dumbarton Oaks Research Library and Collection.

FIG. 1.18.

Mildred Barnes Bliss
with L. Gard Wiggins
and Francis H. Burr of
Harvard University in
the Byzantine Collection
gallery, 1963.

Papers of Robert Woods Bliss
and Mildred Barnes Bliss,
ca. 1860–1969, HUGFP 76.74p,
box 15, Harvard University
Archives.

more speedily and in greater numbers; the other
half continues to develop greater knowledge on
the artistic creation of man. One works for the
development of the most hideous activity of war,
the other for the discovery and preservation of the
beauty of human expression."[83]

In 1943, the research library was reopened
to scholars between ten and four o'clock daily,
except Sundays and holidays, and guided tours of
the gardens were offered to the general public on
Wednesdays and Saturdays. In 1944, the Blisses
arranged for Dumbarton Oaks to serve as the

site of the so-called Dumbarton Oaks Conversations, which were informal discussions, under
the auspices of the Department of State, among
the Americans, British, Russians, and Chinese,
on the question of an international organization for the maintenance of peace and security.
These discussions led to the formation of the
United Nations the following year.[84] In 1945,
the collections were returned and reinstalled,
and the exhibition rooms, including the Music
Room, were formally reopened to the public. In
1946, the Blisses and Thacher finalized plans for

monthly scholarly lectures and musical performances at Dumbarton Oaks.[85] The latter were to be organized by the Friends of Music, which was based on a similar organization at the Library of Congress, of which Mildred Bliss was a longtime member. The Friends offered their first concert series in fall 1946.[86]

The Blisses' vision for the transformation of Dumbarton Oaks into an institution did not stop with the inaugural ceremony in 1940. In 1941, they commissioned Thomas T. Waterman to transform their guest rooms into a reading room and their other bedrooms into spaces for the ever-increasing library, which now numbered over fourteen thousand volumes.[87] With Waterman's addition of a hallway between the Museum Wing and the Main House in 1946, the integration of the institutional components was complete. In 1948, the Blisses financially helped Dumbarton Oaks acquire Hayford Peirce's five-thousand-piece Byzantine coin collection.[88] Mildred Bliss immediately wrote to Royall Tyler, saying: "It is for us a very special flavor that the coin collection should have been inspired by you and made by Hayford. Dumbarton Oaks is now starting on the long road of scholarship—what with the coins, the seals, the library and the Collection, and we are well pleased."[89]

Mildred Bliss was simultaneously shaping a new collection of rare botanical and landscape books and plates, and she began to correspond with antiquarians in an effort to augment it.[90] In 1948, the living room at Dumbarton Oaks was rechristened as the Founders' Room, as it was intended to house her expanding garden research library and her collection of historical correspondence, autographs, holographic documents, and musical scores. The importance of this collection led the Blisses to establish the Dumbarton Oaks Garden Endowment Fund in 1951. They specified that the endowment was for individual fellowships for study in garden design and ornament, for publications on these subjects, and for the maintenance and enlargement of the Garden Library. In making this gift to Harvard University, the Blisses expressed the hope that the Dumbarton Oaks Gardens might in time attain as high a standing in the study and publishing of garden design and ornament as the research library and collection had already attained for its scholarly work in the Byzantine field.[91] At the time of this gift, Harvard University awarded Robert Bliss an honorary doctorate of arts degree.

In the 1950s, Robert Bliss began to contemplate the future of his Pre-Columbian Collection. He had lent it to the National Gallery of Art in 1947, with the intention that the objects would be seen and appreciated as artworks rather than as mere artifacts. In 1957, Robert Bliss published the collection as a full-color art book,[92] and in the same year the Blisses decided that new exhibition and storage spaces were needed to house the Rare Book and the Pre-Columbian collections. Robert Bliss wrote to the president of Harvard University, saying: "For some time past it has been evident that additional space must be provided at Dumbarton Oaks for the exhibition of objects in the Collection, not now on display, as well as to provide suitable rooms for the use and study of a library of books on gardens and related subjects, which Mrs. Bliss has been collecting in recent years."[93] With the university's approval, the Blisses began discussions with Frederic Rhinelander King of the New York City architectural firm Wyeth and King to design and build a Garden Library and Rare Book Room to be modeled in size and materials on the existing Byzantine Collection pavilions. More surprisingly, they engaged the architect Philip Johnson to design a postmodern gallery space for the Robert Woods Bliss Collection of Pre-Columbian Art.[94]

In 1958, the Blisses celebrated their fiftieth wedding anniversary at Dumbarton Oaks, and Igor Stravinsky conducted the *Dumbarton Oaks Concerto* for the occasion. As a gift to the Blisses, the Trustees for Harvard University/ Dumbarton Oaks commissioned Aaron Copland to compose the *Nonet for Solo Strings*. Nadia Boulanger conducted its world premiere in the Music Room on 2 March 1961, just before the museum closed for three years for the construction of the Garden Library and Pre-Columbian Collection pavilions.

Robert Bliss did not live to see the installation of his Pre-Columbian Collection. He died on 19 April 1962. The majority of his residual estate was given to Harvard University for the maintenance of Dumbarton Oaks, and specifically "for purposes directly related to the collection of Pre-Columbian art and the Pre-Columbian library." Mildred Bliss, although now in her eighties, dedicated the remaining years of her life to perfecting what she and her husband had created. She oversaw the installation and opening of the Robert Woods Bliss Collection of Pre-Columbian Art and the Garden Library

FIG. 1.19.
Cecil Beaton, Mildred Bliss, 1966, gelatin print.

Archives, AR.PH.BL.058, Dumbarton Oaks Research Library and Collection.

Rare Book Room, and hosted a meeting of the Harvard Board of Overseers in May 1963 (fig. 1.18). She orchestrated the final design of the Ellipse in the gardens, having accomplished what she termed her "bang-up finale" with the redesign of the tennis court as a rococo-style water garden. She sat for three photographic portraits: the first, a series made in 1963 by Philip Fink in the gardens; a second, by Evelyn Hofer at Dumbarton Oaks (see frontispiece to chapter 7); and the third, a series made in 1966 by Cecil Beaton at her Georgetown house at 1537 28th Street, NW, where the Blisses resided after Dumbarton Oaks was transferred to Harvard University in 1940 (figs. 1.19 and 7.3).[95] She died on 17 January 1969. Her residual estate also went to Harvard University for the maintenance of Dumbarton Oaks and the establishment of a permanent endowment fund for the gardens and Garden Library.

In the preamble to her last will and testament, Mildred Bliss offered an appraisal of what she and Robert Bliss had endeavored to create at Dumbarton Oaks. She wrote:

> In applying these gifts to Harvard, I call upon the present and future President and Fellows of Harvard College and all those who determine its policies, to remember that Dumbarton Oaks is conceived in a new pattern, where quality and not number shall determine the choice of its scholars; that it is the home of the Humanities, not a mere aggregation of books and objects of art; that the house itself and the gardens have their educational importance and that all are of humanistic value. . . . I charge those responsible for carrying forward the life at Dumbarton Oaks to be guided by the standards set there during the lifetime of my husband and me. . . . The fulfillment of this vision of high intellectual adventure seen through the open gates of Dumbarton Oaks will add lustre to Harvard, to the academic tone of our country and to scholarship throughout the world.

Notes

1   The bulk of primary correspondence and other related documents is found in the Papers of Robert Woods Bliss and Mildred Barnes Bliss, ca. 1860–1969, HUGFP 76.xx, HUA. Unless cited otherwise, historical data used in this article comes from this collection. For secondary sources on the Blisses, see Susan Tamulevich, *Dumbarton Oaks: Garden into Art* (New York, 2001); and James N. Carder, "Mildred and Robert Woods Bliss and the Dumbarton Oaks Research Library and Collection," in *Sacred Art, Secular Context: Objects of Art from the Byzantine Collection of Dumbarton Oaks, Washington, D.C., Accompanied by American Paintings from the Collection of Mildred and Robert Woods Bliss*, ed. Asen Kirin, 22–37 (Athens, Ga., 2005).

2   Blissiana files, New York School of Applied Design for Women correspondence, Archives.

3   Marcel Proust, *Lettres à Madame Scheikévitch* (Paris, 1928), 105. Mildred Bliss's attempt to suppress the publication of her name is found in correspondence with her Parisian secretary, Thérèse Malye, 21 November 1927, 20 January 1928, and 2 February 1928, Blissiana files, Malye correspondence, Archives. Marcel Proust met Mildred Bliss for the first time in 1918 at the Paris residence of Mme Jean Hennessy, later the Comtesse Marguerite de Mun. In 1918, he wrote to Louis Hauser that Mildred Bliss "passe pour une femme aussi remarquable que peu simple." Marcel Proust, *Correspondence*, ed. Philip Kolb (Paris, 1970–), 17:264. To their mutual friend, Walter Berry, he wrote: "il paraît que Mme Bliss a toujours sur sa table le dernier Marcel Proust." Ibid., 21:30.

4   Walter Muir Whitehill, *Dumbarton Oaks: The History of a Georgetown House and Garden, 1800–1966* (Cambridge, Mass., 1967); and Tamulevich, *Dumbarton Oaks*.

5   She employed this phase and its variations in her correspondence, e.g., Mildred Barnes Bliss to John S. Thacher, director of Dumbarton Oaks, 27 May 1941, Administrative files, Thacher correspondence, Archives. However, she used it most famously in the preamble to her last will and testament, signed 31 August 1966, which is quoted at the end of this article. Blissiana files, Archives.

6   Papers of Robert Woods Bliss and Mildred Barnes Bliss, HUGFP 76.8, box 47 and 76.36, box 3, HUA.

7   Papers of Robert Woods Bliss and Mildred Barnes Bliss, HUGFP 76.8, boxes 45 and 46, HUA. Robert Bliss had a lifelong interest in opera, which he may have first experienced as a college student. On 10 April 1899, he wrote to his stepsister, Mildred Barnes: "It sounds queer, doesn't it dear, to hear

me going on enthusiastically over music [the opera Charles Gounod's *Roméo et Juliette*], or any thing for that matter, I am such an indifferent, lazy duffer, but I did enjoy this more than words can say . . ." Papers of Robert Woods Bliss and Mildred Barnes Bliss, HUGFP 76.8, box 1, HUA.

8   For the chronology of Robert Bliss's diplomatic postings, see *Dictionary of American Biography, Supplement Seven: 1961–1965*, ed. John A. Garraty (New York, 1981).

9   There is a letter from Robert Bliss to Mildred Barnes dated 3 May 1893. Papers of Robert Woods Bliss and Mildred Barnes Bliss, HUGFP 76.8, box 1, HUA.

10   She was describing the *Très Belles Heures*, Franco-Flemish, 15th century, MS 11060–61, Bibliothèque Royale, Brussels. Papers of Robert Woods Bliss and Mildred Barnes Bliss, HUGFP 76.8, box 45, HUA.

11   Whitehill, *Dumbarton Oaks*, 59.

12   "Demas Barnes's Death," *New York Times*, 2 May 1888; and http://en.wikipedia.org/w/index.php?title=Fletcher%27s_Laxative&oldid=228624147 (accessed 18 August 2008).

13   "Miss Barnes Killed By Fall on Birthday; Suicide the Police Say, but Coroner Feinberg Says 70-Foot Drop Was Accidental; Recently Recovered from a Nervous Breakdown, and Just Returned from an Auto Tour of New England," *New York Times*, 30 September 1911. Although the death—the result of a fall from a fourth-floor window—was eventually recorded as an accident, it was discussed as a suicide in the Blisses' correspondence, e.g., William Bliss to Mildred Barnes Bliss, 11 October 1911, Blissiana files, William H. Bliss correspondence, Archives.

14   "Stepsister of Woman Killed in Fall from Window Receives $4,536,487; Stepmother Gets $42,823," *New York Times*, 8 August 1914.

15   Whitehill, *Dumbarton Oaks*, 60. This textile remains in the House Collection, HC.T.X.xxxx.21.(E).

16   House Collection files, M. Knoedler & Co. and H. Wunderlich & Co. correspondence, Archives.

17   Ethel B. Clark, "The Founders Room Library at Dumbarton Oaks," *Harvard Library Bulletin* 4, no. 2 (Spring 1950): 141; and Whitehill, *Dumbarton Oaks*, 60.

18   The ca. 1734 "Gibson" or "Saint Senoch" viola was made by Antonio Stradivari (1644–1737) and acquired by Mildred Bliss in 1937. http://www.cozio.com/Instrument.aspx?id=264 (accessed 16 November 2009).

19 Lease agreement for Mildred Bliss's property in Sharon, Conn., 1 April 1908, Papers of Robert Woods Bliss and Mildred Barnes Bliss, HUGFP 76.8, box 59, HUA.

20 On 10 January 1909, Mildred Bliss wrote to her stepfather: "Another question of infinite importance has at last been settled. I have told Robert I would sell Sharon. I have acknowledged that course as the only wise one ever since I decided to marry Robert, & mentally I see it right & accept it unreservedly. But you cannot know what it costs my heart & my emotions are aquiver. Sharon has never been mere geography to me & I feel as if I were making a wig of my own hair to put on some other head. I told Robert as soon as I could get the words out so there should be no back sliding. I know the sooner it is over the better . . . " Blissiana files, William H. Bliss correspondence, Archives.

21 Edith Wharton (1862–1937) was an American novelist and short story writer living in Paris. Royall Tyler first met her in February 1913. He wrote to Elisina Tyler on 26 February: "I had a very pleasant time at Koechlin. He lives very snugly indeed—more so than we do, rather, and has most beautiful things. . . . Metman and his wife were there, Mrs. Wharton, the writer, and someone else. . . . I talked a little to Mrs. Wharton, who is an intelligent woman of very near 50, I should think. She asked me to go and see her . . ." On 11 March, he wrote: "This afternoon I went to tea at Mrs. Wharton's. She has a beautiful flat in the rue de Varenne. She is very intelligent, and I think nice woman and she wants very much to meet you. There were lots of people there, all French, but I talked mostly with her and Koechlin . . ." He wrote again on 16 March: "I am going to lunch with Mrs. Wharton and the Blisses on Tuesday and have also accepted for you. Mildred says I have made a conquest of Mrs W. Que tendé." Apparently, Elisina Tyler did not meet Wharton that Tuesday, as an invitation from Wharton of 10 June 1913, inviting her to tea, is annotated in Elisina Tyler's hand: "Invitation to my first meeting with Edith." Edith Wharton mss., William Royall Tyler files, folder 9, Lilly Library Manuscript Collections, Indiana University, Bloomington. In her autobiography, Edith Wharton also remembered first meeting Tyler "before the war at the house of my friend Raymond Koechlin, the distinguished archaeologist and collector . . ." Edith Wharton, A Backward Glance: An Autobiography (New York, 1934), 348. For Raymond Koechlin (1860–1931), see Nelson, chapter 2.

22 William Rieder, A Charmed Couple: The Art and Life of Walter and Matilda Gay (New York, 2000), 124–35 and 212–14.

23 See also Nelson, chapter 2. Born in 1884, Royall Tyler had known Mildred Barnes Bliss since childhood. Although raised in Quincy, Massachusetts, he spent most of his life in Europe, after moving there in 1898, where he was educated at Harrow School, London. He attended New College, Oxford, and the University of Salamanca without taking a degree. In 1910, the Public Records Office of the British Home Office appointed him editor of the Spanish Calendar of State Papers, which included translations of correspondence to English monarchs from their diplomats in Spain. Tyler completed five volumes between 1913 and 1953. After serving in the U.S. Army during World War I, he was appointed to the U.S. delegation to the Commission des Réparations (1920–23); in 1924, he joined the League of Nations as the Deputy Commissioner General of the Financial Committee in Hungary. In 1928, he became the European representative of the Hambros Bank of London. He authored Spain: A Study of her Life and Arts (New York, 1909) and, with Hayford Peirce, Byzantine Art (New York, 1926) and L'art byzantin, 2 vols. (Paris, 1932–34). He was instrumental in organizing the first international exhibition of Byzantine art in Paris in 1931. His last book, The Emperor Charles the Fifth, perhaps left incomplete by his death in 1953, was published posthumously (Fair Lawn, N.J., 1956).

24 See also Nelson, chapter 2. The Blisses' interest in art from cultures and periods outside the "collecting mainstream" was well known to their friends and to dealers. In 1930, for example, their friend, the Crown Prince of Sweden Gustaf Adolf, wrote them of an ancient and "most remarkable piece of woven and embroidered fabric" that he had seen for sale in Cairo. Although he found the asking price "absurd," he sent them a photograph of the textile and wrote: "I just thought that it might interest you to see the photo and that you might possibly think of acquiring it, as I know how you and Mrs. Bliss enjoy these fine and at the same time out of the way pieces." Papers of Royall Tyler, 1902–1967, HUGFP 38.6, box 2, HUA (housed with Tyler correspondence from October–December 1930).

25 S. K. Lothrop, Robert Woods Bliss Collection: Pre-Columbian Art (London, 1957), 7; and Whitehill, Dumbarton Oaks, 60.

26 Royall Tyler to Robert Woods Bliss, 27 May 1912. The bulk of correspondence between the Blisses and the Tylers is in the Papers of Royall Tyler, HUGFP 38.6, box 1, HUA. The French Gothic Madonna and Child sculpture remains in the Byzantine Collection, BZ.1912.2. Gudrun Bühl, ed., Dumbarton Oaks: The Collections (Washington, D.C., 2008), 296f. The Morgan sculpture is probably a French (lower Rhône valley) alabaster Virgin

and Child, 35 in. in height, which was a gift of J. Pierpont Morgan to the Metropolitan Museum of Art in 1917 (17.190.717). This sculpture is dated to the mid-fourteenth century.

27 Tamulevich, *Dumbarton Oaks*, 32; and Papers of Robert Woods Bliss and Mildred Barnes Bliss, HUGFP 76.32, box 1, HUA.

28 Papers of Robert Woods Bliss and Mildred Barnes Bliss, HUGFP 76.8, box 61, HUA.

29 Carol A. Hess, *Enrique Granados: A Bio-bibliography* (New York, 1991), 50.

30 Papers of Robert Woods Bliss and Mildred Barnes Bliss, HUGFP 76.12, box 1, HUA. See also James W. D. Seymour, *History of the American Field Service in France, "Friends of France," 1914–1917* (New York, 1920), 1:18 and 486.

31 The "Service de Distribution Américaine" was established in December 1914. Papers of Robert Woods Bliss and Mildred Barnes Bliss, HUGFP 76.12, box 1, HUA. See also Arthur H. Gleason, *Our Part In The Great War* (New York, 1917), 324.

32 Gleason, *Our Part In The Great War*, 325. See also Ida Clyde Clarke, *American Women and the World War* (New York, 1918), 477.

33 Papers of Robert Woods Bliss and Mildred Barnes Bliss, HUGFP 76.12, box 4, HUA; and Clarke, *American Women and the World War*, 144, 454, 473, and 484.

34 House Collection, HC.P.1918.02.(O). Bühl, *Dumbarton Oaks*, 360f.

35 Roger Valbelle, "La Deuxième Journée de la Vente Edgar Degas," *Excelsior*, 8 May 1918.

36 *Bulletin of the Fogg Art Museum* 9, no. 4 (March 1941): 63.

37 Robin Karson, *A Genius for Place, American Landscapes of the Country Place Era* (Amherst, Mass., 2007), 149–79. See also Karson, chapter 6.

38 Meryle Secrest, *Duveen: A Life in Art* (New York, 2004), 307.

39 House Collection files, Fitzpatrick correspondence, Archives.

40 Dumbarton Oaks History files, Research documents, Archives.

41 Papers of Robert Woods Bliss and Mildred Barnes Bliss, HUGFP 76.36, box 5, HUA.

42 Byzantine Collection, BZ.1924.5. Bühl, *Dumbarton Oaks*, 78f.

43 Byzantine Collection, BZ.1955.18. Bühl, *Dumbarton Oaks*, 80f.

44 Royall Tyler to Mildred Barnes Bliss, 26 January 1924, Papers of Royall Tyler, HUGFP 38.6, box 2, HUA.

45 Robert Woods Bliss to Lawrence Grant White, 20 January 1927, Robert Woods Bliss House, Washington, D.C., call no. 396, McKim, Mead & White Archives, NYHS.

46 Edward W. Forbes to Robert Woods Bliss, 22 April 1932, Dumbarton Oaks History files, Forbes correspondence, Archives. I am indebted to Jennifer Younger and Jeffrey Quilter for sharing their discussion of this material from their unpublished "Archaeology & Dumbarton Oaks."

47 Dumbarton Oaks History files, Fogg Museum and Peabody Museum correspondence, Archives.

48 Fabio Grementieri, *The Bosch Palace, Residence of the Ambassador of the United States to Argentina* (Buenos Aires, 2001), 22–31.

49 Papers of Robert Woods Bliss and Mildred Barnes Bliss, HUGFP 76.14, box 3, HUA.

50 See Carder, chapter 5.

51 Robert Woods Bliss to Robert Abdy (Société Anonyme Ffoulkes [Abdy & Co.], London), 5 December 1927, House Collection files, Guardi correspondence, Archives.

52 Byzantine Collection, BZ.1928.8–17 and BZ.1929.2. Papers of Royall Tyler, HUGFP 38.6, box 2, HUA.

53 Papers of Robert Woods Bliss and Mildred Barnes Bliss, HUGFP 76.32, box 8, HUA.

54 Robert Woods Bliss to Lawrence Grant White, 3 September 1928, Robert Woods Bliss House, call no. 396, McKim, Mead & White Archives, NYHS.

55 Mildred Barnes Bliss to Lawrence Grant White, 9 January 1929, Robert Woods Bliss House, call no. 396, McKim, Mead & White Archives, NYHS.

56 Mildred Barnes Bliss to Geoffrey Dodge, 23 August 1929, House Collection files, Dodge correspondence, Archives.

57 Royall Tyler to Mildred Barnes Bliss, 27 March and 12 April 1929, Papers of Royall Tyler, HUGFP 38.6, box 2, HUA. Byzantine Collection, BZ.1928.6. Bühl, *Dumbarton Oaks*, 118f.

58 Mildred Barnes Bliss to Royall Tyler, 20 October 1930, Papers of Royall Tyler, HUGFP 38.6, box 2, HUA. House Collection, HC.P.1930.04.(O). Bühl, *Dumbarton Oaks*, 328f.

59 *Exposition internationale d'art byzantin: 28 mai–9 juillet 1931*, Paris, Musée des Arts Décoratifs, Palais du Louvre, Pavillon de Marsan, Paris.

60 Mildred Barnes Bliss to Geoffrey Dodge, 18 July 1931, House Collection files, Dodge correspondence, Archives.

61 Hayford Peirce and Royall Tyler, *L'art byzantin*, 2 vols. (Paris, 1932–34).

62 Paul Sachs to Mildred Barnes Bliss, 10 March 1932, and Paul Sachs to Alfred Gregory, 19 July 1932, Dumbarton Oaks History files, Sachs correspondence, Archives.

63 See Jones, chapter 3.

64 "$12,386,000 Estate Left by Mrs. Bliss; Daughter Is Named Residuary Legatee of Bulk of Patent Medicine Fortune," *New York Times*, 23 June 1936.

65 Hawkins, Delafield, & Longfellow, New York, N.Y., to Mildred and Robert Woods Bliss, 4 November 1936: ". . . the Donor (I advisedly omit names) is now definitely committed to a gift . . . to be made in her lifetime, but that the time of making the gift remains indefinite. . . . As you know, I have not been persuaded that the making of so large a gift in the Donor's lifetime is desirable in her interest, but as that matter has now been decided, I mention it only for the purpose of a record on my own letter files." Blissiana files, Gifts correspondence, Archives.

66 Memorandum from Paul Sachs to Harvard University president James B. Conant, 25 November 1936, for use at a dinner meeting with the Blisses on 1 December: "The present Directors [of the Fogg Art Museum] are already heavily burdened and in taking on these important new obligations the financial problems which have faced them each year could be settled once and for all by a further endowment of $1,000,000." Dumbarton Oaks History files, Conant correspondence, Archives.

67 Edward W. Forbes to Robert Woods Bliss, 8 November 1935, Dumbarton Oaks History files, Forbes correspondence, Archives.

68 Royall Tyler to Mildred Barnes Bliss, 4 September 1937, Papers of Royall Tyler, HUGFP 38.6, box 6, HUA. See also Nelson, chapter 2.

69 Royall Tyler to Robert Woods Bliss, 31 July 1937, Papers of Royall Tyler, HUGFP 38.6, box 6, HUA.

70 Mildred Barnes Bliss to Geoffrey Dodge, 15 January 1937, House Collection files, Dodge correspondence, Archives.

71 Robert Woods Bliss to Royall Tyler, 22 May 1937 and 14 September 1938, Papers of Royall Tyler, HUGFP 38.6, box 6, HUA.

72 See Brooks, chapter 4.

73 Royall Tyler to Mildred Barnes Bliss, 22 June 1938, Papers of Royall Tyler, HUGFP 38.6, box 6, HUA.

74 In 1936, the Blisses joined the Committee for the Excavation of Antioch which funded an international archaeological excavation in collaboration with the Syrian government. The sponsors of this project included Princeton University, the Worcester Art Museum, the Baltimore Museum of Art, and the Musées Nationaux de France (on behalf of the Musée du Louvre). Although the Blisses' initial $6,000 contribution in 1936 suggests that they acted as private donors, the committee minutes later record the subscription as from "Fogg Museum-Dumbarton Oaks." 22 October 1937, Byzantine Studies files, Committee for the Excavation of Antioch correspondence, Archives.

75 Royall Tyler to Mildred Barnes Bliss, 17 July 1939, Papers of Royall Tyler, HUGFP 38.6, box 6, HUA.

76 Mildred Barnes Bliss to Royall Tyler, 25 September 1939, Papers of Royall Tyler, HUGFP 38.6, box 6, HUA.

77 Mildred and Robert Woods Bliss to the president and fellows of Harvard College, 2 July 1940, Blissiana files, Gifts correspondence, Archives.

78 *Bulletin of the Fogg Art Museum* 9, no. 4 (March 1941): 63–90. For later reports on Dumbarton Oaks, see also *The Dumbarton Oaks Research Library and Collection, Harvard University, 1940–1950* (Washington, D.C., 1950).

79 Whitehill, *Dumbarton Oaks*, 78.

80 "It touches me deeply that you like the composition of the Dumbarton Oaks Administrative Board, and that you approve of the President's action in appointing me as its Chairman. I hasten to add that he has also appointed Edward [Forbes] and me Directors of the Dumbarton Oaks Museum, and I need hardly assure you, I hope, that no important decision will be taken without securing Edward's advice and sound judgment, for we plan to work at Dumbarton Oaks as we have worked here,—together—these many years." Paul Sachs to Robert Woods Bliss, 19 December 1940, Dumbarton Oaks History files, Sachs correspondence, Archives.

81 Papers of Robert Woods Bliss and Mildred Barnes Bliss, HUGFP 76.16, box 2, HUA.

82 The National Defense Research Committee occupied "the two wings formerly used by the Collection and Research Library as well as the basement floor and certain study rooms on the second floor of the main house" between 1942 and 1 March 1946. "Dumbarton Oaks Research Library and Collection," *Report[s] of the President of Harvard College and Reports of Departments*, 1941–42 through 1945–46.

83 Address by Robert Woods Bliss to the Harvard Club of Washington, D.C., 8 April 1943, Papers of Robert Woods Bliss and Mildred Barnes Bliss, HUGFP 76.16, series 4, box 2, HUA.

84 Robert C. Hilderbrand, *Dumbarton Oaks: The Origins of the United Nations and the Search for Postwar Security* (Chapel Hill, N.C., 1990); and Joachim Wolschke-Bulmahn, with a preface by

Angeliki E. Laiou, *Dumbarton Oaks Conversations, 1944–1994: A Look Behind the Scenes; An Exhibition Catalogue* (Washington, D.C., 1994).

85 For public lecture speakers and topics, see *Twenty-Fifth Anniversary, The Dumbarton Oaks Research Library and Collection: Sunday, October Thirty-First, 1965* (Washington, D.C., 1965) and thereafter the usually annual or biannual reports for the academic years: *Dumbarton Oaks, Trustees for Harvard University, Report for the Academic Year.*

86 John Thacher, *Music at Dumbarton Oaks: A Record, 1940 to 1970* (Washington, D.C., 1977), vi–vii.

87 Whitehill, *Dumbarton Oaks*, 79.

88 See Nelson, chapter 2.

89 Mildred Barnes Bliss to Royall Tyler, 27 October 1948, Papers of Royall Tyler, HUGFP 38.6, box 7, HUA.

90 See O'Malley, chapter 7.

91 Dumbarton Oaks Garden Endowment Fund Number I, 1951, Harvard University.

92 Lothrop, *Robert Woods Bliss Collection.* See also Jones, chapter 3.

93 Mildred and Robert Woods Bliss to the president and fellows of Harvard College, 20 December 1957, Blissiana files, Gifts correspondence, Archives.

94 See Carder, chapter 5.

95 The twenty-four Fink photographs are in the Rare Book Collection, LA.GP.PF.09.C to LA.GP.PF.ZZ.J; the Hofer photograph, HC.PH.2009.01, and three of the four Beaton photographs, HC.PH.BL.058–060, are in the House Collection. The fourth Beaton photograph is in the Papers of Robert Woods Bliss and Mildred Barnes Bliss, HUGFP 76.74p, box 10, HUA.

2

Royall Tyler and the Bliss Collection of Byzantine Art

Because Royall Tyler introduced Mildred and Robert Woods Bliss to Byzantine art in Paris in the 1910s and the 1920s, Dumbarton Oaks is today one of the most important scholarly institutes in the world for the study of Byzantium.[1] American, at least by nationality, Tyler (fig. 2.1) was born in Massachusetts in 1884 and was educated at New College, Oxford. He spoke French, German, Spanish, Catalan, Hungarian, Italian, and some Greek. During his long career, he was a banker, an advisor of the League of Nations to Hungary, the author of books on the art and culture of Spain[2] and international economics,[3] the editor of several volumes of the Spanish State Papers of the British Public Record Office,[4] the coauthor of three books on Byzantine art,[5] and the principal organizer and curator of the first international exhibition of Byzantine art.[6] Left initially with an adequate income by his parents, Tyler lived in Europe from the beginning of the past century and became European in all but fact, never returning to the United States for more than a few months for the rest of his life. He died in 1953. His last volume of the Spanish State Papers and a study of the Emperor Charles V,[7] a logical outgrowth of this larger project, appeared posthumously.

After adolescence, his childhood friendship with Mildred Barnes developed into something more serious, so it was a shock when she informed him in 1908 that she was marrying Robert Bliss. Nevertheless, Royall and his eventual wife Elisina remained close friends of the Blisses for the rest of their lives. We know about their relationship

from an extraordinary correspondence that began in 1902, when Royall Tyler was studying at Oxford, and continued until his death in 1953. This correspondence, preserved in the Harvard University Archives, reveals that Royall Tyler was the principal advisor to the Blisses on the formation of their Byzantine Collection until its donation to Harvard University in 1940. These letters provide an unparalleled glimpse into the market for medieval art and record the enthusiasms of collectors at a time, not seen since, when it was possible to acquire objects from major, long-established collections.

In November 1903, after a year and a half at New College, Royall Tyler left or "went down from Oxford" and traveled to France and Spain. His mother died in January, but he, nonetheless, kept to his plan and began studying at the University of Salamanca in February 1904.[8] Enamored of Spanish art and culture, Tyler often wrote Mildred Barnes about works of art of various periods, but especially the medieval. In his unpublished autobiography written some years later, he recalled that the Middle Ages seemed nearer in Spain than in other countries.[9] At the suggestion of his publisher, Grant Richards, Tyler developed his thoughts about Spain in his first book, *Spain: A Study of her Life and Arts* (1909). One clue to his aesthetic preferences was his selection of a late Gothic Madonna and Child (fig. 2.2) as the book's frontispiece. Meanwhile, Tyler continued to travel extensively, learning German in that country and working on his French in Paris, where he took an apartment in 1906.[10] In

NUESTRA SEÑORA LA BLANCA, TOLEDO CATHEDRAL.

1910, the Public Record Office of the British Home Office appointed him editor of the Spanish State Papers, a collection of official papers between the Spanish and English monarchs, and he eventually produced several volumes between 1912 and 1916.[11] Paris remained his base, and there he acquired additional expertise that would be of great value to the Blisses.

In April 1912, the Blisses sailed to Paris, where Robert took up a post at the U.S. Embassy, much to the pleasure of Royall and Elisina Tyler. Soon Royall Tyler was introducing Robert Bliss to Parisian dealers. Forty-five years later, Robert Bliss remembered that they went together to see Pre-Columbian objects. Although often quoted, Bliss's remarks remain essential: "I had just come from the Argentine Republic, where I had never seen anything like these objects, the temptations offered there having been in the form of colonial silver. Within a year, the *antiquaire* of the Boulevard Raspail, Joseph Brummer, showed me an Olmec jadeite figure [see fig. 3.6]. That day the collector's microbe took root in—it must be confessed—very fertile soil."[12]

Robert Bliss's enthusiasm for the Olmec figure is informative, because it reveals his abiding interest in the tactile surface qualities of sculpture. The same aesthetic would motivate his later Byzantine purchases.[13] For example, his love of low relief prompted the purchase of an Early Byzantine stone relief of an antelope (fig. 2.3) and a small ivory of the Incredulity of Thomas (fig. 2.4) in 1936 and 1937, respectively.[14] Also in 1936, the Blisses bought the early medieval equivalent of the Olmec man in a small statuette about four inches tall. Made of solid gold in Gaul in the late fourth or fifth century, this unique piece from the Migration period owes much to the pre-Christian traditions of Gaul (fig. 2.5).[15] Both men stand stiffly, and their facial expressions have an odd kinship. Motivating both acquisitions was a regard for small, finely wrought objects in precious materials and for the pleasures of what the Germans call *Kleinkunst*—art that can be held easily in the hand and displayed gracefully amid the fine furniture of a well-appointed room, and thus the aesthetics also of the Cabinet des Médailles in Paris, about which more shortly.

The Blisses were also motivated by their deep fascination for Byzantium. When welcoming the Harvard Club to Dumbarton Oaks in 1943, Robert Bliss expressed his wish that Dumbarton Oaks would be a research center "in the Fine Arts and the Humanities, with emphasis upon

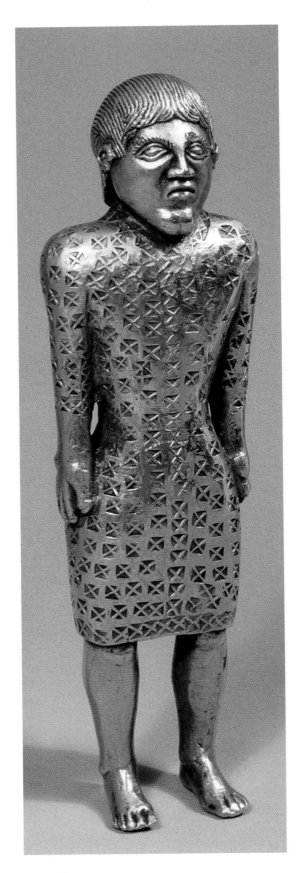

Byzantine Art and the history and culture of the Eastern Empire in all its aspects."[16] How do we get from an Olmec figure bought in Paris by an inexperienced collector to this grand vision of Dumbarton Oaks centered on Byzantine art in 1943? One answer is Royall Tyler.

In their collecting, the Blisses followed the lead of their friend for many years. In 1911, Royall Tyler wrote that he was only knowledgeable about "two things—Persian pottery and French medieval sculpture..."[17] Six months later, he added a third category, remarking that he never missed "a chance of seeing Gothic sculpture or Persian pottery, or as far as I can, early Chinese things."[18] All were then popular among collectors in Paris and London due to a heightened regard for objets d'art during the Arts and Crafts and Art Nouveau movements. His autobiography suggests how he came by his significant skills as a connoisseur:

> The Paris art-trade drew me inevitably. Shily [*sic*], for I had little money to spend, I gradually made terms with one dealer after another: all sorts and kinds, from him who ran a junk-shop to the magnate of the Plâce Vendôme. What I bought did not matter so much to me as just to be admitted, to see the wares coming in, to hear the gossip of the market....
>
> At first, indeed, I knew no rich collectors ... Gradually, I came to know a few, and later many, among whom [a] friend [possibly Mildred Barnes Bliss] of my family whom I had known all my life, though hitherto not on that particular ground. These people often asked me to visit the dealers with them. Why not improve such opportunities? ... [However] I found I could only enjoy the marvels of the market if I kept my independence on both sides. I made it a rule, which once taken I never broke, not to accept anything, in any shape or form, from either dealer or amateur....
>
> But I was someone to whom it was worth-while to display the best they had. The amateurs realised that though I might commit errors of judgment or of taste, I did know the market, and the opinions I expressed were not influenced by hope of profit. What I did gain was many an opportunity to see and to fondle objects which were jealously hidden away from the general view.[19]

Royall Tyler's fondness for touching art was shared with Robert Bliss. A curator once remarked that Bliss liked to carry in his pocket a small piece of highly polished Olmec jade: "It was his 'lucky piece,' a fine object to be played with and caressed in the hand."[20] These were tactile values enacted.

One collector that Tyler met before the Blisses arrived in Paris was Raymond Koechlin (1860–1931). In her autobiography, the expatriate American novelist Edith Wharton (1862–1937) remembers that she first met Tyler "before the war at the house of my friend Raymond Koechlin, the distinguished archaeologist and collector. . . ."[21] Their friendship was long lasting. In 1926, the Tylers entertained Koechlin at their château in Burgundy.[22] A generation older than Tyler, Koechlin was precisely the sort of well-informed *amateur* or *connoisseur* that Tyler was in the process of becoming.[23] A collector of Chinese, Japanese, Islamic, and medieval art, Koechlin also acquired works by the Impressionists and Post-Impressionists. He displayed his collection crowded together in a small apartment on the Boulevard Saint-Germain.[24] Although this *grand amateur* wrote a number of books about the arts he collected, he is best known for his studies of French Gothic sculpture (mainly ivories), Islamic ceramics, and Japanese art.[25]

At the end of his life, Koechlin wrote a memoir about French collectors of Asian art, titled *Souvenirs d'un vieil amateur d'art de l'Extrême-Orient* (fig. 2.6). The memoir and the pattern of Koechlin's broad interests suggest a larger context for Tyler's enthusiasm for French Gothic sculpture, Persian ceramics, and early Chinese art.[26] During the later nineteenth century, famine in Persia and the activities of dealers in Paris and London brought quantities of Persian ceramics and carpets to the West.[27] Not only connoisseurs but also the merely wealthy filled their houses with them.[28] For example, Koechlin began collecting Islamic art about 1890.[29] A decade later, he turned to what he called "ancient" Chinese art: objects that had appeared on the Parisian market after excavations for railroads in China cut through T'ang tombs.[30] Because of the efforts of dealers in Paris, early Chinese art supplanted the widely influential *Japonisme*;[31] Chinese painting, which had long been neglected, became the subject of several books between 1905 and 1912.[32]

Always aware of contemporary tastes, Royall Tyler wrote Mildred Bliss in January 1912: "I never have cared very much for Japanese art, and Chinese porcelain also leaves me cold. But Chinese painting of periods earlier than Ming (which begins you probably know when—I believe about the early XV) is tremendous stuff, and a lot of it has come through Paris lately."[33]

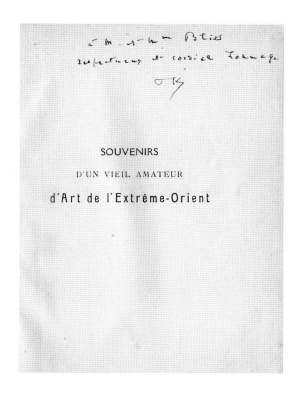

That spring, the Blisses arrived in Paris, and soon Royall Tyler was leading Robert Bliss to the shops of Parisian dealers. Their collecting followed the tastes of their guide and his dealers, and included Tyler's three early favorites, Gothic sculpture, Persian pottery, and early Chinese art. In 1912—the same year that Robert Bliss saw his Olmec figure—they bought a characteristically French Gothic statue of the Virgin and Child (fig. 2.7),[34] and later acquired a rather more impressive Madonna, "arguably the finest Riemenschneider in the United States" (fig. 2.8).[35]

The Persian ceramics (fig. 2.9) in the Bliss Collection are likely the consequence of their general availability and the strong interest of Tyler, Koechlin, and others, who lived in what has justly been called the "capital of the arts of Islam" at the turn of the century.[36] Tyler joined a number of luminaries, such as Roger Fry and Henri Matisse, who traveled to Munich to see the great Islamic exhibition of 1910.[37] Dumbarton Oaks retained some of the founders' Persian ceramics, but sold most of its Chinese and Persian objects to acquire Byzantine art and build endowment after the donation of the Bliss Collection to Harvard University in 1940. Thus, a sixth-century head of Buddha, acquired in 1925 (fig. 2.10), must stand for what was

deaccessioned. French collectors fully accepted Robert and Mildred Bliss and their Chinese and Islamic collection, as shown by Koechlin's description of an "American couple who felt at home amongst us and who we welcomed into our circle. They entrusted the Louvre with a portion of their treasures during the long absences from Paris a diplomatic career demanded. The Bliss's [*sic*] valuable holdings 'mingled' with our national collections, and they held pride of place in the Islamic and Chinese rooms where they were installed."[38]

The combination of early Chinese sculpture and Persian art, seen in the Bliss Collection, was popular elsewhere during the period. Bernard Berenson, for example, had been interested in Chinese art from 1910; in 1912, he wrote that he bought "only Chinese and Persian" objects, nothing Japanese. His enthusiasm for Asian art, however, was brief, and his purchases were confined to 1912–17.[39] Today, Berenson's collection of Chinese sculpture is one of the highlights of the collection displayed at his Villa I Tatti, which was also donated to Harvard University. Berenson's personal library, fortunately, is still intact and contains a copy of Koechlin's *Souvenirs*, with a personal dedication from the author, indicating that Berenson (like the Blisses) was a part of the French circle of learned, amateur collectors of Asian art.[40] Dumbarton Oaks and the Villa I Tatti share at least one other similarity: when I Tatti fellows adjourn for lunch in the private quarters, they pass by an elegant Egyptian cat not unlike the one that Mildred and Robert Bliss purchased in 1921 and is today in the collection of Dumbarton Oaks (fig. 2.11).[41]

Royall Tyler's decisive turn toward Byzantium came the year after the Blisses' arrival in Paris. On 11 March 1913, he wrote Mildred Bliss in a state of great excitement, having just bought an Early Byzantine silver chalice (fig. 2.12) that would remain important to him and his family for the rest of his life: "Dear Mildred, I can't wait any longer to tell you that the chalice is

here. I waited, sweating great drops of blood, in Brummer's back shop yesterday afternoon, while Stoclet made him an offer for the Egyptian relief, the chalice, and most of the other good things in the shop."[42] When Joseph Brummer (1883–1947) rejected the offer from the far wealthier Adolph Stoclet (1871–1949), the patron of Josef Hoffmann and Gustav Klimt, Tyler immediately bought the chalice. Tyler wrote that, five minutes after Stoclet left the shop, he had his chalice and was running home, dodging the cars in the street "with la santissima under my arm. I have got to find 6,500 francs now, and selling in a hurry is a bore—however, the joy of having the thing leaves no room for care—I don't care what I sell. . . . Not a word to a soul except Robert."[43]

Tyler's enthusiasm for "Byzantine things" (as he described them in a 1905 letter to Mildred Bliss)[44] may have begun as early as a family trip to Venice in 1900,[45] but probably had a more immediate stimulus in his visit to Venice and Ravenna in 1912 with the British art historian Eric Maclagan (1879–1951).[46] Then a medievalist in the Department of Architecture and Sculpture at the Victoria and Albert Museum in London, Maclagan would become its director in 1924. During World War I, Maclagan served in Paris, and (like Tyler) participated in the negotiations for the peace treaty. Tyler introduced Maclagan to the Blisses in January 1913, and vouched for his aesthetic judgments and hence utility to them.[47] Joining this set of connoisseurs of Byzantine

FIG. 2.10.

Head of a Pratyeka Buddha, Chinese, ca. 581–617, stone.

House Collection, HC.S.1925.005.(S), Dumbarton Oaks Research Library and Collection.

FIG. 2.11.

Cat, Egyptian, ca. 944–525 BCE, bronze.

House Collection, HC.S.1921.001.(B), Dumbarton Oaks Research Library and Collection.

FIG. 2.12.

Silver Chalice from Riha (or Kaper Koraon), Early Byzantine, ca. 527–65, silver with gold and niello.

Byzantine Collection, BZ.1955.18, Dumbarton Oaks Research Library and Collection.

art in Paris during the teens were the older British aesthete Matthew Prichard (1865–1936), who supplied the philosophical aesthetics that these collectors absorbed,[48] and the U.S. Army Captain Hayford Peirce (1883–1946), who joined Major Tyler's intelligence unit in 1918. Peirce also caught the Byzantine microbe and began to collect Byzantine art, especially coins. After the war, he and Tyler collaborated on books about Byzantine art.[49]

Given the Byzantine expertise available to the Blisses, one might have thought that their first purchase in this general area might have gone better. In the same year that Tyler bought his chalice—which was arguably one of the finest pieces of sixth-century silver then known—the

Blisses acquired a silver bowl (fig. 2.13) that was initially thought to be Post-Sassanian and was exhibited as such in London in 1931.[50] Today, it is considered rather more Post-Sassanian than the Blisses would have wanted. In the catalogue of the Dumbarton Oaks Collection, Marvin Ross compares it to sixteenth-century silver from the Adriatic port of Ragusa.[51]

Although World War I brought these students of Byzantine art together in Paris, it did not provide the necessary leisure to visit dealers and pursue scholarship. Thus, the consequences of these lessons and liaisons would not be seen until later. At the end of the war, Maclagan, Tyler, and Robert Bliss stayed to work on the peace negotiations, but at the end of 1919, Bliss returned to

FIG. 2.13.
Silver Bowl with Central Boss, Dalmatian (?), 16th century (?), silver.

Byzantine Collection, BZ.1913.3, Dumbarton Oaks Research Library and Collection.

the United States and in April became the chief of the Division of Western European Affairs at the State Department in Washington, D.C. The Blisses kept their apartment in Paris, and Mildred returned to the city she loved in the summer of 1920.[52] At the same time, they began negotiations to buy Dumbarton Oaks, completing the purchase that fall, and beginning the renovations that James Carder describes in this volume. Meanwhile, Robert's career advanced. In 1921, he was promoted to third assistant secretary of state, and while they lived in Washington, D.C., Mildred returned often to Paris, so that correspondence with Royall Tyler is limited in these years.

In 1921, the Blisses made their first significant Byzantine acquisition: several pieces of an eleventh-century silver cross with figural decoration.[53] Although fragmentary, this is a first-class object that compares well with the beautiful processional crosses that were so well displayed at the Metropolitan Museum of Art's 1997 exhibition The Glory of Byzantium.[54] Tyler's role is to be suspected, but there are no letters about the cross, perhaps because he had discussed it with Mildred Bliss when she was in Paris. In 1923, Robert Bliss was appointed U.S. minister to Sweden; the appointment was a fortunate turn for his career and also for the history of the Byzantine Collection, as his distance from Tyler generated many letters about Byzantine objects.

In 1924, Robert and Mildred bought the famous Riha paten (see fig. 1.13). Tyler could not have been more enthusiastic, writing: "It is unquestionably right . . . [and] to me is perhaps the most moving thing—possibly excepting my chalice—I've ever seen for sale. . . . If you do get it, live with it for a good long time anyway. It will teach you a great deal about the age when Santa Sophia and the great churches of Ravenna were built, when the most perfect Byzantine enamels were made and the throne of Maximian was carved."[55] Tyler advised the Blisses that some day they should donate their paten to "the Cabinet des Médailles [in Paris], the only place in the world I know of that's fit to receive it. . . . [It is] the one museum that has an atmosphere in which works of art live, grow sleek and glossy and are patently as happy as they would be in any well-appointed private house."[56] He told the Blisses that he planned to give his chalice to the Cabinet des Médailles. In a telling remark that underscores the human-like quality of this chalice and its ability to serve as a substitute for himself, Royall Tyler concluded in the same letter with the wish that it "would be a happiness for life to think that the two pieces would one day be joined together and live happily ever after."

Here and throughout his correspondence, Tyler responded viscerally and passionately to works of art. Though American by birth, he had acquired the traits of what the French knew as the amateur, a learned but non-professional art expert. In a small book of 1939, Georges Salles (1889–1966), the French curator and museum director, wrote about amateurs and represented Raymond Koechlin as a typical example of the distinguished genre. After the book appeared, Walter Benjamin reviewed Salles's book, praising this "enchanting work" for the "beauty" of "its happy formulations" expressed in Proustian language.[57] Salles himself was an example of the amateur that he described. Some were collectors; others were curators. A few like Royall Tyler were both, for in a sense he was the informal and thus amateur curator of the Blisses' Byzantine Collection in its formative years.

In the end, the Blisses did not give their art to the Cabinet des Médailles, but instead created a similar institution: Dumbarton Oaks. As Robert Bliss remarked at its inauguration as a Harvard institution on 2 November 1940: "During the years of professional nomadism, Mrs. Bliss and I dreamed of having a home of our own—a country home near a city. A kindly star led us to Dumbarton Oaks. The dream grew. We should find a way to make the old house and noble trees productive of beauty and enlightenment. And,

gradually from our old enjoyment of mediaeval art, a strong sense of the value of continuity, the conception of a small and modest, but specialized, cabinet des médailles took form; a research collection to illustrate the books—a library to interpret the objects."[58] His enthusiasm for a collection of small, exquisite objects, modeled on the Parisian institution, must have been inspired by the Tylers, who were recorded as visitors to the Cabinet des Médailles during the 1920s. The Blisses, in contrast, do not appear in the institution's registers for that decade.[59]

In September 1924, Tyler wrote that he had been asked to go to Hungary as deputy commissioner general for the League of Nations.[60] His wife, Elisina, stayed behind in Paris, and—having also caught the collecting microbe—she too visited art dealers, now on behalf of her husband and the Blisses. Hayford Peirce was often in Paris, and, at the end of October 1926, he accompanied her on a visit to the dealer Kalebdjian Frères. After seeing photographs of a treasure of Byzantine silver found in Syria, Elisina Tyler wrote to the Blisses: "I considered these objects so beautiful and interesting, that I told him to send the photographs for you. . . . You see the likeness to our two objects [the Riha chalice and paten], don't you."[61] Mildred Bliss responded from Stockholm the next month: "First I must tell you that the Kalebdjian photographs are most upsetting. Bless you for having them sent. The likeness to your and our 'family' features is so close that we must surely wander up this alluring trail in the hope of increasing the family!"[62]

Royall, Elisina, and their son William Royall Tyler travelled to Cairo with Hayford Peirce to look carefully at the silver hoard, but were ultimately disappointed.[63] Peirce and Tyler thought that the silver had been overcleaned to make it more attractive to buyers and advised against the purchase. The hoard was bought by Henry Walters, and today resides in the Walters Art Museum in Baltimore.[64]

Meanwhile, Robert Bliss was transferred from Sweden to Argentina, where he served as U.S. ambassador from 1927 to 1933. Tyler's letters and their growing collection barely compensated for the difficult situation of being so far from the Parisian dealers.[65] From 1928 to 1932, Royall Tyler worked in Paris as the representative for Hambros Bank, London, and was thus again well positioned to help the Blisses.[66] And it was during the 1920s that his self-taught knowledge of Byzantine art became public. He published the

well-regarded *Byzantine Art* with Hayford Peirce in 1926; two years later, they were busy working on an article on the same subject commissioned by the *Encyclopedia Britannica*.[67]

In fall 1929, two French curators—the afore-mentioned Georges Salles and the Islamic art specialist Eustache de Lorey—approached Royall Tyler to collaborate on what was to be the first international exhibition of Byzantine art.[68] Held at the Musée des Arts Décoratifs in Paris, the exhibition was a critical and a popular suc-cess. Tyler wrote a heavily illustrated overview of the show for the French art magazine *Cahiers d'Art*.[69] His circle lent more objects to the show than other private collectors: he and Hayford Peirce each contributed eighteen items, while the Blisses contributed fifteen mainly higher

quality works, including two recent acquisitions brokered by Tyler. Tyler described one item as a "ravishing Coptic necklace, gold and lapis-lazuli, with . . . a little gold Venus . . ." (fig. 2.14). Because he enjoyed the complete confidence of the Blisses, he wrote: "Cable me only if you <u>don't</u> want it, as otherwise I shall not let it escape. As a matter of fact, I have no doubt Hayford would jump at it if he had the chance," showing where his first loyalty lay.[70]

The Blisses' second major contribution to the exhibition was a large Egyptian textile of Hestia, the goddess of the hearth (fig. 2.15).[71] When it arrived in Paris, Tyler examined it with Salles and the other French collaborators and wrote the Blisses: "Their enthusiasm knows no bounds. [Paul] Alfassa, who was inclined to be doubtful

about our ability to get together a Byz. Exhibition of the first order, simply boiled over with delight, and proclaimed that it beat all the Gothic tapestries in the world into a cocked hat."[72] In reviewing the exhibition, Tyler predicted that visitors would be struck by the "stupefying display of Byzantine textiles," beginning with this grand piece with its "incredible burst" of color.[73]

Edith Wharton, an old friend of the Tylers and the Blisses, wrote Mildred Bliss: "You will have heard so much about the Byzantine Exhibition and its overwhelming success, that there is little left for me to tell you. Royall has received all the credit which he so richly deserves, for Metman and the other members of the Arts Décoratifs have outdone each other in saying that the whole thing was due to his initiative and his energy.

The objects were most beautifully arranged by Jacques Guérin, and your vitrine with the lovely jewels attracted a great deal of attention. The whole thing was really a triumph for every one concerned."[74] The Blisses were disappointed that their duties in Buenos Aires prevented them from seeing the exhibition in Paris. They also missed the increased market for high-quality Byzantine artifacts in its aftermath. Tyler wrote them about an early fourteenth-century miniature mosaic icon of the Forty Martyrs of Sebasteia, but they were unmoved, and Hayford Peirce eventually bought it (fig. 2.16).[75] The Blisses never showed much interest in icons or in Byzantine painting generally. Those icons that Dumbarton Oaks does possess were acquired after the collection passed to Harvard University.

In 1933, Robert Bliss retired from the State Department, and he and Mildred moved from the grand U.S. Embassy in Buenos Aires to their hardly humble home in Washington, D.C. Now they had time to devote themselves to their art collection. The period from 1933 to 1940 and the Harvard donation offered extraordinary opportunities for collectors of means. In 1930 and 1931, Royall Tyler wrote from Paris about the bank failures, the sale of the collections of bankrupt individuals, the dearth of objects at the auction houses, and the generally falling prices due to the "slump on Wall Street."[76] After 1929, the Blisses' income was reduced but still substantial. Yet Robert Bliss was cautious. He wrote Royall Tyler in 1934 that they wanted to save their funds for truly important objects that "may possibly appear in the market as the times grow worse throughout the world . . . though there is always the fear that as time goes on we may not have the wherewithal to purchase anything . . ."[77] By 1937, Robert was worried about new taxes and "possible legislation which may result at any time in necessary curtailment of industrial dividends."[78] Nonetheless, they kept their "powder for straight Byz.,"[79] as Royall Tyler advised, and did well in the changing art market.

Tyler wrote frequently about new material. He reported that some items in the 1932 exhibition of treasures from Mainz Cathedral were for sale,[80] and that Stalin was rumored to be selling Van Eycks—these rumors turned out to be correct, if slightly exaggerated.[81] Through intermediaries, the Russians sold an exquisite *Annunciation* by Jan Van Eyck to Andrew Mellon, along with other masterpieces that are currently in the National Gallery of Art in Washington, D.C.[82] A January 1935 letter speculated about other treasures that might be "loosed" and included a list of illuminated Byzantine manuscripts that they should try to buy from Russia.[83]

Tyler's letters about what had been the "comparatively inaccessible" Trivulzio Collection in Milan offered greater promise.[84] Most of these treasures were bought by the city of Milan in 1935,[85] but individual items had previously come on the market, including a consular diptych that Tyler first saw at a dealer in August 1934. On 5 September 1934, he wrote Mildred Bliss about its "most lovely patina and . . . style."[86] Twenty days later, the Blisses agreed on the aesthetic merits of the diptych, but decided against the purchase—a wise move financially. By May 1935, the diptych had dropped in price from 300,000

to 125,000 francs, but Robert Bliss, who had a deserved reputation for driving a hard bargain, did not commit to the purchase immediately. He took an option on the diptych, pending the receipt of photographs, and bought it by August.[87] Thus, long distances could be an advantage as well as a disadvantage.

Since 1932, Royall Tyler had served as a financial advisor to Hungary for the League of Nations, and he therefore was spending less time visiting Parisian dealers. But they, of course, knew how to tempt the Blisses, who made purchases on their own. Some were not to Tyler's liking, as he wrote in a stern letter of September 1937:

> Precious Mildred, I'm apalled [*sic*] by your list of things to be acquired. [I am] a bit reassured when you told me you don't want to scatter too much, and that Byz[antium] remains the main thing. But I do beg you to consider that if you go in for all you mention in that list you'll be in grave danger of scattering, and of getting a lot of things of no relevancy to your central subject—and perhaps even not of first quality. I'll confess to you that I don't care much for the ivory part of the Melk reliquary (I admit the top is attractive). I'd be very chary of getting Germanic stuff. It's very costly, and often very poor, in my opinion.[88]

He was referring to an eleventh-century German reliquary with plaques of walrus ivory.[89] It came from the abbey of Melk, which perches so grandly above the Danube River in Austria. Because of inflation and the loss of assets during the interwar years, the abbey was forced to sell some of its great treasures, including a Gutenberg Bible now at Yale University.[90] Nonetheless, Tyler firmly opposed the acquisition of the German reliquary—admittedly, its walrus carvings do appear less finely wrought than the subtle surface detailing of tenth-century Byzantine ivories. He continued: "We'll see what Fiedler says about the Dresden-Hannover diptych. . . . And, who knows—Limburg might be pried loose. That would be a haul."

These last items in Dresden, Hannover, and Limburg an der Lahn are tantalizing and surprising. Tyler was referring to an exchange about German acquisitions that began in March 1937. He had written excitedly to the Blisses about the possibility of acquiring what is perhaps the greatest of all Byzantine enamels: the Limburg True Cross Reliquary.[91] After all, if other German and Austrian churches and abbeys were selling their treasures, why not this cathedral also? While the Limburg reliquary would remain only a dream, the tenth-century diptych, divided between Dresden and Hannover, was another matter.[92] In the same letter, Tyler sent a list of the four most desirable Byzantine objects to be acquired from Germany. At the top was the diptych, which featured four scenes from the life of Christ from the Crucifixion to the Resurrection. To obtain the diptych and the other objects, he would work with their "Roman friend," their code name for Wolfgang Fritz Volbach (1892–1988), a German medievalist trained primarily in Berlin by Adolph Goldschmidt, then the leading connoisseur of ivories. Volbach had to leave his post at the Berlin Museum because of the Nazi racial laws—his mother was of Jewish descent. He moved to Rome, and became associated with the Vatican Museum in 1934.[93] Tyler had known him since at least 1931, when he visited the Paris exhibition, and Volbach had coauthored a book about Byzantine art in 1933 with George Salles and Georges Duthuit, who had worked on the exhibition with Royall Tyler.[94]

Despite Volbach's exile in Italy, he maintained contacts with former colleagues in Germany, as Tyler indicated in the same letter of 1 March 1937: "The Roman friend's plan of campaign, which I think is probably a good one, would be for him to send his wife on the errand. She is on good personal terms with Prince Philip of Hesse, Göring's Aide-de-Camp, who is a former art dealer himself. I do not know her personally, but he tells me that she is thoroughly-versed in all these questions." Philipp von Hessen (1896–1980) was indeed close to Göring, at least until 1943 when Hitler had Philipp arrested. Thereafter he spent the rest of the war in concentration camps. Philipp studied art history at Darmstadt between 1920 and 1922 without receiving a degree and worked briefly at the Kaiser Friedrich Museum in Berlin. In 1925, he married a daughter of the king of Italy and settled in a villa in Rome.[95] There he became Hitler's personal emissary to King Vittorio Emanuele III, his father-in-law, and to Mussolini, dealt with Pope Pius XII, and helped arranged Hitler's Italian visit in 1938.[96] More importantly for the present purposes, Prince Philipp acquired art for one of Hitler's favorite projects, the Führermuseum in Linz. Thus, he enjoyed excellent connections among high Nazi officials as well as the museum establishment.[97] It is reasonable to imagine, therefore, that Volbach, a Vatican curator, would have had contacts with the prince.[98]

In the same letter of 1 March, Tyler wrote the Blisses that the "Roman friend" had sent them "photographs of three sculptures belonging to Prince Leopold of Prussia." The subjects were an emperor, an angel, and the Virgin Mary. He continued: "The owner is at present living in Switzerland, but our friend thinks he could arrange to get three objects, which are still in Potsdam, out of Germany."[99] On 6 April, Tyler reported that "Our friend V[olbach] has just been to Switzerland, where he has seen one Fiedler, whom he thinks able to deliver the goods."[100] The person mentioned was Hermann Fiedler, not otherwise identified to date. Volbach quoted prices for the stone reliefs of the emperor and the Virgin Mary (presently at Dumbarton Oaks)[101] and for the aforementioned ivory diptych in Dresden and Hannover. Among the difficulties to be solved was the decided inconvenience that the relief medallion of the emperor was immured in the wall of a princely villa in Berlin, but we know from other sources that Prince Leopold had asked to have a plaster copy made of this object, then substituted the copy and smuggled the original to Switzerland.[102] The stone relief of the Virgin Mary, Tyler reported, was in the Kaiser Friedrich Museum, "but the family thinks they can get it out."[103] The Blisses would buy both.

The Dresden-Hannover diptych was more difficult to acquire. Tyler wrote that the Hannover diptych leaf, "alas, belongs not to the Museum, but to the city of Lüneburg, which won't hear of selling." The Dresden authorities, however, were willing to negotiate and offered as well a stunning ivory of Saint Paul and John the Evangelist.[104] Ultimately, these negotiations did not succeed, but Tyler nonetheless ended the remarkable year of 1937 by writing to the Blisses about the rumored sale of a great enameled reliquary in Esztergom.[105] He and Peirce had published it in their book of 1926.[106] Because a work of such significance might become available, he stressed once more the importance of saving their funds for major purchases—not minor works like the Melk reliquary, which had so angered him a few months earlier. These were indeed exciting times.

In addition to the reliefs of the Virgin Mary and the emperor, the Blisses also purchased the aforementioned ivory of the Incredulity of Thomas (fig. 2.4) in 1937.[107] It came from the Germanisches Museum in Nuremberg via an established dealer. The Blisses also acquired a tenth-century diptych wing with the portrait of an emperor at the center of a cross from a private collection in Lucca, Italy.[108] Its mate in Gotha, Germany, was well known,[109] and immediately Tyler began working with Fiedler and Volbach to purchase it as well. When Tyler met with Fiedler in September 1937, Fiedler was optimistic about getting the Gotha and Dresden ivories, and Tyler concluded the same after he saw Fiedler the next summer.[110]

As war approached, the correspondence about art objects dwindled. Tyler had other problems. In February 1938, he wrote that his job in Hungary was ending and that he had only the prospect of a temporary job at reduced salary with the League of Nations. He must have been desperate, because he broached selling his beloved chalice to the Blisses:

> You asked me some time ago about our Riha chalice, & said you would like to know if we ever wanted to part with it.
>
> Well—I think we must consider doing so now. . . . The very heavy charges we have had in connexion with the settlement of Edith [Wharton]'s estate . . . have created an awkward problem, just at a time when it is particularly awkward. If things had so shaped as to allow it, what we should have liked best would have been to bequeathe [*sic*] the chalice to the Oaks. We have always wanted it to come to rest beside the paten. But things have turned out differently.
>
> It would be very hard for me to put a price on the chalice. If you want it, would you tell me what you are prepared to give for it?[111]

Robert Bliss was interested, of course, because it was the mate for their paten, but in the end, the matter was dropped.

On 18 May 1940, Tyler wrote Mildred Bliss that Fiedler died a couple of weeks earlier. "All of our questions of course in suspense, for the time being."[112] And they would forever remain in suspense, for Germany had invaded France eight days earlier. Tyler had a passage to the States booked for 1 June 1940, but on 17 May, he cabled the Blisses from Geneva that he had to "abandon journey indefinitely terribly distressed but no choice, Love Tyler."[113] Tyler tried to remain involved with the Blisses' acquisitions, but matters were different after the collection was transferred to Harvard University. Back in the States for a few months in 1941, he saw an exhibition of Coptic art at the Brooklyn Museum and a relief of the Sacrifice of Isaac that he subsequently

recommended to the Dumbarton Oaks acquisition board (fig. 2.17).[114] When they turned him down, he appealed to Mildred Bliss. At her urging, the director approached the Islamic art expert Richard Ettinghausen of the Freer Gallery of Art, and after he vouched for the panel, Dumbarton Oaks acquired it.[115]

During the war, Tyler stayed in Geneva, while his wife took care of their château in Burgundy, thereby saving it and all their possessions—including their art collection and library—from being looted.[116] They seldom saw each other. Officially, Tyler worked for the League of Nations, but his extensive network of contacts in Eastern Europe and France proved helpful for other matters. Under the code name Anderson or source 477, Tyler supplied intelligence to Allen Dulles and the American Office of Strategic Services in Bern.[117] Dulles, who later became the longtime head of the Central Intelligence Agency, coordinated American intelligence activities in Switzerland during World War II. He reported to his superiors that Tyler had "extraordinary personal influence" and, "more than any other American, enjoys the confidence of the Hungarians."[118]

After Dulles returned to the United States at the conclusion of the war, he wrote Tyler, remembering their time together:

> I miss Switzerland and look back on those exciting days when we worked together as certainly among the most interesting that I have had or probably will have. I don't feel that I was ever able to fully express to you what a joy and a comfort it was to have your constant advice and help. I have told many here of the outstanding contributions you made. I feel that whatever success I may have had is in a very major degree due to your constant help.
>
> Bob Bliss was in the other day and you were the first topic of conversation . . .[119]

In his own way, Royall Tyler had been working in intelligence for years, but now it was in the service of his country—not the Blisses' collection of Byzantine art. In both cases, he took no compensation for his efforts.

After the war, Tyler's employment was not secure, and he sought Dulles's help in finding another position. Eventually he managed to secure a job with the World Bank in Paris, where he continued to work in what long since had become his profession, international finance. At the same time, he looked forward to resuming his old art historical activities on the side. But

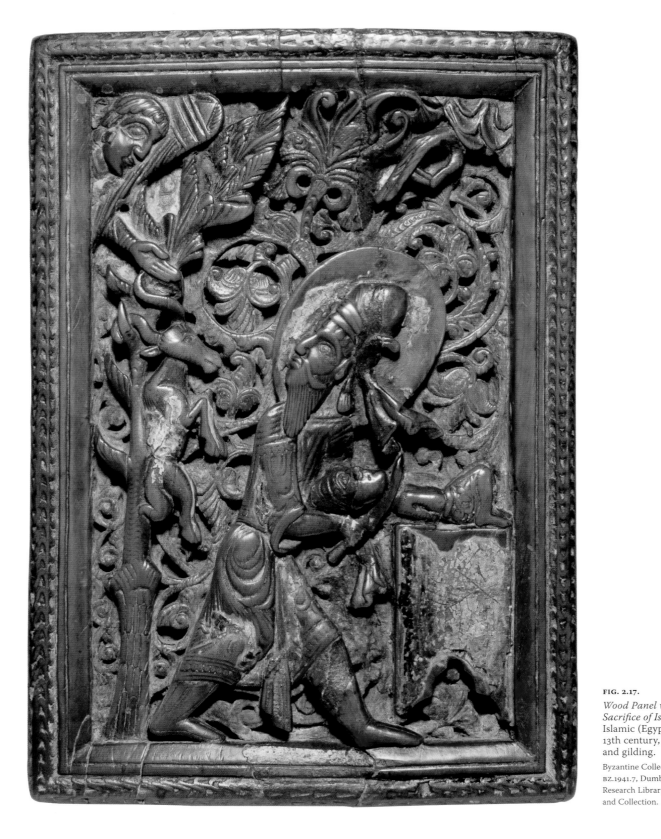

times had changed. Dumbarton Oaks was now a fully professionalized institution with its own academically trained faculty and advisors. The era of the amateur—who specialized in the arts, cultures, and histories of many countries, and who loved art with visceral passion—was ending. The death of Hayford Peirce in 1946 was "a great blow" to Tyler,[120] and he chose not to continue to produce *L'art byzantin,* their history of Byzantine art. The series had been a source of disappointment since the 1930s. Volume three (of a projected five) had been finished in 1936 but was never published.[121] After considerable delay, publication was anticipated for the summer of 1940,[122] hardly a propitious time to bring out a large-format, expensive art book in France.

The 1950s brought other closures. One year after Peirce's death, his widow, Polly, at Tyler's urging, gave Dumbarton Oaks in her husband's memory the miniature mosaic that the Blisses had once rejected (fig. 2.16).[123] In 1948, Dumbarton Oaks purchased Peirce's large collection of Byzantine coins, something that Tyler had contemplated as early as 1937, when he wrote to Mildred Bliss: "I've never breathed a word to him, but I've often thought we might make an effort to secure [the coins] for the Oaks. It's a grand collection, with many *unica* in it, and hardly any important gaps."[124] Before his death in 1953, Tyler turned to other writing projects, including the thirteenth volume of the Spanish State Papers and a related study of the Emperor Charles the Fifth, which were published posthumously.[125] As an act of filial piety, his son struggled to find a publisher for the book after several rejections.[126] One problem, according to reviewers, was that the text was not well polished or edited.[127] Evidently unfinished, the book was not up to the standards of Royall Tyler, who valued form as well as content in all aspects of a life lived well and with style.

Arthur Salter—a friend, colleague at the League of Nations, Oxford professor, and member of Parliament—lamented Tyler's death and described him thus: "There was a curious affinity between Peter Tyler's [his nickname to his friends] unequalled subtlety of appreciation of a good wine or a good food—and of a work of art. In an exclusive French restaurant where all who served and all who supped did so with the devoutness of participants in a religious service, all looked to Peter Tyler as one of special authority. So too if his judgment were asked as to the dating of a picture he would seem to sniff at it just as he might have done at a wine of quality—and his verdict would be accepted as final by those professionally engaged in such identifications."[128]

Such were the characteristics of the amateur. Three decades earlier, Georges Salles had similarly equated the conviction of an amateur's eye with a gourmand's sense of taste, for both shared a common sensibility, refinement, and "the same shock of an impression" that might confuse others but instantly struck them with clarity and conviction.[129]

Tyler was aware of this reputation, as suggested by his 1946 letter to Allen: "I can't help smiling at the thought that, when you received from me a letter . . . [all] you found in it was a breathless paean about those little winter trout from the Lake of Zug. Shall I ever be able to re-establish a reputation for valuing anything above the joys of the table? I'm frequently told by the initiated that eating is the only thing I really care for. See how unjust the world can be, and appearances, how misleading."[130] Those qualities that he feared would be adversely judged were much admired by his friends, as the social activist Violet Markham acknowledged in the obituary she wrote for *The Times*: "A fluent linguist with a knowledge of half a dozen tongues, art critic, scholar, historian, archaeologist, a connoisseur of food—to be ranked in his mind with other works of merit—Royall Tyler, witty and charming, carried a great weight of learning as lightly as though it were thistle-down. . . . At his beautiful home in Burgundy, Peter and his brilliant wife . . . would gather round them a circle of friends for whom the hours were golden as we listened to the incomparable conversation of our host."[131]

Such was the devoted friend of the Blisses and the collection and institution they created. That relationship survived his death. In 1955, Elisina and William Royall Tyler presented his beloved chalice to Dumbarton Oaks, and thus it ultimately did join the Blisses' paten, as he had put it in 1924, in "an atmosphere in which works of art live, grow sleek and glossy and are patently as happy as they would be in any well-appointed private house . . ."[132]

Notes

1   I explored the relationship between the Tylers and the Blisses in an earlier paper, "Private Passions Made Public: The Beginnings of the Bliss Collection," in *Sacred Art, Secular Context: Objects of Art from the Byzantine Collection of Dumbarton Oaks, Washington, D.C., Accompanied by American Paintings from the Collection of Mildred and Robert Woods Bliss*, ed. Asen Kirin, 38–51 (Athens, Ga., 2005). James Carder and I are also preparing an edition of the Bliss-Tyler correspondence that is the basis of this and my previous article.

2   Royall Tyler, *Spain: A Study of her Life and Arts* (New York, 1909).

3   Royall Tyler, *The League of Nations Reconstruction Schemes in the Inter-War Period* (Geneva, 1945).

4   *Calendar of Letters, Despatches, and State Papers, Relating to the Negotiations between England and Spain, Preserved in the Archives at Simancas, Vienna, Brussels, and Elsewhere* (London, 1904–54). Tyler took over the editing of volume nine (1547–49; London, 1912) at the death of his predecessor, Martin Andrew Sharp Hume, and was solely responsible for volumes ten (1550–52; London, 1914) and eleven (1553; London, 1916). Four decades later, he edited volumes twelve (January–July 1554; London, 1949) and thirteen (July 1554–November 1558; London, 1954), the last posthumously.

5   Hayford Peirce and Royall Tyler, *Byzantine Art* (London, 1926) and *L'art byzantin*, 2 vols. (Paris, 1932–34).

6   *Exposition internationale d'art byzantin: 28 mai–9 juillet 1931, Musée des Arts Décoratifs, Palais du Louvre, Pavillon de Marsan* (Paris, 1931).

7   Royall Tyler, *The Emperor Charles the Fifth* (Fairlawn, N.J., 1956).

8   Royall Tyler to Mildred Barnes, 8 November and 5 December 1903, 5, 17, and 26 January 1904, and 18 February 1904, Papers of Royall Tyler, 1902–1967, HUGFP 38.1, box 1, HUA.

9   When the text was written is not known, but it breaks off about 1914. I thank James Carder for alerting me to this source.

10   Royall Tyler to Mildred Barnes, 12 January 1906, Papers of Royall Tyler, HUGFP 38.6, HUA.

11   See note 4.

12   S. K. Lothrop, *Robert Woods Bliss Collection: Pre-Columbian Art* (London, 1957), 7; and Walter Muir Whitehill, *Dumbarton Oaks: The History of a Georgetown House and Garden, 1800–1966* (Cambridge, Mass., 1967), 7. According to Miriam Doutriaux, exhibition associate in the Pre-Columbian Collection, while Robert Bliss

remembered seeing the Olmec figure in 1912, he only purchased it in 1914.

13   Nelson, "Private Passions Made Public," 47.

14   Gary Vikan, *Catalogue of the Sculpture in the Dumbarton Oaks Collection from the Ptolemaic Period to the Renaissance* (Washington, D.C., 1995), 79–82; and Kurt Weitzmann, *Catalogue of the Byzantine and Early Medieval Antiquities in the Dumbarton Oaks Collection*, vol. 3, *Ivories and Steatites* (Washington, D.C., 1972), 43–48.

15   Marvin C. Ross, *Catalogue of the Byzantine and Early Medieval Antiquities in the Dumbarton Oaks Collection*, vol. 2, *Jewelry, Enamels, and the Art of the Migration Period*, 2nd ed. (Washington, D.C., 2005), 126–28.

16   Address by Robert Woods Bliss to the Harvard Club of Washington, D.C., 8 April 1943, Papers of Robert Woods Bliss and Mildred Barnes Bliss, ca. 1860–1969, HUGFP 76.16, series 4, box 2, HUA.

17   Royall Tyler to Mildred Barnes Bliss, 26 June 1911, HUA.

18   Royall Tyler to Mildred Barnes Bliss, 22 January 1912, HUA.

19   Tyler autobiographical manuscript, section IV, Walter Muir Whitehill papers, N-2177, carton no. 70, Massachusetts Historical Society.

20   Elizabeth P. Benson, "The Robert Woods Bliss Collection of Pre-Columbian Art: A Memoir," in *Collecting the Pre-Columbian Past: A Symposium at Dumbarton Oaks*, ed. Elizabeth H. Boone (Washington, D.C., 1993), 23–24.

21   Edith Wharton, *A Backward Glance: An Autobiography* (New York, 1934), 348.

22   Tyler wrote that Koechlin had stayed with them at their Antigny home for a week. Royall Tyler to Mildred Barnes Bliss, 28 September 1926, HUA.

23   Another is Henri Vever (1854–1942), a jeweler by trade and a major collector of Islamic art. Glenn D. Lowry and Susan Nemazee, *A Jeweler's Eye: Islamic Arts of the Book from the Vever Collection* (Washington, D.C., 1988). In 1909, Tyler wrote enthusiastically about what he called the "modern amateur" in "Essays on Masterpieces, I," *The Englishwoman* 1, no. 1 (1909): 72–78.

24   Georges Salles, *Le Regard: La collection, le musée, la fouille, une journée, l'école*, 2nd ed. (Paris, 1992), 17; and Marcel Guérin, "Raymond Koechlin et sa collection," *Bulletin des Musées de France* 4 (1932): 66–88. See also Paul Alfassa, *Raymond Koechlin (1860–1931), notice lue à l'assemblée generale annuelle de la Société des Amis du Louvre, le 30 Avril 1932* (Paris, 1932).

25 Michele Tomasi, "L'objet pour passion: Remarques sur la démarche intellectuelle de Raymond Koechlin (1860–1931), historien de l'art," *Histoire de l'art* 58 (2006): 133–44.

26 Raymond Koechlin, *Souvenirs d'un vieil amateur d'art de l'Extrême-Orient* (Chalon-sur-Saône, 1930), 73–117. Koechlin's little book was privately printed in an edition of 220 copies and "non mis dans le commerce," which explains why relatively few American libraries have a copy. Neither of the two in which I regularly work, Yale University and the University of Chicago, own the title. Upon requesting it through interlibrary loan, I was sent a copy from the University of Maryland, which, it so happens by the serendipity of scholarship, was dedicated to "M. et Mme Bliss" by the author. Some or all of the Bliss library passed to Harvard University with the donation of Dumbarton Oaks, but over the years, books from that collection were regrettably sold off, and the University of Maryland was the fortunate beneficiary.

27 Stephen Vernoit, "Islamic Art and Architecture: An Overview of Scholarship and Collecting, c. 1850–c. 1950," in *Discovering Islamic Art: Scholars, Collectors and Collections 1850–1950,* ed. Stephen Vernoit (New York, 2000), 12–13.

28 Cf. the Persian carpets and ceramics in the collection of Emily Crane Chadbourne, an American living in Paris and London before World War I. Robert S. Nelson, "The Art Collecting of Emily Crane Chadbourne and the Absence of Byzantine Art in Chicago," in *To Inspire and Instruct: A History of Medieval Art in Midwestern Museums,* ed. Christina M. Nielsen (Newcastle, UK, 2008), 136–37.

29 Max Put, *Plunder and Pleasure: Japanese Art in the West, 1860–1930* (Leiden, 2000), 39.

30 Jan Fontein and Tung Wu, *Unearthing China's Past* (Boston, 1973), 16.

31 Put, *Plunder and Pleasure,* 16 and 97–101.

32 Michael Sullivan, *Symbols of Eternity: The Art of Landscape Painting in China* (Stanford, Calif., 1979), 5.

33 Royall Tyler to Mildred Barnes Bliss, 22 January 1912, HUA.

34 Vikan, *Catalogue of the Sculpture in the Dumbarton Oaks Collection,* 123–26.

35 Ibid., 133–35.

36 Rémi Labrusse, "Paris, capitale des arts de l'Islam? Quelques aperçus sur la formation des collections françaises d'art islamique au tournant du siècle," *Bulletin de la Société de l'histoire de l'art français* (1997–98): 275–311.

37 Royall Tyler to Mildred Barnes Bliss, 26 August 1910, HUA. On Matisse in Munich, see Alfred H. Barr Jr., *Matisse: His Art and His Public* (New York, 1951), 109; and Rémi Labrusse, *Matisse: La condition de l'image* (Paris, 1999), 68. Roger Fry reviewed the exhibition in "The Munich Exhibition of Mohammedan Art," pts. 1 and 2, *The Burlington Magazine for Connoisseurs* 17, no. 89 (August 1910): 283–90; 17, no. 90 (September 1910): 327–33. The review was republished in *Vision and Design,* ed. J. B. Bullen (New York, 1981), 81–91.

38 Put, *Plunder and Pleasure,* 102–3.

39 Laurance P. Roberts, *The Bernard Berenson Collection of Oriental Art at Villa I Tatti* (New York, 1991), 7.

40 I thank Joseph Connors for checking the dedication of Berenson's copy.

41 Gudrun Bühl, ed., *Dumbarton Oaks: The Collections* (Washington, D.C., 2008), 292–93. According to Joseph Connors and Giovanni Pagliarulo of Villa I Tatti, it is not known when or where Berenson purchased his cat. I am grateful for their checking.

42 Royall Tyler to Mildred Barnes Bliss, 11 March 1913, HUA.

43 Royall Tyler to Mildred Barnes Bliss, 11 March 1913, HUA.

44 Royall Tyler to Mildred Barnes, 3 June 1905, HUA.

45 Tyler autobiographical manuscript, section II, Walter Muir Whitehill papers, N-2177, carton no. 70, Massachusetts Historical Society.

46 Elisina Tyler to Mildred Barnes Bliss, 2 October 1912, HUA. On Maclagan, see Trenchard Cox, "Maclagan, Sir Eric Robert Dalrymple (1879–1951)," rev. Anne Pimlott Baker, in *Oxford Dictionary of National Biography*, eds. H. C. G. Matthew and Brian Harrison (Oxford, 2004), http://www.oxforddnb.com/view/article/34772 (accessed 1 September 2008).

47 Royall Tyler to Robert Woods Bliss, 4 January 1913, HUA.

48 Robert S. Nelson, *Hagia Sophia, 1850–1950: Holy Wisdom Modern Monument* (Chicago, 2004), 159–64. Prichard was important to this group only before World War I, because he spent the war as a German prisoner of war. His relationship with T. S. Eliot has lately been discussed by James E. Miller Jr., *T. S. Eliot: The Making of an American Poet, 1888–1922* (University Park, Pa., 2005), 135–39.

49 To date, little is known about Peirce. Obituaries are in the *New York Times*, 5 March 1946, and *American Journal of Archaeology* 50 (1946): 293. He came from a wealthy family and left an estate of $1.9 million. *New York Times*, 5 September 1946.

50 *Catalogue of the International Exhibition of Persian Art*, 2nd ed. (London, 1931), 48.

51 Marvin C. Ross, *Catalogue of the Byzantine and Early Medieval Antiquities in the Dumbarton Oaks Collection*, vol. 1, *Metalwork, Ceramics, Glass, Glyptics, Painting* (Washington, D.C., 1962), 29–30. According to Marta Zlotnick, registrar and curatorial assistant, Byzantine Collection (e-mail of 7 September 2004), the invoice from Claude Anet for the silver bowl is dated 22 July 1913.

52 Susan Tamulevich, *Dumbarton Oaks: Garden into Art* (New York, 2001), 35.

53 Byzantine Collection, BZ.1921.8. Ross, *Catalogue of the Byzantine and Early Medieval Antiquities*, 1:26–27.

54 Helen C. Evans and William D. Wixom, eds., *The Glory of Byzantium: Art and Culture of the Middle Byzantine Era, A.D. 843–1261* (New York, 1997), 55–67.

55 Royall Tyler to Mildred Barnes Bliss, 26 January 1924, HUA. Few today would agree that the "most perfect Byzantine enamels" are from the sixth century. On the paten (BZ.1924.5), see Bühl, *Dumbarton Oaks*, 78–79.

56 Royall Tyler to Mildred Barnes Bliss, 26 January 1924, HUA.

57 Salles, *Le Regard*, 11–28. Walter Benjamin saw similarities in the book to the argument of his famous essay, "The Work of Art in the Age of Mechanical Reproduction," in *Illuminations*, trans. Harry Zohn (New York, 1968), 217–51. See also "Walter Benjamin: 1940 Survey of French Literature," *New Left Review* 51 (2008): 42–44. I thank Martha Ward for first directing me to Salles's book.

58 2 November 1940, Papers of Robert Woods Bliss and Mildred Barnes Bliss, HUGFP 76.16, series 4, box 2, HUA.

59 "Registres contenant la liste des personnes auxquelles des monuments ont été communiqués," Cabinet des Médailles, Paris. I thank Cécile Morrison for her kind assistance in this research.

60 Royall Tyler to Mildred Barnes Bliss, 4 September 1924, HUA.

61 Elisina Tyler to Mildred Barnes Bliss, 31 October 1926, HUA.

62 Mildred Barnes Bliss to Elisina Tyler, 22 November 1926, HUA.

63 Nelson, "Private Passions Made Public," 45–46.

64 Marlia M. Mango, *Silver from Early Byzantium: The Kaper Koraon and Related Treasures* (Baltimore, 1986), 26–27.

65 Frustrated by their distance from Paris, but "hyper-excited" about a silver dish (that eventually was also found wanting), Mildred Barnes Bliss wrote Royall Tyler on 31 January 1928: "This Argentine chapter is simply ruinous, and we would rather barter our souls for such a majestic object as the Strogonoff dish than acquire four or five lesser pieces, however alluring they may be." HUA.

66 Royall Tyler to Mildred Barnes Bliss, 6 September 1928, HUA.

67 Royall Tyler to Mildred Barnes Bliss, 5 January 1928, HUA.

68 Royall Tyler to Mildred Barnes Bliss, 23 October 1929, HUA.

69 Royall Tyler, "Exposition internationale d'art byzantin," *Cahiers d'art* 6 (1931): 173–92.

70 Royall Tyler to Mildred Barnes Bliss, 27 March 1929, HUA. Ross, *Catalogue of the Byzantine and Early Medieval Antiquities*, 2:18–19.

71 Byzantine Collection, BZ.1929.1. Bühl, *Dumbarton Oaks*, 62–63.

72 Royall Tyler to Mildred Barnes Bliss, 30 April 1931, HUA. Alfassa was a curator of decorative arts, a translator of Robert Browning into French, and the author of an aforementioned memoir about the collector Raymond Koechlin.

73 Tyler, "Exposition internationale d'art byzantin," 176.

74 Edith Wharton to Mildred Barnes Bliss, 8 August 1931 and 31 August 1931, Beinecke Library, Yale University.

75 Ross, *Catalogue of the Byzantine and Early Medieval Antiquities*, 1:103–4.

76 Royall Tyler to Mildred Barnes Bliss, 3 November 1930, 1 May 1931, 21 October 1930, and 6 March 1930, HUA.

77 Robert Woods Bliss to Royall Tyler, 25 September 1934, HUA.

78 Robert Woods Bliss to Royall Tyler, 22 May 1937, HUA

79 Royall Tyler to Mildred Barnes Bliss, 10 August 1938, HUA.

80 Royall Tyler to Mildred Barnes Bliss, 3 June 1932, HUA.

81 Royall Tyler to Mildred Barnes Bliss, 21 October 1930, HUA.

82 John Walker, *The National Gallery of Art, Washington* (New York, 1975), 32–33.

83 Royall Tyler to Mildred Barnes Bliss, 2 January 1935, HUA.

84 Eric Maclagan was unable to see an ivory in the Trivulzio Collection for a study he published: "An Early Christian Ivory Relief of the Miracle of Cana," *The Burlington Magazine for Connoisseurs* 38, no. 217 (April 1921): 181–82.

85 Clelia Alberici, *Capolavori di arte decorativa nel Castello Sforzesco* (Milan, 1975), 12.

86 Royall Tyler to Mildred Barnes Bliss, 5 September 1934, HUA.

87 Royall Tyler to Robert Woods Bliss, 15 May 1935 and 10 August 1935, HUA.

88 Royall Tyler to Mildred Barnes Bliss, 4 September 1937, HUA.

89 Weitzmann, *Catalogue of the Byzantine and Early Medieval Antiquities*, 89–93.

90 Ernst Bruckmüller, et al., *900 Jahre Benediktiner in Melk: Jubiläumsausstellung 1989 Stift Melk* (Melk, 1989), 486–87; and Andrew Keogh, "The Gutenberg Bible as a Typographical Monument," *Yale University Library Gazette* 1, no. 1 (1926): n.p.

91 Royall Tyler to Mildred and Robert Woods Bliss, 1 March 1937, HUA. Tyler had been to Rome and had spoken with Wolfgang Fritz Volbach. They discussed acquiring the Limburg reliquary: "He will investigate and report. Where it is a question of objects in State possession, the matter is much simpler, and he thinks that, if the right time is chosen and the deal is properly prepared, there should be no insurmountable difficulty." On the reliquary, see Klaus Wessel, *Byzantine Enamels: From the 5th to the 13th Century* (Greenwich, Conn., 1967), 75–78.

92 Adolph Goldschmidt and Kurt Weitzmann, *Die byzantinischen Elfenbeinskulpturen des X.-XIII. Jahrhunderts*, 2 vols., 2nd ed. (Berlin, 1979), 37; and Evans and Wixom, *Glory of Byzantium*, 146–47.

93 On Wolfang Fritz Volbach, see Ulrike Wendland, *Biographisches Handbuch deutschsprachiger Kunsthistoriker im Exil: Leben und Werk der unter dem Nationalsozialsmus verfolgten und vertriebenen Wissenschaftler*, 2 vols. (Munich, 1999), 2:716–23; and Peter Betthausen, *Metzler Kunsthistoriker Lexikon: Zweihundert Porträts deutschsprachiger Autoren aus vier Jahrhunderten* (Stuttgart, 1999), 431–33.

94 Royall Tyler to Mildred Barnes Bliss, 12 August 1931, HUA. Wolfgang Fritz Volbach, Georges Duthuit, and Georges Salles, *Art byzantin* (Paris, 1933).

95 Jonathan Petropoulos, *Royals and the Reich: The Princes von Hessen in Nazi Germany* (New York, 2006), 2–3 and 61–82.

96 Ibid., 177–88 and 275.

97 Ibid., 231–39.

98 One problem here is Volbach's wife, Maria Luise Adelung. In his brief autobiography, Volbach records that his wife died in 1936 and that he remarried in 1948. *Wissenschaft und Turbulenz: Der Lebensweg des W. F. Volbach aus Mainz* (Mainz am Rhein, 1972), 30 and 36. This is repeated in Wendland, *Biographisches Handbuch deutschspranchiger Kunsthistoriker im Exil*, 716.

99 These objects were in the "Klosterhof," a part of a princely villa in Glienicke, Berlin, that has been studied by Gerd-H. Zuchold, *Der "Klosterhof" des Prinzen Karl von Preussen im Park von Schloss Glienicke in Berlin*, 2 vols. (Berlin, 1993). On these sculptures and the villa in the 1930s, see 1:69–72.

100 HUA.

101 Vikan, *Catalogue of the Sculpture in the Dumbarton Oaks Collection*, 99–108.

102 See note 99.

103 Royall Tyler to Mildred and Robert Woods Bliss, 8 September 1937, HUA.

104 Goldschmidt and Weitzmann, *Die byzantinischen Elfenbeinskulpturen des X.–XIII. Jahrhunderts*, 2:39; and Evans and Wixom, *Glory of Byzantium*, 143–44.

105 Royall Tyler to Mildred and Robert Woods Bliss, December 1937, HUA. Evans and Wixom, *Glory of Byzantium*, 81.

106 Peirce and Tyler, *Byzantine Art*, 47.

107 Weitzmann, *Catalogue of the Byzantine and Early Medieval Antiquities*, 43–48.

108 Ibid., 55–58.

109 Goldschmidt and Weitzmann, *Die byzantinischen Elfenbeinskulpturen des X.–XIII. Jahrhunderts*, 2:36.

110 Royall Tyler to Mildred Barnes Bliss, 10 July 1938, HUA.

111 Royall Tyler to Robert Woods Bliss, 15 February 1938, HUA. Tyler's finances had gotten worse a year later, when his son, William Royall Tyler, reported that his allowance had been cut in half and that his father was "living in a small room in a second-rate Hotel in Geneva, alone." William

Royall Tyler to Violet Markham, 15 January 1939, Papers of Violet Markham, MARKHAM/25/84, London School of Economics.

112 Royall Tyler to Mildred Barnes Bliss, 18 May 1940, HUA.

113 HUA.

114 *Pagan and Christian Egypt: Egyptian Art from the First to the Tenth Century A.D., Exhibited at the Brooklyn Museum by the Department of Ancient Art, January 23–March 9, 1941* (New York, 1941), 31.

115 Royall Tyler to Mildred Barnes Bliss, 3, 4, and 13 September 1941, HUA. *Handbook of the Byzantine Collection* (Washington, D.C., 1967), 86.

116 Circumstances described in letter from William Royall Tyler to Violet Markham, 5 October 1940, Papers of Violet Markham, MARKHAM/25/84, London School of Economics.

117 Allen W. Dulles, *From Hitler's Doorstep: The Wartime Intelligence Reports of Allen Dulles, 1942–1945*, ed. Neal H. Petersen (University Park, Pa., 1996), 7, 9, and 567.

118 Ibid., 199 and 203.

119 Allen Dulles to Royall Tyler, 28 November 1945, Allen W. Dulles Papers, 1845–1971, box 55, folder 19, Princeton University Library.

120 Royall Tyler to Allen Dulles, March 1946, Allen W. Dulles Papers, box 55, folder 19, Princeton University Library.

121 Royall Tyler to Robert Woods Bliss, 20 August 1935, HUA. "Volume 3 is nearly finished." Royall

Tyler to Mildred Barnes Bliss, 28 June 1936, HUA. "The whole of our Vol. III text is now in the publishers' hands, and as they've had all the photographic material, complete, for 9 months, I hope the vol. may appear in October . . ."

122 Royall Tyler to Mildred and Robert Woods Bliss, 2 August 1939, HUA.

123 Ross, *Catalogue of the Byzantine and Early Medieval Antiquities*, 1:103–4.

124 Royall Tyler to Mildred Barnes Bliss, 4 September 1937, HUA.

125 *Calendar of Letters, Despatches, and State Papers*, vol. 13 (London, 1954); and *The Emperor Charles the Fifth*.

126 William Royall Tyler to Violet Markham, 26 December 1953 and 10 September 1954, Papers of Violet Markham, MARKHAM/25/84, London School of Economics.

127 Reviewed by Garrett Mattingly in *The Journal of Modern History* 29, no. 3 (1957): 260 and by H. G. Koenigsberger in *The English Historical Review* 72, no. 285 (1957): 741–42.

128 Arthur Salter, *Slave of the Lamp: A Public Servant's Notebook* (London, 1967), 93.

129 Salles, *Le Regard*, 12.

130 Royall Tyler to Allen Dulles, 16 January 1946, Allen W. Dulles Papers, box 55, folder 19, Princeton University Library.

131 *The Times*, 9 March 1953.

132 See note 56.

3

Mildred and Robert Woods Bliss and the
Pre-Columbian Collection at Dumbarton Oaks

In December 1963, the Pre-Columbian wing at Dumbarton Oaks opened to the public (fig. 3.1). Designed by Philip Johnson, the noted Harvard-educated American architect then at the height of his career, the wing was a significant departure in style from the prevailing Georgian revival buildings of Dumbarton Oaks. The transformation of a Victorian house, purchased in 1920, into an institution with a Georgian revival "campus" had taken Mildred and Robert Woods Bliss much time, thought, and effort to accomplish.[1] But after forty years, a decision was made to try a new architect. Philip Johnson, inspired by the compartmentally organized buildings he had seen in Istanbul early in his career, designed a building of eight circular, one-story, domed pavilions joined together.[2] Glass, marble, teak, and bronze made a structure of great elegance and transparency, one that was meticulously finished and discretely set into a wooded area adjacent to the Byzantine galleries (fig. 3.2). Reviewers saw the building and the art it contained differently. Some described the new Pre-Columbian wing as "one of the most beautiful little museums in the world,"[3] and as a beauty in which there was "no competition between the container and the things contained."[4] Others found the building postmodern and "alluring" but "so delightful that it competes with the pre-Columbian art."[5]

The very transparency of the building ruled out a more traditional installation, such as that of the adjacent Byzantine Collection.[6] As the structure was distinctive, so the Pre-Columbian

installation would be as well. The installation of the Byzantine and Pre-Columbian galleries make it clear to all but the most inattentive visitors that distances of time and space exist between the works of art displayed in them. Yet Robert Woods Bliss and his wife, Mildred Barnes Bliss, became interested in the two art fields more or less simultaneously. It happened in Paris in the early teens of the twentieth century, when the Blisses arrived with Robert Bliss's posting to the U.S. Embassy in 1912.

The art scene in Paris was particularly lively then, as it had been for some two decades, when interest in innovation in visual culture was current with the questioning of the imitation of nature as the appropriate aesthetic goal. Artists, critics, dealers, and collectors of avant-garde circles cast off the conventions of nineteenth-century naturalism, and all types of earlier and non-Western art forms were scrutinized.[7] Pre-Columbian art was perhaps the earliest non-Western art to be publicly visible in Paris. In 1850, almost one thousand works, primarily from Mexico and Peru, were exhibited in the Louvre.[8] They remained there until French ethnographic collections were united in the Musée d'Ethnographie du Trocadéro after 1878.[9]

The most well-known non-Western aspect of the primitivist reevaluation is the role African art played in the redirection of form in painting and sculpture in France.[10] African sculpture was initially collected by French scientific missions, colonial administrators, clergy, and commercial agents in Africa in the nineteenth century. By

Robert Woods Bliss (right) with an unidentified man examining a Teotihuacan limestone mask that Bliss acquired in 1940.

Papers of Robert Woods Bliss and Mildred Barnes Bliss, ca. 1860–1969, HUGFP 76.74p, box 15, Harvard University Archives.

53

the very early twentieth century, African objects were not only found in European museums but in private collections, including those of artists such as Matisse, Braque, and Picasso. Picasso's famous 1906–7 work, *Les Demoiselles d'Avignon*, a transformative painting in terms of conceptual changes of form, was much influenced by works he and his fellow artists owned, as well as by the impressive collections on view at the Musée d'Ethnographie du Trocadéro.[11]

While primitivist thought focused primarily on African art in France, in England the critic Clive Bell, known for his early defense of abstract art, wrote in his much reprinted 1914 book titled *Art:* "In primitive art you will find no accurate representation; you will find only significant form. Yet no other art moves us so profoundly. Whether we consider Sumerian sculpture or pre-dynastic Egyptian art, or archaic Greek . . . [or] primitive Byzantine art of the sixth century . . . [or] that mysterious and majestic art that flourished in Central and South America before the coming of the white man, in every case we observe three common characteristics—absence of representation, absence of technical swagger, sublimely impressive form."[12] Fellow British critic Roger Fry noted as early as 1897 that Byzantine art marked a return to an elementary symbolism after the literalness of late Roman art.[13] Fry, an early art historian, subsequently said of ancient American art: "[W]e have come to recognize the beauty of Aztec and Maya sculpture, and some of our modern artists have even gone to them for inspiration. This is, of course, one result of the general aesthetic awakening which has followed on the revolt against the tyranny of the Graeco-Roman tradition."[14]

It was in this period of ongoing critical reexamination and redirection in art and aesthetics that the Blisses were introduced to many of the visual attractions of Paris by their friend, Royall Tyler.[15] The American-born Tyler lived in Europe for much of his life and was a serious enthusiast of its cultural heritage. He had a particular attachment to Byzantine art, which he had discovered in 1900 when he visited Venice for the first time. He described how Venice "opened the door leading to Byzantine art, the central point from which I approached other domains. For the time being, the Byzantine vision alone held me."[16]

Pre-Columbian art, however, did not escape Royall Tyler's notice. Having quickly taken on the role of art advisor to the Blisses, Tyler wrote with great excitement to Robert Bliss in 1913 to report on a group of gold and silver objects then in the hands of the Parisian art dealer Joseph Brummer. Tyler had introduced Bliss to the dealer the year before, not long after the Blisses had arrived in Paris. Tyler wrote to Bliss, who was away from Paris at the time, "Brummer, who but Brummer? has just got hold of a great treasure of Inca gold and silver objects. . . . They are of a grand, somber beauty that defies description, and [are] of the utmost rarity." Tyler had set aside a large number of objects for Bliss and a small group for himself. His letter continued: "I hate advising anyone to buy without seeing, God knows, but I think it would be an ill turn not to advise you to buy now."[17] Bliss cabled back affirmatively, and the objects were acquired.[18]

The works Tyler purchased for Bliss that December were Peruvian antiquities, which had come to Europe as part of the collection of Eduard Gaffron, a German doctor who had lived in Peru for twenty years. From 1892 onwards, Gaffron accumulated thousands of antiquities, most of which have made their way into the museum collections of Germany.[19] Many of the gold and silver works that Bliss bought in 1913 are currently in the Pre-Columbian Collection at Dumbarton

Oaks. The most significant object among them is a tall silver figure (fig. 3.3). Of Inca date, and unusually large for its type, it has lost its clothes. In Inca times, it would have been elegantly clothed with garments that were specifically woven for it, and would have worn a bright feathered headdress so large that it would have obscured its face. The 1913 purchase also included gold cups (fig. 3.4), fourteen Chimú gold feline faces and six Chimú silver bird ornaments thought to be textile ornaments, and an inlaid tin-bronze knife and staff finial of Inca date.[20] For himself, Tyler bought five works that were duplicates of objects in the Bliss group, plus a silver mask and a plain gold cup.[21]

The Parisian art dealer that sold the Gaffron objects to Bliss and Tyler, Joseph Brummer, was Hungarian. He had gone to Paris as an art student, and became an art dealer in about 1908. In his small shop at 3 Boulevard Raspail, Brummer dealt in many areas of the world's art and became an important participant in the "primitivist market" for African sculpture in the years before World War I.[22] He also took a chance on Peruvian antiquities when the opportunity arose. It was in his shop, in spring 1912, that Robert Bliss had his first experience with Pre-Columbian art, about which he later wrote: "I had just come from the Argentine Republic, where I had never seen anything like

these objects . . . [and] . . . that day the collector's microbe took root in . . . very fertile soil."[23]

Bliss soon acquired two other objects that are milestones in the Pre-Columbian Collection. According to Dumbarton Oaks records, the first Pre-Columbian acquisition was a ten-inch-high stone hacha from Veracruz, Mexico, purchased from Joseph Brummer in 1913 (fig. 3.5). A year later—the same year the Peruvian objects of gold and silver were acquired—Bliss bought a Mexican figure of deep green jadeite. The sculpture is so well known today that it has become virtually the symbol of the Dumbarton Oaks Pre-Columbian Collection (fig. 3.6). It is a standing figure with

a large, elongated head, goatee-like beard, and powerful shoulders, and now is identified as Olmec in style.[24] Smoothly finished, the figure is carefully balanced, standing on its own small feet with its arms extended forward. Aside from the unusual shape of its head, with its constricted and domed top, it has few revealing attributes.

The Olmec purchase took place in 1914—the year World War I began. The Blisses remained in Paris throughout the ensuing conflict, but life was markedly different for them. Art collecting and other personal pleasures, while not completely forgotten, were significantly diminished during those years. There would be no further

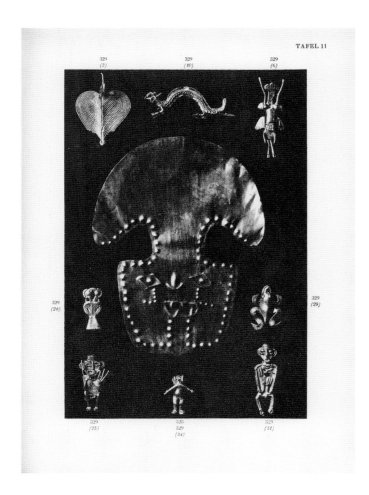

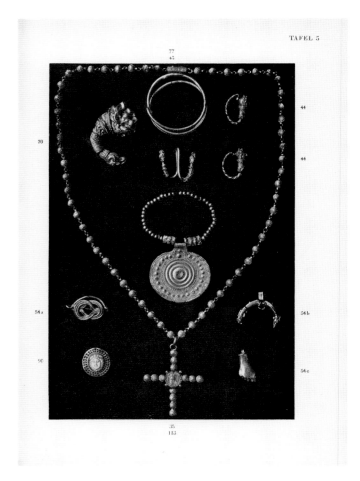

Pre-Columbian purchases until 1929—a full fifteen years after the excitement of the first acquisitions. By this time, the Blisses were in Buenos Aires, where Robert Bliss was U.S. ambassador to Argentina. Royall Tyler kept them in touch with the European art scene and alerted them to purchasing opportunities. One such opportunity was the impending sale of the collection of Marc Rosenberg, a noted German authority on goldworking techniques. The Rosenberg collection was auctioned in Berlin in November 1929. It included Pre-Columbian, Byzantine, and many other ancient works of gold (figs. 3.7 and 3.8).[25]

Marc Rosenberg had been a serious student of goldworking techniques in a wide array of early civilizations and had personally acquired examples of the kinds of objects he had studied. His multivolume publication, *Geschichte der Goldschmiedekunst auf technischer Grundlage*, began to appear in Germany in 1908. By 1929, the sale of the Rosenberg collection was of great interest in Europe. The preciousness of gold used for high-status objects in both the Byzantine and Pre-Columbian worlds was an important link between these cultures in those years. Objects of gold, silver, and precious and semiprecious stones were integral to the large, long-lived civilizations, where royalty and kings, churches, temples, and palaces existed and where beautiful objects of rich materials were made. High-quality materials, grand in design and outstanding in craftsmanship, were particularly appealing to Royall Tyler and, through him, to the Blisses. They were successful purchasers at the Berlin auction. Tyler wrote to Mildred Bliss after the sale about the Pre-Columbian pieces: "You will like these objects, there are birds, frogs, little people, all sorts of things, all in gold (fig. 3.9)."[26]

The 1920s saw the growth of informed interest in the art of ancient America. The decade began with An Exhibition of Objects of Indigenous American Art at the venerable Burlington Fine

FIG. 3.7.

Pre-Columbian gold objects from Colombia.

Reprinted from *Sammlung Marc Rosenberg* (Berlin, 4 November 1929), auction catalogue, plate 11, lot 329.

FIG. 3.8.

Gold objects of various sources and dates, including Byzantine cross and chain.

Reprinted from *Sammlung Marc Rosenberg* (Berlin, 4 November 1929), auction catalogue, plate 5, lot 113 (bottom).

FIG. 3.9.

Human Figure, Muisca, 900–1500 CE, gold.

Pre-Columbian Collection, PC.B.418, Dumbarton Oaks Research Library and Collection.

Arts Club in London, of which Royall Tyler was a member. The prefatory note to the catalogue stated that the "Committee of the Burlington Club may lay claim . . . to the distinction of being first in the field with an exhibition of an American art which owes nothing to any other continent. . . . [The] art, is here seen grouped together for the first time, at any rate, in this country."[27] The catalogue included a lengthy introduction by the British Museum's T. A. Joyce, then a noted authority on ancient America. Near the end of the decade, a larger exhibit took place in Paris.[28] Les Arts Anciens de l'Amérique was on view at the Musée des Arts Décoratifs in the spring of 1928. The Paris show was large with many lenders. Royall Tyler and his wife loaned four Pre-Columbian objects, including three works of gold and a small stone relief, said to be from Oaxaca.[29] Tyler had lent the relief to the Burlington Fine Arts Club exhibit eight years previously.

Royall Tyler purchased a final group of Pre-Columbian objects for the Blisses in 1937. In June, a Sotheby & Co., London, auction offered more than fifty lots of Mexican antiquities from the collection of Mrs. Jean Holland.[30] Tyler contacted the Blisses enthusiastically about the Mexican gold, silver, and jadeite objects being offered (fig. 3.10).[31] He thought it a wonderful opportunity and requested permission to spend up to two thousand pounds on his chosen pieces. Bliss replied by telegraph the same day, saying that "although Aztec is not Byzantine [we] have complete confidence as always [in] your judgment but [the] objects must be whales to justify . . . [a] limit as you suggest."[32] Tyler secured an important Aztec gold necklace and ear ornaments together with other works for the Blisses.[33] He also secured several for himself.[34] Even in brief international cables sent from distant places, his ardor and enthusiasm for works of art were compelling. He was generous with his admiration and opinions and was distinctive in his tastes. A connoisseur of art objects, he taught Mildred and Robert Bliss to be connoisseurs too. And he would on occasion remind them both not to stray from the straight and narrow path, that is to say, not to stray too far from Byzantine art.

But to return to the 1912 beginnings of Robert Bliss's interest in Pre-Columbian art, it is interesting to speculate on what specifically intrigued him about the Peruvian antiquities he saw in Joseph Brummer's shop, those that had so activated the "collector's microbe." The Blisses had just come to Paris after three years in Argentina, where they had seen no Andean antiquities. But

they had seen objects of colonial silver from the silver-rich areas of the Andean Altiplano and the Río de la Plata in private collections in Buenos Aires. Even on their trip to Argentina in 1909—when they made stops in Lima, Peru, and Santiago, Chile—they had seen no Peruvian antiquities.

Robert Bliss's experience with Latin America, if not with its Pre-Columbian antiquities, actually had begun after graduation from Harvard University in 1900, when he went to Puerto Rico as a clerk to William H. Hunt, a judge who subsequently became the governor of the island. Puerto Rico was Bliss's first experience with a foreign country. He had not been outside, much less lived outside, of the United States previously. His first months in Puerto Rico were difficult. He wrote to Mildred Barnes, then his stepsister, that he spent time learning Spanish and trying to find his vocation (fig. 3.11).[35] Three years later, he had reached those goals and had become a member of the U.S. Foreign Service.

FIG. 3.10.

Mexican objects from the collection of Mrs. Jean Holland.

Reprinted from *Egyptian, Greek, Roman, Indian and South American Antiquities, Native Art* (Sotheby & Co., London, 6 June 1937), plate 3, lots 163–68.

When Robert Bliss was assigned to Argentina in 1909, he was already an established Foreign Service officer and had married Mildred Barnes. Their trip to Buenos Aires was highly personal and somewhat unconventional. They took a long way round by going east to west through Panama, where canal building was underway. They traveled through the Culebra Cut, a valley-sized excavation being dug across the Isthmus, and then went south along the west coast of South America, passing through Lima and Santiago. From Santiago, they crossed the southern Andes, reportedly on muleback,[36] before continuing to Buenos Aires. Even now, a century later, that would be an impressive trip. Unfortunately, no diaries provide insights into what the Blisses saw and experienced on their journey. After completing it, the Blisses

remained in Buenos Aires until 1912, when Robert was posted to Paris, where he would marvel at the Peruvian antiquities in Joseph Brummer's shop and subsequently buy pieces in gold and silver.

The Blisses were to live again in South America, as Robert Bliss was appointed U.S. ambassador to Argentina in 1927. The following six years in Buenos Aires were challenging but rewarding, as he had considerable success at improving the reputation of the United States.[37] From Europe, Royall Tyler kept the Blisses informed of art-world activities and Byzantine and Pre-Columbian works being offered for sale. In late 1928, the Blisses briefly returned to Paris, visiting old friends and making the rounds of art dealers. Unfortunately, they missed Les Arts Anciens de l'Amérique at the Musée des Arts Décoratifs, as

FIG. 3.11.

Robert Woods Bliss in San Juan, Puerto Rico, ca. 1900–3.

Photograph by R. Colorado. Papers of Robert Woods Bliss and Mildred Barnes Bliss, ca. 1860–1969, HUGFP 76.74p, box 9, Harvard University Archives.

it had been on exhibit earlier in the year. In 1933, Robert Bliss retired from the Foreign Service, and the couple returned to Washington, D.C., where they finally became residents in their own house at Dumbarton Oaks.

Robert and Mildred Bliss took many new directions in the 1930s. They began the formation of a research center at Dumbarton Oaks, started talks with Harvard University about it, and furthered their knowledge of institutional attitudes and conventions at the Harvard museums. They continued to renovate the house and enlarge the gardens, and, late in the decade, collected art—both Byzantine and Pre-Columbian—more attentively. Robert Bliss furthered his substantial engagement with Pre-Columbian art and archaeology. He traveled to southern Mexico and

Guatemala to see Maya ruins in the mid-1930s. The trip to the Guatemalan Highlands was made with Frederic Walcott, a trustee of the Carnegie Institution of Washington (figs. 3.12 and 3.13). The Carnegie Institution, founded in 1902, was dedicated to scientific discovery. For much of the first half of the twentieth century, it was actively engaged in the excavation of ancient Maya sites in Mexico and Central America. It was a major force in Maya studies at the time. Bliss and Walcott traveled in February and March 1935, and met with archaeologists, expatriates, hotel keepers, and local clergy, among many others. Near the highland Guatemalan town of Hueheutenango, they visited the ruins of the Maya site of Zaculeu, where the main buildings dated from the fifth through the seventh centuries. Bliss described

Fig. 3.12.

Robert Woods Bliss
in the Guatemalan
Highlands, 1935.

Pre-Columbian Collection,
PC.RWB.1935.154, Dumbarton
Oaks Research Library and
Collection.

Fig. 3.13.

Frederic C. Walcott seated
on Altar O, Copán, 1935.

Pre-Columbian Collection,
PC.RWB.1935.167, Dumbarton
Oaks Research Library and
Collection.

Fig. 3.14.

Unidentified man beside
Stela F, Copán, 1935.

Pre-Columbian Collection,
PC.RWB.1935.159, Dumbarton
Oaks Research Library and
Collection.

the site in his travel diary, which he meticulously kept during this part of the journey: "the centre temple has been restored by the Guat[emalan] Gov[ernment] around it are about 8 mounds, the whole on a broad piece of land between two deep ravines. . . . There is no hewn stone in the construction of Zaculeu (no carving & decoration as at Chichenitzá [*sic*]. The walls are rough stone & rubble faced with thick mortar or plaster."[38] Earlier in the trip, Robert Bliss visited the excavations at Chichén Itzá in Yucatán.

Toward the end of their journey, the men moved eastward down through the Highlands to see Copán, where the Carnegie Institution was clearing the site prior to excavation. Copán was, and is, a Maya center renowned for the quality of its sculpture (fig. 3.14). Now in the nation-state of Honduras, a powerful Maya dynasty flourished there from the fifth to the eighth century. During those centuries, relief-carved monuments in honor of the ruling dynasty were erected, and buildings were enlarged and elaborated sumptuously with more sculpture. When Frederic Walcott and Robert Bliss arrived in the town of Copán, they found its inhabitants preparing for a fiesta. Bliss wrote in his journal: "Copán annual fair was due the next day, so that [the] plaza was beginning to fill up with people from [the] surrounding

country. Booths [were] on three sides, fires burned all round them before which women were mixing punch for sale. . . . Games of chance, a raffle etc. were in full swing. Night noise, people on plaza . . . talking, laughing, singing (some), making music. About 3 am Fred was swearing loudly, the ever grinning attendants at the fair were still awake & voluble, pigs were squealing, cock crowing, rocket bomb . . . exploding, when a dog fight broke loose under our window—I burst out laughing."[39] In the morning, they visited the site.

Gustav Strömsvic, in charge of the excavations for the Carnegie Institution, showed the two men around the ruins of ancient Copán: "We return with Strömsvic to the ruins, to the citadel & various courts, all overgrown with trees, the bush has been fairly well cleared. The hieroglyph stairway is unique, with god or idol in centre, very few stones in place but many are found giving hopes of its restoration fairly complete. Stelae very good most of them on ground; a sculptured seat at opposite end of court to glyph stairway; numerous carved heads and faces. . . . The fine altar, a commemorative stone appearing to represent a conference between the chiefs with their counselmen . . . described and illustrated by Stevens [sic] in his book 'Incidents of Travel' following his visit to Cent[ral] Am[erica] in 184–."[40] The Carnegie Institution excavations, which were just beginning at the time of the Bliss-Walcott visit, were significant. They had the support of the government of Honduras, and lasted for seven years, resulting in the restoration of many buildings and re-erection of many monuments. The Carnegie Institution of Washington was one of the many organizations engaged in the study of ancient America that Robert Bliss would support then and in subsequent years.

During the months of discussion with Harvard University about Dumbarton Oaks and its research center, the level of professionalism in Washington grew. Advice and expertise was sought from, and given by, many authorities at the university and its two museums, the Fogg Art Museum and the Peabody Museum of Archaeology and Ethnology. Acquisitions of Byzantine art increased, while Robert Bliss's Pre-Columbian holdings enlarged only slowly. With the exception of the Mexican objects bought at the London Sotheby sale of 1937, purchases were few. A jadeite object (fig. 3.15) of ancient Mexican origin was acquired from Joseph Brummer in 1935, twenty years after the purchase of the first jadeite figure from him (see fig. 3.6). The new jadeite

FIG. 3.15.
Pendant, Olmec,
900–300 BCE,
diopside-jadeite.

Pre-Columbian
Collection, PC.B.023,
Dumbarton Oaks
Research Library and
Collection.

object was a large pendant incised with a trefoil emblem symbolic of maize. In ancient Mexican thought, maize was associated with agricultural plenty and rulership.[41] The pendant is Olmec in style, as is the standing figure. The ancient Olmec peoples thrived along the coast of the Gulf of Mexico—and made objects of precious materials such as jadeite—in the early first millennium BCE (if not earlier). Precious objects were a consistent Bliss interest. As his collection grew, several more Olmec jadeite objects were purchased.[42]

In early 1940, the Peabody and Fogg museums mounted an important Pre-Columbian exhibition in Cambridge. The planners of the exhibit were fortunate in being able to include objects from Mexico's national collections that had just been shown in the Mexican Pavilion of the 1939 World's Fair in New York. Also in the exhibition were Mexican and Peruvian works from the Dumbarton Oaks Collection, several objects from Joseph Brummer (who had become a naturalized citizen of the United States in 1921 and had opened a shop in New York), and pieces from Alfred Tozzer and his wife. Alfred Tozzer, the chief organizer of the exhibition and noted Mayanist at Harvard University, was a university classmate and friend of Robert Bliss. The introduction to the exhibition catalogue stated: "It seems fitting to pay tribute to the magnificent artistic heritage of the Americas. . . . It is hoped that the present exhibition of objects, selected primarily on an artistic basis, will show how great is this heritage and how it may with justice be compared with the finest objects of any

civilization."[43] These sentiments were echoed by Robert Bliss many times over.

Robert and Mildred Bliss's initial gift to Harvard University was formalized with the official inauguration of the Dumbarton Oaks Research Library and Collection on 1 November 1940. After the event, the Byzantine Collection gained a public face in Washington, D.C., and Dumbarton Oaks found its first director, John Thacher, a man sympathetic to the Blisses' goals. He too envisioned Dumbarton Oaks as a vital center of distinguished and productive scholarship, and he worked positively to achieve this end during his long tenure at the institution.

As the Dumbarton Oaks Research Library and Collection was then in good hands and functioning, the Blisses returned to California. They had the habit of spending time in Southern California, particularly during summers, when the climate was better than in Washington, D.C. As the Blisses had experienced war directly while living in Paris during World War I, they were distressed at the news of yet another war approaching in Europe. California was at a greater distance from the dismaying reports. Robert Bliss took the opportunity to acquaint himself with local art dealers, particularly those who dealt in Pre-Columbian art. Chief among them was Earl Stendahl of the Stendahl Art Galleries in Los Angeles.[44] Stendahl was the main source of Bliss's Pre-Columbian purchases from 1940 until the end of the war. A number of significant works, notably the Teotihuacan net-jaguar mural,[45] were added to the collection during those years.

When the United States entered the war, Robert Bliss returned east and went back to work for the government.

The Dumbarton Oaks property itself was put to work, and—among its many uses—it was the venue for discussions that led to the founding of the United Nations in 1945. When the fighting was over, Robert Bliss once again left government service. The art world in the United States revived, eager to make up for lost time. In 1947, a big, historically important show of Early Christian and Byzantine art, one that surveyed all the centuries of that art, was organized by the Walters Art Gallery in Baltimore.[46] Dumbarton Oaks was a significant participant in the event. Robert Bliss, meanwhile, had been looking for a venue in which to show his Pre-Columbian Collection. After several years of lending generously to exhibitions in museums throughout the United States,[47] he found one in Washington, D.C. The National Gallery of Art—then still a new museum, as it was inaugurated only in 1941—"opened its doors" to Robert Bliss's Pre-Columbian Collection in 1947.[48] While pleased with this opportunity, Bliss knew that in order to exhibit his objects intelligently, he had to have them knowledgeably catalogued. He unsuccessfully approached his old classmate Alfred Tozzer with the project, but a younger, Harvard-trained archaeologist with a substantial reputation, Samuel Lothrop, was available and interested in doing the catalogue.[49]

Samuel Lothrop was a well-born, Harvard-educated American archaeologist, a bibliophile, and an object man.[50] He was on the staff of the Museum of the American Indian in New York for a decade before its research branch closed in 1930, when he began his affiliation with Harvard's Peabody Museum of Archaeology and Ethnology. An archaeologist whose specialty was Central and South America, Lothrop brought into Bliss's circle of advisors archaeologists with Mexican experience, which Lothrop thought he lacked. The first Mexicanist Lothrop recommended was Matthew Stirling of the Smithsonian's Bureau of American Ethnology. Stirling took part in the initial cataloguing of the Bliss Collection and was thanked (with Lothrop) in the acknowledgments to the first catalogue, *Indigenous Art of the Americas: Collection of Robert Woods Bliss*.[51] The Bliss Collection went on view at the National Gallery of Art in 1947, in an installation that was intended to show the works as art objects (fig. 3.16). No attempt was made to contextualize them, as was the practice in natural history museums.

Short years after the *Indigenous Art of the Americas* exhibition and catalogue were in place, an opportunity arose for Robert Bliss to fund a Peabody Museum excavation.[52] Lothrop, an experienced excavator who had previously worked for Harvard's Peabody, principally in Central America, was to conduct the work. His best-known excavation had been at Sitio Conte in the Coclé Province of Panama, a rich burial site that had been washing out of the banks of the Río Coclé when it was brought to the Peabody's attention.[53] Lothrop worked at Sitio Conte for three seasons in the early 1930s, excavating many rich graves with worked gold objects. He was pleased to have the opportunity to return to the area to excavate further.

The excavation in Coclé Province that was to be funded by Robert Bliss never took place. Lothrop had to choose a smaller site in Panama at Venado Beach in the Canal Zone. He excavated there in the early 1950s, when archaeologically excavated objects were still shared with the excavators.[54] Thus, in return for Bliss's support of the project, Venado Beach objects entered the Bliss Collection in 1953.[55] Lothrop continued to advise Bliss on his collection. While he was not the only authority Bliss consulted on objects, books, or people, he was a significant contributor to the Bliss Collection from 1946 onward. The two men became good friends, and, despite a mutual, inherent formality, they eventually called one another "Bob" and "Sam."[56]

The Bliss Pre-Columbian Collection grew during the fifteen years it had a public presence at the National Gallery of Art (fig. 3.17). Pieces were added to the collection from many sources.[57] Some do not have a source recorded,[58] unusual for meticulous record keeper Robert Bliss. Others came with a more immediate source history, such as the important group from Joseph Brummer that was purchased after the dealer's death in 1947. Brummer retained many pieces for several years, considering them part of his private collection. This included works lent to the Fogg exhibition of 1940, like the beautiful small Teotihuacan mask[59] and the Aztec stone sculpture of a rabbit with the head of an eagle warrior at its waist.[60] Also in the group was the so-called birth-giving deity (now known as Tlazoltéotl),[61] a figure that has had a certain amount of controversy associated with it.[62] Another noteworthy acquisition was the maize deity from Copán that Robert Bliss had been particularly anxious to include in his collection. The Peabody Museum had acquired the

over two-foot-high head, along with other Copán sculptures, as the excavator's share for work done at the site in the 1890s. Robert Bliss was able to trade the Peabody for it in 1953.[63]

Public interest in the art of the ancient Americas increased substantially during the 1950s. Robert Bliss continued to promote the field of Pre-Columbian art and archaeology, as he had done since the late 1930s. More museums and collectors were attracted to the field, and more special exhibitions were contemplated. The greater public interest, in turn, increased competition among collectors. Requests from friends who were unable to visit Washington, D.C., particularly those who lived in "countries in which the objects originated," led Bliss to publish his collection with a flourish.[64] Samuel Lothrop was charged with producing the catalogue and was also the principal author of various introductory texts and catalogue entries. The majority of illustrations were in color—many with patterned or backlit backgrounds. The Robert Woods Bliss Collection was presented to the reading public with the authoritative title *Pre-Columbian Art* in 1957. It was the first grand coffee-table book on the topic.

The Dumbarton Oaks Research Library and Collection was also growing, and in 1957, Robert Bliss wrote to the president of Harvard University about the need for additional space at Dumbarton Oaks. The Byzantine Collection wanted to house its coins and seals, the Garden Library—which Mildred Bliss had been assiduously gathering—needed suitable rooms for use and study, and more stack space was required generally. Soon the Pre-Columbian Collection needed its own home. The Blisses saw to it that these things happened. Robert Bliss transferred his Pre-Columbian Collection to Harvard University in 1960, and with the help of John Thacher, the director of Dumbarton Oaks, chose Phillip Johnson to design a structure to house the collection.

FIG. 3.18.

Robert Woods Bliss studying a Pre-Columbian gold object, 1950s.

Archives, AR.PH.BL.002, Dumbarton Oaks Research Library and Collection.

The addition of a new research field and gallery space to the Dumbarton Oaks establishment meant that staff for the Pre-Columbian Collection was required. Elizabeth Benson, who had worked with the collection at the National Gallery of Art, was sought. Robert Bliss knew her work from the gallery years. In a letter to Lothrop when Benson was about to leave the gallery in 1961, Bliss commented: "You will be sorry to hear that Miss Benson leaves the National Gallery to-morrow, for good. I shall miss her very much because she took such an interest in the collection and knew it almost as well as I do!"[65] Elizabeth Benson did take the job with the Pre-Columbian Collection. When the new Pre-Columbian pavilion was completed, she worked with John Thacher to install the works of art in the new transparent building. Benson became the first curator of the Pre-Columbian Collection at Dumbarton Oaks, and a new archaeological advisor was named: Harvard-trained, Yale University professor Michael Coe. Coe collaborated with Benson on the new *Handbook of the Robert Woods Bliss Collection of Pre-Columbian Art*, which was issued at the time of the building's opening in 1963.

Robert Bliss would not see his Pre-Columbian wing finished. He died before it was complete, leaving his residual estate to Harvard University for the continued maintenance of Dumbarton Oaks and his beloved Pre-Columbian Collection. As John Thacher noted in the foreword to the *Handbook of the Robert Woods Bliss Collection of Pre-Columbian Art*, "The Robert Woods Bliss Collection of Pre-Columbian Art was formed by the strong personal interest of a man deeply engaged in his subject." He was "eager to have the indigenous arts of the Americas represented permanently in the capital of this country."[66] Mildred Bliss, who previously left the collecting of Pre-Columbian art to her husband (fig. 3.18), acquired significant works after his death with the assistance of Elizabeth Benson and Michael Coe. Many of the acquisitions were quickly published.[67] As Benson has written, when making purchases, they always bore in mind the aesthetic and technical qualities that Robert Bliss held dear.[68] One significant purchase, made before the opening of the Pre-Columbian wing, was a relief panel from the Maya site of Palenque in Chiapas, Mexico (fig. 3.19). Acquired by Mildred Bliss and Dumbarton Oaks in honor of Robert Woods Bliss, it depicts an eighth-century Maya king performing a ritual dance while impersonating the deity Chahk, the maker of storms. In one hand, the king holds high a hafted axe, a symbol of lightening, while in the other hand, he holds a small jar containing dark thunderstorms. He is flanked by his parents. On his right, his father, a great Palenque king, dedicates a temple to his dancing son.[69]

The Pre-Columbian wing at Dumbarton Oaks opened to the public on 10 December 1963. During the remainder of the decade, attitudes towards the collecting of archaeological objects began to change in the world at large, as did certain laws in the United States relating to the importation of antiquities. After 1970, Dumbarton Oaks no longer purchased archaeological objects. Accordingly, it turned its attention in other directions—to publications, symposia, and fellowships in Pre-Columbian art and archaeology. Today, the Pre-Columbian Studies program at Dumbarton Oaks occupies a singular place in the field of ancient American research and interests. The early public exposure of the Robert Woods Bliss Collection combined with the ongoing research activities of the institution—now of more than forty years duration—have made Pre-Columbian Studies at Dumbarton Oaks a vital center of distinguished and productive scholarship on ancient America. It has become prominent within the learned international community and holds a unique position within it for the stewardship and sharing of its many resources. Robert Woods Bliss would be well pleased.

ACKNOWLEDGMENTS

I would like to thank those who offered help with this paper: James Carder of Dumbarton Oaks, who has been most particularly generous with information; Helen C. Evans of the Metropolitan Museum of Art, who offered insights into the world of Byzantine scholarship; and Yaëlle Biro also of the Metropolitan, for awareness of Joseph Brummer. Two previously published articles on the topic of Robert Woods Bliss and his Pre-Columbian Collection should be mentioned as well: Elizabeth P. Benson, "The Robert Woods Bliss Collection of Pre-Columbian Art: A Memoir," in *Collecting the Pre-Columbian Past* (Washington, D.C., 1993) and Elizabeth Hill Boone, "Robert Woods Bliss and Pre-Columbian Art," in *Andean Art at Dumbarton Oaks* (Washington, D.C., 1996). Both added immeasurably to the substance of the current paper.

Notes

1 See Carder, chapter 1.

2 Franz Schulze, *Philip Johnson: Life and Work* (New York, 1994), 277–78; and Hilary Lewis and John O'Connor, *Philip Johnson: The Architect in His Own Words* (New York, 1994), 52–61.

3 Karl E. Meyer, "A Jewel Case for Pre-Columbian Gems," *Art News* (February 1964): 36.

4 Frank Getlein, "Model Museum: Glass at Dumbarton Oaks," *The New Republic* (28 December 1963): 28.

5 "Pre-Columbian Art in a Post-Modern Museum," *The Architectural Forum* 120 (March 1964): 110.

6 Elizabeth P. Benson, "The Robert Woods Bliss Collection of Pre-Columbian Art: A Memoir," in *Collecting the Pre-Columbian Past,* ed. Elizabeth Hill Boone (Washington, D.C., 1993), 26–29.

7 William Rubin, "Modernist Primitivism: An Introduction," in *"Primitivism" in 20th Century Art: Affinity of the Tribal and the Modern,* ed. William Rubin (New York, 1984), 1:1–81.

8 Adrian de Longpérier, *Notice des monuments exposés dans la salle des antiquités américaines (Mexique et Pérou), au Musée du Louvre* (Paris, 1850).

9 Elizabeth A. Williams, "Art and Artifact at the Trocadero: Ars Americana and the Primitivist Revolution," in *Objects and Others: Essays on Museums and Material Culture,* ed. George W. Stocking Jr. (Madison, Wis., 1985), 146–66. See also Elizabeth A. Williams, "Collecting and Exhibiting Pre-Columbiana in France and England, 1870–1930," in *Collecting the Pre-Columbian Past,* 124–27.

10 See Jean-Louis Paudrat, "From Africa," in *"Primitivism" in 20th Century Art,* 125–75.

11 See William Rubin, "Picasso," in ibid., 243ff.

12 Clive Bell, *Art* (London, 1914), 22–23.

13 Roger Fry, "Transition from Classical to Modern Art" lecture, 1897, discussed by Christopher Green in "Roger Fry's Canon from African Sculpture to Vlaminck: Byzantine Art," *Art Made Modern: Roger Fry's Vision of Art*, ed. Christopher Green (London, 1999), 142–43.

14 Roger Fry, "American Archaeology," review of *South American Archaeology, Mexican Archaeology, and Central American Archaeology,* by Thomas A. Joyce, *The Burlington Magazine for Connoisseurs* 33, no. 188 (November 1918): 156. The review was reprinted as "Ancient American Art," in Roger Fry, *Vision and Design* (London, 1920), 71.

15 For further discussion on Royall Tyler, see Robert S. Nelson, "Private Passions Made Public: The Beginnings of the Bliss Collection," in *Sacred Art, Secular Context: Objects of Art from the Byzantine Collection of Dumbarton Oaks, Washington, D.C., Accompanied by American Paintings from the Collection of Mildred and Robert Woods Bliss,* ed. Asen Kirin, 38–51 (Athens, Ga., 2005); and Nelson, chapter 2.

16 Nelson, "Private Passions Made Public," 40n6.

17 Royall Tyler to Robert Woods Bliss, 3 December 1913, Brummer file, Pre-Columbian Collection.

18 Robert Woods Bliss to Royall Tyler, 26 December 1913, Brummer file, Pre-Columbian Collection.

19 For the Eduard Gaffron Collection, see Claudia Schmitz, *Geschenke der Ahnen: Peruanische Kostbarkeiten aus der Sammlung Eduard Gaffron; Konstruktion und Wirklichkeit einer Kultur* (Leipzig, 2001).

20 Pre-Columbian Collection, PC.B.444, PC.B.475, PC.B.482, and PC.B.483. See Elizabeth Hill Boone, ed., *Andean Art at Dumbarton Oaks* (Washington, D.C., 1996), 1:plates 66, 69, 92, and 90.

21 Royall Tyler to Robert Woods Bliss, 3 December 1913, Brummer file, Pre-Columbian Collection.

22 Paudrat, "From Africa," 143–44. See also Krisztina Passuth, "Plus qu'un marchand, une eminence grise: Joseph Brummer, ami d'Henri Rousseau," in *Tribus contemporaines: explorations exotiques des artistes d'Occident; Actes du colloque de Dijon, 5 et 6 mai 2000,* ed. Valérie Dupont, 43–64 (Dijon, 2002).

23 Robert Woods Bliss, preface to *Robert Woods Bliss Collection: Pre-Columbian Art,* by Samuel K. Lothrop (London, 1957), 7–8. In this preface, Robert Bliss conflates the events of 1912 with 1914 vis-à-vis his introduction to Joseph Brummer by Royall Tyler. The introduction took place in 1912, whereas the purchase of the Olmec jadeite figure occurred in 1914.

24 Karl A. Taube, "Standing Male Statuette," in *Olmec Art at Dumbarton Oaks* (Washington, D.C., 2004), 67–73.

25 *Sammlung Marc Rosenberg* (Berlin, [1929]).

26 Royall Tyler to Mildred Barnes Bliss, 8 November 1929, Papers of Royall Tyler, 1902–1967, HUGFP 38.6, box 2, HUA.

27 C. H. R., prefatory note to *Catalogue of an Exhibition of Objects of Indigenous American Art* (London, 1920), vii.

28 See Elizabeth A. Williams, "Collecting and Exhibiting Pre-Columbiana in France and England, 1870–1930," in *Collecting the Pre-Columbian Past,*

135–37, for a brief discussion of the reception of the two exhibits.

29 *Les arts anciens de l'Amérique: Exposition organisée au Musée des Arts Décoratifs, Palais du Louvre, Pavillon de Marsan, mai–juin 1928* (Paris, 1928), cats. 118, 478, 727, and 730.

30 Sotheby & Co., London, "A Fine Collection of Mexican Pre-Conquest Carvings in Jade, Jadeite, Hardstones, Crystal, Alabaster, Obsidian and Gold Ornaments," in *Egyptian, Greek, Roman, Indian and South American Antiquities, Native Art* (London, 9 June 1937), 19–28, plates 3–5, lots 137–92.

31 Royall Tyler to Mildred and Robert Woods Bliss, 4 June 1937, Papers of Royall Tyler, HUGFP 38.6, box 4, HUA.

32 Robert Woods Bliss to Royall Tyler, 4 June 1937, Papers of Royall Tyler, HUGFP 38.6, box 4, HUA.

33 Royall Tyler to Mildred and Robert Woods Bliss, 9 June 1937, Papers of Royall Tyler, HUGFP 38.6, box 4, HUA.

34 Sotheby & Co., London, "Prices and Buyers' Names," in *Egyptian, Greek, Roman, Indian and South American Antiquities, Native Art* (London, 9 June 1937), [33–35].

35 Robert Woods Bliss to Mildred Barnes, 26 October 1900, Papers of Robert Woods Bliss and Mildred Barnes Bliss, ca. 1860–1969, HUGFP 76.8, box 1, HUA.

36 Walter Muir Whitehill, *Dumbarton Oaks: The History of a Georgetown House and Garden, 1800–1966* (Cambridge, Mass., 1967), 59.

37 Ibid., 67–68.

38 Robert Woods Bliss, Guatemala Diary, 5 March 1935, Papers of Robert Woods Bliss and Mildred Barnes Bliss, HUGFP 76.8, box 48, HUA.

39 Ibid., [18] March 1935.

40 Ibid., 19 March 1935. See also John Lloyd Stephens, *Incidents of Travel in Central America, Chiapas, and Yucatan* (London, 1842), 1:140–42, and illustrations facing p. 142 for the altar mentioned.

41 Taube, "Celt Pendant," in *Olmec Art at Dumbarton Oaks,* 132–35.

42 See Taube, *Olmec Art at Dumbarton Oaks.*

43 Introduction to *An Exhibition of Pre-Columbian Art, January 15 Through February 10, Arranged by the Peabody Museum and the William Hayes Fogg Art Museum* (Cambridge, Mass., 1940), 5. For a brief look at the Peabody/Fogg exhibit within the context of special exhibits in 1940, see Holly Barnet-Sanchez, "The Necessity of Pre-Columbian Art in the United States," in *Collecting the Pre-Columbian Past,* 192–93.

44 Michael D. Coe, "From *Huaquero* to Connoisseur: The Early Market in Pre-Columbian Art," in *Collecting the Pre-Columbian Past,* 279–81.

45 Pre-Columbian Collection, PC.B.062. *Handbook of the Robert Woods Bliss Collection of Pre-Columbian Art* (Washington, D.C., 1963), cat. 7. See also Gudrun Bühl, ed., *Dumbarton Oaks: The Collections* (Washington, D.C., 2008), 198–99.

46 *Early Christian and Byzantine Art: An Exhibition Held at the Baltimore Museum of Art April 25– June 22, [1947]; Organized by the Walters Art Gallery, in Collaboration with the Department of Art and Archaeology of Princeton University and Dumbarton Oaks Research Library and Collection of Harvard University, and Forming Part of Princeton's Bicentennial Celebration* (Baltimore, 1947).

47 Elizabeth Hill Boone, "Robert Woods Bliss and Pre-Columbian Art," in *Andean Art at Dumbarton Oaks,* 1:9.

48 Robert Woods Bliss, acknowledgments in *Indigenous Art of the Americas: Collection of Robert Woods Bliss* (Washington, D.C., 1947), 4.

49 Robert Woods Bliss to Samuel Lothrop, 23 April 1946; Samuel Lothrop to Robert Woods Bliss, 25 April 1946; Robert Woods Bliss to Alfred Tozzer, 8 May 1946; and Alfred Tozzer to Robert Woods Bliss, 11 May 1946, Lothrop and Tozzer files, Pre-Columbian Collection.

50 See Gordon Randolph Willey, "Samuel Kirkland Lothrop," in *Portraits in American Archaeology: Remembrances of Some Distinguished Americanists* (Albuquerque, N. Mex., 1988), 195–216.

51 Bliss, *Indigenous Art of the Americas,* 3.

52 Robert Woods Bliss to J. O. Brew, director of the Peabody Museum, 7 July 1949, Peabody file, Pre-Columbian Collection.

53 Samuel Kirkland Lothrop, *Coclé: An Archaeological Study of Central Panama*, Memoirs of the Peabody Museum of Archaeology and Ethnology, Harvard University 7–8 (Cambridge, Mass., 1937–42). See also Eleanor Lothrop, *Throw Me a Bone: What Happens When You Marry an Archaeologist* (New York, 1948).

54 Robert Woods Bliss to Alfred Tozzer, secretary of the Peabody Museum, 5 January 1951, Tozzer file, Pre-Columbian Collection.

55 Samuel K. Lothrop, *Robert Woods Bliss Collection: Pre-Columbian Art* (London, 1957), 267–69, cats. 263–72. See also Samuel K. Lothrop, "Jewelry from the Panama Canal Zone," *Archaeology* 9, no. 1 (1956): 34–40, for a discussion of works that were unearthed at Venado Beach after the Lothrop excavation closed.

56 Lothrop's obituary of Robert Woods Bliss ended with these words: "Robert Woods Bliss not only assembled a unique American collection, but he helped to direct, or himself sponsored, a large amount of field research. To those who knew him, he will be remembered for his multiple interests, his unfailing courtesy and kindness, and his gift for friendship." Samuel K. Lothrop, "Robert Woods Bliss, 1875–1962," *American Antiquity* 29, no. 1 (1963): 92–93.

57 For the Andean collection, see Elizabeth Hill Boone, "Robert Woods Bliss and Pre-Columbian Art," in *Andean Art at Dumbarton Oaks*, 1:1–10, and specific catalogue entries by multiple authors, vols. 1 and 2. For the Olmec objects, see the catalogue entries in Taube, *Olmec Art at Dumbarton Oaks*.

58 See Ann Pollard Rowe and John Howland Rowe, "All-T'oqapu Tunic," in *Andean Art at Dumbarton Oaks*, 2:457–65. The tunic is one of the most significant Andean works in the Dumbarton Oaks Collection, and there is no information about its source. It was acquired by Bliss before 1954.

59 Lothrop, *Robert Woods Bliss Collection*, cat. 37, plate 29; and *Exhibition of Pre-Columbian Art*, cat. 165, illustrated.

60 Lothrop, *Robert Woods Bliss Collection*, cat. 53, plates 38–39; and *Exhibition of Pre-Columbian Art*, cat. 32.

61 Lothrop, *Robert Woods Bliss Collection*, cat. 52, plates 36–37.

62 Jane MacLaren Walsh, "The Dumbarton Oaks Tlazolteotl: Looking Beneath the Surface," *Journal de la Société des Américanistes* 94, no. 1 (2008): 7–43.

63 Coe, "From *Huaquero* to Connoisseur," 284–86.

64 Robert Wood Bliss, preface to *Robert Woods Bliss Collection*, 8.

65 Robert Woods Bliss to Samuel Lothrop, 2 February 1961, Lothrop file, Pre-Columbian Collection.

66 John Thacher, foreword to *Handbook of the Robert Woods Bliss Collection of Pre-Columbian Art*, vii.

67 Michael D. Coe, *An Early Stone Pectoral from Southeast Mexico*, Studies in Pre-Columbian Art and Archaeology 1 (Washington, D.C., 1966); Michael D. Coe and Elizabeth P. Benson, *Three Maya Relief Panels at Dumbarton Oaks*, Studies in Pre-Columbian Art and Archaeology 2 (Washington, D.C., 1966); Michael D. Coe, *Classic Maya Pottery at Dumbarton Oaks* (Washington, D.C., 1975); and Elizabeth P. Benson, *An Olmec Figure at Dumbarton Oaks*, Studies in Pre-Columbian Art and Archaeology 8 (Washington, D.C., 1971).

68 Benson, "The Robert Woods Bliss Collection of Pre-Columbian Art," 31.

69 Pre-Columbian Collection, PC.B.528. *Handbook of the Robert Woods Bliss Collection of Pre-Columbian Art*, cat. 47, illustrated as frontispiece. See also Mary Miller and Simon Martin, *Courtly Art of the Ancient Maya* (San Francisco, 2004), 218–19, plate 117; and Beatriz de la Fuente, "Multiple Languages of a Single Relief," in *Courtly Art of the Ancient Maya*, 244–46, fig. 77.

4

Collecting Past and Present
Music History and Musical Performance at Dumbarton Oaks

8 MAY 1938:

The date figures in the title of the first printed edition of Igor Stravinsky's Concerto in E♭ for chamber orchestra, which was premiered at Dumbarton Oaks on that day.[1] The piece was commissioned by Mildred and Robert Woods Bliss to celebrate their thirtieth wedding anniversary, and the commission was brokered by the French musician and composition teacher Nadia Boulanger, whom the couple knew from their years in Paris during the First World War. On a lecture tour in spring 1937—her first transatlantic trip since 1925—Boulanger visited Mildred Bliss in Washington, D.C., apparently to discuss the possibility of commissioning a new work. Stravinsky was also in the United States for a concert tour culminating in the premiere of his ballet *Jeu de cartes* at the Metropolitan Opera on 27 April. It is unlikely that Stravinsky visited Dumbarton Oaks himself, though he already knew Mildred Bliss, and Boulanger had probably discussed the project with him when they were both in New York (fig. 4.1).[2] But whether she was acting with his knowledge, and whether the idea was entirely hers or initially suggested by Mildred Bliss, Boulanger was able to fix the terms of the commission with Stravinsky when they sailed on the same crossing back to Europe on 5 May. In early June, she sent a telegram to the Blisses confirming Stravinsky's acceptance.[3]

The Blisses met Boulanger while posted in Paris in 1912–19, probably in the context of war charity work. In early 1915, Boulanger and her sister, Lili, founded the Comité Franco-Américain

du Conservatoire de Paris to organize war relief for musicians, with the Blisses' close friend, the composer-diplomat Blair Fairchild, as head of the American effort. Work with Fairchild and renowned conductor Walter Damrosch during the war and the subsequent foundation of the Conservatoire Franco-Américain at Fontainebleau in 1921 brought Boulanger in contact with the community of Francophile American philanthropists in which the Blisses were active. Boulanger used her connections to solicit support for her most promising composition students, and Mildred Bliss was among the most reliable patrons of young American composers in the "Boulangerie." In addition to financing scholarships to the Conservatoire Franco-Américain that were taken up by Boulanger's pupils, Mildred Bliss regularly disbursed funds—often anonymously—to individual pupils at Boulanger's request.[4]

But although they had supported musical activities and institutions for decades, the Blisses were relative newcomers to the world of new music patronage. They entered an arena profoundly influenced by women's work in private commissions that counterpointed with the often much more visible activities of large musical institutions. Here Mildred Bliss was following in the footsteps of notable American music patrons such as Isabella Stewart Gardner, whose work at Fenway Court set a significant precedent for the Dumbarton Oaks project, and Elizabeth Sprague Coolidge, the doyenne of Washington music patrons. Coolidge had, in fact, already

FIG. 4.1.

Igor Stravinsky. Inscribed in upper right corner: Pour Madame Robert Woods Bliss témoignage d'une sympathie très respectueuse Igor Stravinsky Paris Avril/36.

House Collection, HC.PH.1936.01, Dumbarton Oaks Research Library and Collection.

commissioned a piece from Stravinsky: the ballet *Apollon musagète*, which had received its world premiere at the Library of Congress almost exactly ten years earlier on 27 April 1928.[5]

For her part, Boulanger was building on her experience in negotiating commissions with that most formidable of Parisian patrons of the musical avant-garde, Winnaretta Singer, Princesse de Polignac. The princess had been a major backer of the Ballets Russes in Paris, and was an important early sponsor for Stravinsky's work. After the death of Serge Diaghilev in 1929, Boulanger had gradually become her main musical advisor, regularly organizing concerts in her Paris salon after 1933, and providing advice and guidance on new commissions.[6] Mildred Bliss was well-connected in East Coast and Parisian music circles, and knew both Elizabeth Sprague Coolidge and Winnaretta Singer; she had attended some of the princess's private premieres in the salon of her Greek revival mansion in Paris, where new works were performed for a select audience of invited guests. In commissioning the *Dumbarton Oaks Concerto* from Stravinsky and hosting its first performance in their home, the Blisses were following an established pattern in French contemporary music circles. At the same time, the public dimension to their work—particularly the relationship of the commission to their plans to give the house and its Music Room to Harvard University, already well underway by 1938—linked their activity to American patterns of philanthropy.[7]

As James Carder has remarked in connection with the Blisses' acquisition of modern art, they were not per se collectors of modern music.

They were, however, keenly interested in music and musical performance. Mildred Bliss was a competent player of the piano and violin. The Blisses were avid concertgoers, and were involved in the sponsorship of performing groups and educational institutions, including the Conservatoire Franco-Américain at Fontainebleau, where Nadia Boulanger taught composition.[8] Mildred was an energetic organizer of small, usually private concerts, which sometimes featured internationally acclaimed performers but were not usually associated with the cutting edge of new musical composition. The Blisses remained involved in concert activity at Dumbarton Oaks after the house was turned over to Harvard University. The chamber music concerts they held while in residence metamorphosed into the regular series still held today under the aegis of the Friends of Music at Dumbarton Oaks. In addition, the house saw one further Stravinsky premiere (of the *Septet*) in 1954, as well as the first performance of Aaron Copland's *Nonet*, commissioned to celebrate the Blisses' fiftieth wedding anniversary in 1958.[9] Their musical activism was relatively modest when compared to that of women like Polignac or Coolidge, who put large fortunes principally into music, regularly commissioned new works, and founded or underwrote public concert series and festivals. Nevertheless, their music patronage, which entailed mounting concerts of historical repertory as well as commissioning a small number of new works, added an important dimension to their aspirations for Dumbarton Oaks, aspirations for which the first performance of the Stravinsky concerto can in some ways be considered emblematic.

According to the initial plans for the Concerto in E♭, Stravinsky would travel to the United States to conduct the premiere. But poor health kept him in Europe, and Boulanger directed the concert in his place.[10] The event was a high point in her career. She had remained a passionate advocate for Stravinsky during the previous two decades, when many others were lamenting his turn away from the colorful Russian style of his early ballets. Stravinsky's works of the 1920s and 1930s—those generally grouped under the rubric "neoclassical"—were marked instead by sustained engagement with the tonal and formal conventions of the European musical past. The *Dumbarton Oaks Concerto* sits squarely in this phase of Stravinsky's preoccupations. The commission specified a work of Baroque *concerto grosso* dimensions, a stipulation Boulanger no doubt knew the composer

would find congenial. The piece dialogues with Baroque style and concerto form generally, and with Bach's Brandenburg Concertos in particular, in its musical textures and the disposition of its movements. It is a prime example of what Martha Hyde has termed "heuristic imitation" in Stravinsky's work; it "advertises its dependence on an earlier model, but in a way that forces us to recognize the disparity, the anachronism, of the connection being made." As Hyde observed, Stravinsky uses this procedure to open "a transitive dialogue with the past that allows him to take—and take responsibility for—his place in music history."[11] It was a mode of creative appropriation of the past that many at the time condemned as retrogressive academicism (a charge several critics leveled against the *Dumbarton Oaks Concerto*), but which Boulanger had defended from the early 1920s as a form of innovation.[12]

The change in conductor was not the only difference between the concert as originally planned and what happened in May 1938. In late 1937, Mildred Bliss asked Boulanger for advice on two draft concert programs.[13] The choice of works is slightly different in each draft, but both were for all-Stravinsky concerts, which aimed to show the composer's range and development through music chosen from different moments of his career. Stravinsky's reputation as a conductor was based principally on authoritative renditions of his own works—he was not especially admired as a performer of others' music—and the programs may reflect a moment in the planning when it was still thought that he would direct the Dumbarton Oaks premiere. Such retrospective programs, conducted by others as well as Stravinsky himself, had become common by the 1930s, when the then fifty-year-old composer's position among the most influential figures in twentieth-century music was firmly established. It was on just such an all-Stravinsky program, with the composer on the podium, that the *Dumbarton Oaks Concerto* received its European premiere in June.[14]

But this is not what happened at Dumbarton Oaks at the world premiere a month earlier (fig. 4.2). Boulanger convinced Mildred Bliss to adopt a program in which Stravinsky's Concerto in E♭ and his Duo Concertant for Violin and Piano, composed in 1931–32, alternated with selections from cantatas by Johann Sebastian Bach. The program allowed Boulanger to perform a particular relationship between past and present, one strikingly resonant with the setting

I. Wie will ich mich freuen   *J. S. Bach*
   Mein Gott, verwirf mich nicht.   1685-1750
   Wie zittern und wanken
   Wohl aber dem
   Lass, Seele, kein Leiden.
          HUGHES CUÉNOD and DODA CONRAD

II. Duo Concertant for violin and piano   *Igor Stravinsky*
    Cantiline   1882
    Eglogue I
    Eglogue II
    Gigue
    Dithyrambe
          SAMUEL DUSHKIN and BEVERIDGE WEBSTER

III. Beglückte Heerde, Jesu Schafe   *J. S. Bach*
     Der Tod'bleibt doch—Selig sind die Toten
     Es ist genug
          HUGHES CUÉNOD and DODA CONRAD

IV. Dumbarton Oaks Concerto in Eb major   *Igor Stravinsky*
    for small orchestra (1937-1938)
    First performance
                          Allegro
                          Allegretto
                          Con moto

         1 Flute   3 Violins
         1 Oboe   3 Violas
         1 Clarinet   2 Celli
         1 Bassoon   2 Double basses
         2 Horns

                 Under the direction of
                    NADIA BOULANGER
Dumbarton Oaks
May 8, 1938

FIG. 4.2.
Program for the
premiere of
Igor Stravinsky's
Concerto in Eb at
Dumbarton Oaks,
8 May 1938.
Collection of the Fondation
Internationale Nadia et Lili
Boulanger, Paris.

FIG. 4.3.
Program for
Nadia Boulanger's
solo organ recital
at the Grand Court
of Wanamaker's,
Philadelphia,
9 January 1925.
Collection of the Fondation
Internationale Nadia et Lili
Boulanger, Paris.

of the Dumbarton Oaks Music Room and more broadly with the Blisses' project of making their house a "home of the Humanities." Here I aim to explore how the first performance—and not only the composition itself—can be read as an exemplar of the dramatized relation to the past that characterized French neoclassicism between the wars, and to investigate how this vision of history relates to other aspects of the Blisses' collecting.

I begin with a flashback to an earlier point in Boulanger's career, before the intense activity of the 1930s that established her in the public eye as a conductor. For a brief period after the First World War, Boulanger spent several years as

an active music journalist, contributing regular concert reviews to *Le monde musical*. In a review from December 1921, she criticized one leading concert series for poor programming, and provided a rationale for non-chronological and non-linear programs that used the metaphor of the museum to make her point:

It is obviously not a matter of seeking a chronological order, which would have a useless and pedantic character, but indeed of finding, as much by the law of contrasts as by the demands of harmony, the general idea that allows for the most audacious juxtapositions without destroying unity. . . . It is easy

Nadia Boulanger—*Organist—Composer*

Mlle. Boulanger at her own organ in her home in Paris

THOUGH still in the years of her youth, Nadia Boulanger is by virtue of her genius the ranking woman organist of Europe. Her visit this winter to America is her first, and the first organ keys which her gifted fingers will touch in a public performance in this country will be those of the Wanamaker Grand Organ, the largest in the world, on January 9th. Walter Damrosch says of Mlle. Boulanger: "Among women, I have never met her equal in musicianship and indeed there are very few men who can compare with her. She is one of the finest organists of France."

Mlle. Boulanger was born in Paris, of musical parentage. Her father was a professor in the Conservatory, a position which her father had held before him; while her mother was a daughter of Mychetzky. At an early age she entered the Conservatory, where she attained the highest honors, graduating at the age of 16. Soon afterward she became assistant to Dallier, professor of harmony at the Conservatory, and

also as his assistant at the great organ of the church of La Madeleine. From the Conservatory she received, in 1898, first medal in solfeggio; in 1903, first prize in harmony; in 1904, first prize in piano accompaniment, organ, counterpoint and fugue, and in 1908, second Grand Prix de Rome.

She is professor of harmony at the American Conservatory, Fontainebleau; professor of organ, harmony, counterpoint and fugue at the Normal Music School of Paris; critic of the "Monde Musical," and is the author of a number of striking musical compositions. Of these one of the most notable is "La Villa Morte," produced by her in collaboration with the late Raoul Pugno. It is a four-act tragedy by d'Annunzio, who wrote for them a special version of his celebrated drama.

A course of lectures in modern music, to be delivered in the English language by Mlle. Boulanger, in various American cities, is being arranged by the Symphony Society of New York.

PROGRAM

"And the night shall be filled with music"
—Longfellow

1. FINALE FROM THE FIRST SONATA . . . *A. Guilmant*

2. a PIECE IN D MINOR. . . . .*D. Scarlatti*
   b SISTER MONICA. . . . .*Franc. Couperin*
   Transcribed by A. Guilmant
   c TOMB OF COUPERIN. . . . .*Maurice Ravel*
   Forlane
Rigaudon
Toccata

3. a PRELUDE AND FUGUE IN E MINOR. . . . .*J. S. Bach*
   b PRELUDE AND FUGUE ON BACH. . . . . . .*Franz Liszt*

4. a PIECE FOUNDED ON POPULAR FLEMISH AIRS
      Nadia Boulanger
   b CRADLE SONG AND FINALE FROM "THE FIRE-BIRD". . . . .*Strawinsky*
      Transcribed by Maurice Begby
   c PIECE IN B MINOR. . . . .*M. de Falla*
   d CORTEGE. . . . .*Lili Boulanger*

5. FINALE, FIRST SYMPHONY. . . . .*L. Vierne*

PROGRAM NOTE—Among the numbers on this program are several which have been transcribed for organ from piano and orchestral scores by Mlle. Nadia Boulanger, including works by Ravel, de Falla, and Lili Boulanger, the talented sister of Mlle. Boulanger, who in her brief life revealed the fire of real genius—a flame which was unhappily quenched at the early age of twenty-four.

---

to represent through vision the error thus committed: certain paintings cannot be brought together without doing harm to each other, whether by too great a contrast, by too marked a similarity, or by a crushing superiority. Sometimes one attracts to itself everything that cannot then be given to the others that surround it—sometimes they mutually weaken each other and become monotonous, sometimes they destroy each other a little. Though each work is a fixed and tangible thing whose beauty seems unchangeable—yet, not only does their setting help us to see them, to understand them, to feel them, it also gives off an atmosphere of which each ray seems to cast a favorable harmony over the entire group.

A demonstration of this, alas, can be made in the majority of museums. The abundance of works, the lack of space explains it—but does not alter the feeling of regret any more than it

diminishes that of fatigue, leaving in the heart the sense of melancholy at a joy for which only a little silence, respect and solitude was missing.[15]

What Boulanger meant by "the general idea that allows for the most audacious juxtapositions without destroying unity" can be partly inferred from the organ recitals she performed during her first tour of the United States in 1925 (fig. 4.3).[16] Her program began with the Finale of Alexandre Guilmant's First Symphony, and continued with a piece by Domenico Scarlatti, followed by arrangements of François Couperin's *Soeur Monique* and sections from Maurice Ravel's *Le tombeau de Couperin*. The third group juxtaposed a Bach prelude and fugue with Franz Liszt's Prelude and Fugue on B–A–C–H. After another group of Boulanger's *Airs populaires flamands*, extracts from Stravinsky's *The Firebird*, Manuel

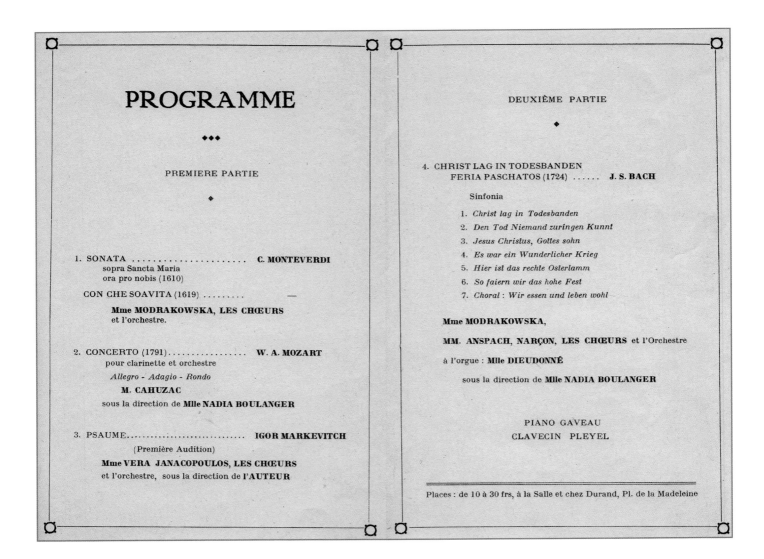

PROGRAMME

♦♦♦

PREMIERE PARTIE

♦

1. SONATA .... **C. MONTEVERDI**
   sopra Sancta Maria
   ora pro nobis (1610)

   CON CHE SOAVITA (1619) .... —

   Mme MODRAKOWSKA, LES CHŒURS
   et l'orchestre.

2. CONCERTO (1791)............... **W. A. MOZART**
   pour clarinette et orchestre
   Allegro - Adagio - Rondo
   M. CAHUZAC
   sous la direction de **Mlle NADIA BOULANGER**

3. PSAUME............................ **IGOR MARKEVITCH**
   (Première Audition)
   Mme VERA JANACOPOULOS, LES CHŒURS
   et l'orchestre, sous la direction de l'**AUTEUR**

DEUXIÈME PARTIE

♦

4. CHRIST LAG IN TODESBANDEN
   FERIA PASCHATOS (1724) ...... **J. S. BACH**

   Sinfonia

   1. *Christ lag in Todesbanden*
   2. *Den Tod Niemand zuringen Kunnt*
   3. *Jesus Christus, Gottes sohn*
   4. *Es war ein Wunderlicher Krieg*
   5. *Hier ist das rechte Osterlamm*
   6. *So faiern wir das hohe Fest*
   7. *Choral : Wir essen und leben wohl*

Mme MODRAKOWSKA,

MM. ANSPACH, NARÇON, LES CHŒURS et l'Orchestre

à l'orgue : **Mlle DIEUDONNÉ**

sous la direction de **Mlle NADIA BOULANGER**

PIANO GAVEAU
CLAVECIN PLEYEL

Places : de 10 à 30 frs, à la Salle et chez Durand, Pl. de la Madeleine

De Falla's Piece in B Minor, and Lili Boulanger's *Cortège*, the concert closed with the Finale of Louis Vierne's First Symphony. Striking elements of this program include not only the juxtaposition of chronologically distant pieces, but also a concern for formal symmetry. Note the use of the Guilmant and Vierne finales to open and close the concert, and the framing of the central Bach-Liszt pillar with two groups of short pieces with correspondences between them—for example, the mirror placement of the Boulanger *Cortège* and Ravel's *Le tombeau de Couperin*.

Such patterns became the basis for programs Boulanger directed in the following decade, when her conducting career first began to take off.[17] Her concerts typically featured one or more recent works, often in first performances. As in her earlier solo recitals, she invariably surrounded

these new pieces with a heterogeneous mix of much earlier music—even for series where all-contemporary programs were the rule. The 1934 premiere of her pupil Igor Markevitch's *Psaume* at the Salle Gaveau in Paris was typical (fig. 4.4). The concert was the tenth for La Sérénade, a society founded expressly to promote new music—it was La Sérénade, in fact, that would host the first European performance of the *Dumbarton Oaks Concerto* a little over a month after its world premiere in Washington, D.C. Markevitch conducted his *Psaume* as the centerpiece of a program otherwise directed by Boulanger, who began with two works by Claudio Monteverdi and Mozart's Clarinet Concerto K. 622 and concluded with a Bach cantata. This resembles today's well-known ruse of slotting premieres just before the intermission of a concert otherwise made up of

FIG. 4.4.

Program for La Sérénade at the Salle Gaveau, Paris, 9 June 1934.

Collection of the Fondation Internationale Nadia et Lili Boulanger, Paris.

older pieces to comfort audiences who may be wary of new music. But it broke completely with normal practice for La Sérénade, whose programs were uniformly devoted to recent works.[18]

This was the sort of program that Boulanger exported to the United States for her tours in 1937, 1938, and 1939, and directed during her wartime residence in the country from 1940 to 1946. The formal programs she conducted at Dumbarton Oaks for Mildred Bliss, which began a few months before the *Dumbarton Oaks Concerto* in 1938, fit smoothly into the pattern. In February 1938, for example, Boulanger directed a concert that juxtaposed compositions by Monteverdi, Claude Debussy, and Gabriel Fauré (fig. 4.5). The following year (fig. 4.6), she mixed Monteverdi and Fauré with Marc-Antoine Charpentier, in a concert that included a signature set, in which a recent work by Stravinsky was framed by sixteenth- and eighteenth-century pieces. For another concert in 1939, she devised a palindromic program, in which songs by Francis Poulenc and Fauré surrounded medieval and Renaissance vocal music around an axis formed by Fauré's Sonata in A Major for Violin (fig. 4.7).

Boulanger had been producing this kind of program for the Princesse de Polignac's salon since 1933, and it is instructive to compare the Dumbarton Oaks concerts—particularly the premiere of Stravinsky's concerto—with the December 1938 concert featuring the private premiere of Poulenc's Organ Concerto that she devised for the princess (fig. 4.8). This program began with a suite by Henry Purcell and continued with a Bach ensemble sonata framed by two sets of songs by Poulenc, so that the Purcell-Bach-Poulenc instrumental chamber music sequence was symmetrically punctuated by two groups of recent songs. In contrast, for the public premiere for La Sérénade at the Salle Gaveau on 21 June 1939, Roger Désormière conducted the same musicians—the Orchestre de Chambre de la Société Philharmonique de Paris, with soloist Maurice Duruflé—but matched Poulenc's piece with recent works by Darius Milhaud, Vittorio Rieti, and Arthur Honegger.[19]

Boulanger's programs were strikingly different from those of most of her contemporaries. Although the performance of early music was in itself nothing new, it was typical to compartmentalize works from different eras. That is, organizers and performers devoted individual programs or entire series to single periods, genres, or composers, or presented "historical concerts"

in overtly didactic chronological arrangements. New music was generally performed in all-contemporary concerts. In cases where both old and new pieces were featured on the same program, the early music was almost invariably segregated in the first part of the concert to provide a teleological trajectory from past to present. Boulanger not only defied this trend, but went to extremes both in the chronological span she covered and in the frequency of her shifts between epochs. The engagement with music history implicit in any performance of early music was simultaneously foregrounded and problematized by her rapid seesawing between chronologically distant pieces. Her programs were performative demonstrations of the claims she had made in relation to Stravinsky's music for well over a decade. For example, she praised Stravinsky's *Octet*, which was often described as his first unambiguously "neoclassical" work and which confused some listeners familiar with his earlier music. Like the *Dumbarton Oaks Concerto*, if in a more free-wheeling and less systematic way, the *Octet* employs both forms and textures drawn from much earlier music, and mixes classical and Baroque allusions and imitations with Stravinsky's characteristically inventive experiments in pitch structure.[20] Boulanger's glowing review of the work's 1923 premiere praised the *Octet's* geometrical construction, classical form, simplicity, and clarity—all values that would be attached to the new neoclassical aesthetic—and asserted its affinity with the masterpieces of Renaissance polyphony and the works of Bach.[21]

Boulanger's postwar concert criticism and her concert practice of the 1920s and 1930s were interventions in some of the most intensely debated aesthetic issues in interwar France. The polemic around the "retour à Bach" and particularly Stravinsky's neoclassicism brought opposing positions into sharp relief: Was the invocation of musical forms and materials from the distant past a symptom of debilitating nostalgia or a paradigmatically modern creative impulse? How was the relationship between musical tradition and innovation to be understood?

To appreciate how Boulanger's concerts engaged with these debates, we can begin with the explanations she supplied herself. In November 1936, she was approached by the British Broadcasting Corporation (BBC) to present five concerts of French vocal music from the Middle Ages to the present for the music-historical program "Foundations of Music." When the BBC

I. (a) Hor ch'el ciel   *Claudio Monteverdi*
                                (1567-1643)

       L'Ensemble Vocal et Instrumental

(b) Lamento della Ninfa
       Ctesse. de Polignac
       Mme. Irène Kédroff
       MM. Cuénod et Conrad

(c) Lasciatemi morire
       L'Ensemble Vocal

II.   Pelléas et Mélisande (fragments)
            Claude Debussy (1862-1918)
       Mélisande : Ctesse. de Polignac
       Geneviève : Mme. Nathalie Kédroff
       Le petit Yniold : Mme. Peyron
       Pelléas : M. Cuénod
       Golaud ⎫
       Arkel ⎬ M. Conrad
       Le Berger ⎭

III. (a) Chiome d'oro   *Claudio Monteverdi*
       Mmes. Peyron et de Polignac
       et l'Ensemble Instrumental

(b) Romanesca
       MM. Cuénod et Conrad

(c) Ecco mormorar l'onde
       L'Ensemble Vocal

(d) Il Ballo dell'Ingrate
       L'Ensemble Vocal et Instrumental

IV. (a) Nocturne de Shylock   *Gabriel Faure*
                               (1845-1924)
       Violon solo : M. Jacobsen

(b) Celle que j'aime
       M. Cuénod

(c) Madrigal
       Mmes. de Polignac et Irène Kédroff
       MM. Cuénod et Conrad

(d) Dieu qu'il la fait bon regarder
(e) Yver, vous n'estes qu'un villain
                     Claude Debussy
       L'Ensemble Vocal

Under the direction of
MELLE. NADIA BOULANGER

NOËMIE PERUGIA, Soprano
NATHALIE KEDROFF, Contralto
HUGUES CUENOD, Tenor
DODA CONRAD, Bass

Assisted by
THE MUSICAL ART QUARTET
and FRANK ENEY, Double-bass

Dumbarton Oaks   *April 14, 1939.*

I. 1. Hor ch'el ciel   *Claudio Monteverdi*
                               (1567-1643)
   2. Romanesca   "   "
   3. Maledetto   "   "
   4. Il ballo delle ingrate   "   "

II. Pelléas et Mélisande   *Gabriel Fauré*
     a) Prélude   *(1845-1924)*
     b) Fileuse
     c) Molto adagio
     d) Nocturne (Shylock)

III. Air de Jocaste (Oedipus Rex) *Igor Strawinsky*
                                 (1882-
    O Nata Lux   *Thomas Tallis*
                         (1520-1585)
    Benedictus   *Joseph Haydn*
                         (1732-1809)

IV. La Peste de Milan   *Marc-Antoine Charpentier*
                               (1634-1704)

Under the direction of

MELLE. NADIA BOULANGER

❧

NOËMIE PERUGIA, Soprano
NATHALIE KEDROFF, Contralto
HUGUES CUENOD, Tenor
DODA CONRAD, Bass
PAUL MAKANOWITZKY, Violin

Dumbarton Oaks   *April 16, 1939.*

I. Airs chantés (Moréas)	Francis Poulenc (1899-
Tel jour, telle nuit (Elvard)	" "
Avant le cinéma (Apollinaire)	" "
II. Cassez mes yeulx (1558)	Créquillon
Quand ce beau printemps (Ronsard) (1561)	Adrian Le Roy
Tant que vivray (Clément Marot (1519)	d'après Claudin de Sermizy
III. Sonate en la majeur pour piano et violin	Gabriel Fauré (1845-1924)
IV. A prié qu'en chantant plour (Canso (Chanson de Troubadour)	Anonyme
Quel deuil immense (planh sur la mort de Richard Coeur de Lion)	Gaucela Faidit (1199)
Chanterai pour mon courage (Chanson de Croisade)	Anonyme (1197)
Ici commence tout un roman	(Environ XIIIe)
V. Fêtes Galantes (Verlaine)	
Mandoline	Gabriel Fauré
Fantoches	Claude Debussy (1862-1918)
Clair de Lune	Fauré
Le Faune	Debussy
Colloque sentimental	"

attempted to impose a chronological pattern—in which each program in the series was devoted to one historical period, with the final broadcast containing premieres and recent works—Boulanger resisted with all her considerable strength. Eventually the BBC capitulated and allowed her to construct five heterogeneous broadcasts that mimicked her Paris concerts. When asked to prepare a short introduction to the programs, Boulanger leapt at the chance to explain her goals:

What have we tried to do? How have we done it? The purpose was to give an idea of the different aspects vocal ensemble music has had and still has in France, what it has meant and means. What it has been and is, as a medium of expression.

In order to succeed, was it necessary to follow a chronological order? At first one would say so, but considering the question from another angle, we came to another conclusion, and that for two reasons: the first, if built in successive periods, each recital would only let appear one isolated part of the ensemble we had the purpose to display in its entirety: the second, certainly the more important, refers to the real relationship in art; in looking for it, one makes associations which

seem at first strange to the mind, but are clear to the deeper understanding.

She then returned to the painting metaphor she had applied in her earlier concert reviews, saying that "some modern painting is infinitely nearer to the 14th century than to a painting of 50 years ago." She closed the broadcast by re-emphasizing the continuities that justified her rejection of segregation or chronology:

It is not for the sake of variety or contrast that DEBUSSY, RAVEL and POULENC are inserted in the midst of Renaissance masters, that Francis POULENC'S Litanies and PREGER'S Motet are surrounded with medieval and early Renaissance music.

There is in the grouping one intention, our purpose; works of the most striking periods having been chosen. The point was . . . to demonstrate that the past lights the present, but also the present the past, and they have thus created new links between them.[22]

Seemingly wildly divergent works are not juxtaposed for difference, but because they are

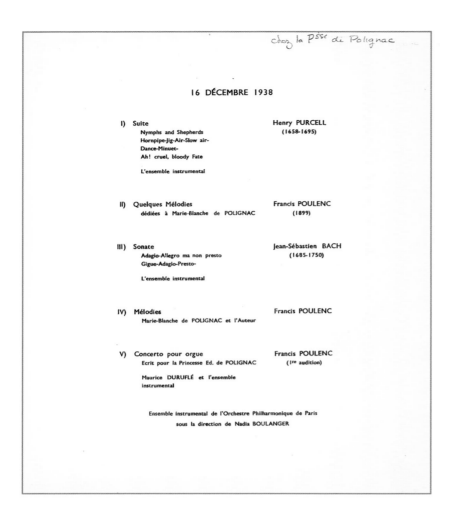

FIG. 4.8.
Program conducted by Nadia Boulanger for Winnaretta Singer, Princesse de Polignac, 16 December 1938.

in some fundamental sense the same. Careful placement can bring out essential similarities between pieces that at first glance would seem to have nothing in common. The key passage here is Boulanger's claim that "the past lights the present, but also the present the past." That is, the benefit works both ways: early music does not simply provide a historical imprimatur for departure from common-practice techniques or signify a break from romanticism—it is itself changed when juxtaposed with later repertories. Because of Stravinsky, we listen differently to Bach; and this is a way of rescuing Bach from the museum as well as anchoring Stravinsky in history.

This position is consistent with important Parisian intellectual currents of the early twentieth century, and particularly reflects the work of thinkers such as Henri Bergson, Charles Maurras, and Paul Valéry—all of whom Boulanger regularly cited in her teaching and concert criticism. It is characteristic of a strain of modernism that rejected many elements of nineteenth-century historicism—particularly its positivistic and scientific dimensions—while at the same time avoiding a complete refusal of the past, as was the case in other modernist movements, such as futurism. As Christopher Butler has observed, Stravinsky's neoclassical music was firmly anchored in this intellectual tradition, whose hallmarks include an acute consciousness of the past and a sense of meaningful relationships between the techniques and structures of music, literature, and art.[23] This brand of "conservative modernism," as Butler has described it, was an important force in the social and artistic circles in which all the protagonists of my story moved. The Blisses' friend and advisor Royall Tyler was steeped in this philosophy, and it is the intellectual environment in which Mildred and Robert Bliss began collecting with Tyler's guidance[24] and in which Nadia Boulanger's music journalism and early performing career unfolded. Butler's remarks about Stravinsky in this context are equally pertinent to Boulanger's aesthetic of performance and to aspects of the Blisses' collecting.

Boulanger's consistent analogies with graphic art—and particularly with museum installations—emphasize how her own understanding of the relationship between tradition and innovation in music echoed and built upon debates in the arena of visual culture. In what follows, I will briefly review some of these before returning to explore their application to Boulanger's reading of Stravinsky and the Music Room at Dumbarton Oaks. For Boulanger, a key text was Paul Valéry's 1923 essay "Le problème des musées," a brief but influential attack on contemporary museum practice that manifested the same opposition to chronological placement—as well as advocacy of thematic and formal connections between adjacent works—that Boulanger applied to music. Valéry was not only one of the most influential cultural figures in France, he was also Boulanger's friend and close neighbor. His wife, a pianist, was a pupil of Boulanger's mentor Raoul Pugno, and Boulanger took charge of his son François's musical education (roughly a decade after she took over the same responsibility for Stravinsky's son Soulima). Throughout the 1930s, Stravinsky and Valéry met socially at Boulanger's house in Gargenville, and Stravinsky consulted Valéry while staying there in the summer of 1939 when he was finishing the text of his *Poétique musicale*.[25]

In "Le problème des musées," Valéry claimed that only a civilization neither rational nor sensual could have conceived a "house of incoherence" as insane as an art museum. The visitor, initially attracted by the desire to experience beauty, is soon stunned by the profusion of competing works; portraits and seascapes jostle for attention with still life and history paintings of completely different dimensions, until the hapless visitor is reduced to stumbling between them like a drunkard from bar to bar:

> The more beautiful [the works] are, the more they are the exceptional effects of human ambition, the more they should be distinct. They are rare objects which their creators would have wished to be unique. "This painting," people sometimes say, "KILLS all the others around it. . . ."
>
> I am sure that neither Egypt, nor China, nor Greece, which were wise and sophisticated, knew this system of juxtaposing creations that devour each other.[26]

The system Valéry condemned is the arrangement of artworks in successive rooms by period and style, which he calls a "strange organized disorder." It imposes time as a controlling principle—the chronology Boulanger labeled "pointless" and "pedantic" when applied to music—without regard for thematic or formal harmony.

For Valéry, the sense-making frame that art required to release its meanings—the frame that the museum had disastrously replaced with historical science—was architecture: "Painting and Sculpture, the demon of Explanation tells me, are abandoned children. Their mother is dead, their mother Architecture. While she lived, she gave them their place, their function, their constraints. The freedom to wander was denied them. They had their place, their well-defined light, their topics, their alliances. . . . While she lived, they knew what they wanted."[27]

Valéry's protests were, in part, a reaction to the development of art history as a critical frame for museum practice. Rather than placing paintings and sculptures in relation to furnishings, mirrors, and other domestic objects (as was common in private settings), public museums organized their collections by artist, school, or region, and the overall sequence of rooms was governed by chronology. According to Philip Fisher, the "subject" of the art museum in this arrangement—the narrative that renders the objects meaningful and valuable—is art history, whose linking forward motion is replicated physically by the movement of the visitor through the museum space.[28] Chronological installations encourage a walk-by viewing aimed at producing a historical account—"this" leads to "that"—rather than an attentive engagement with a single object. Given the progressive assumptions of nineteenth-century historiography, the chronological hang irresistibly evoked an evolutionary understanding of the relationship between earlier and later works. Such an understanding was fundamentally incompatible with the notion of a timeless masterpiece, and the historical sequence necessarily prevented any object from simultaneously occupying multiple moments of linear time.[29]

That Boulanger, like Valéry, was acutely aware of the conflict between the aesthetic of the masterpiece and the technology of the series is demonstrated by her concert practice. In Krzysztof Pomian's analysis, the museum is a semiosphere in which visible objects are assigned value through their relationship to an invisible realm of signification—such as "nation" or "the past"—for which they are taken metonymically to stand.[30] To extend his analysis from visual display to sound, the concert might be understood as organizing an exchange between the audible and inaudible. Concerts can be distinguished from one another by the ways in which they mediate this exchange through, among other things, program choice and order. The temporal nature of music means that—even more inevitably than the museum—the concert constructs a before-and-after sequence, in which each piece, in turn, becomes the "before" of the work in the frame. The chronological concert could, thus, be read as an implicit authorization of the values of evolutionary music history, as it aligned the forward motion of the audible sequence to the temporal progression of the inaudible historical narrative that underpins it. The concert audience listens through a condensed history—just as the museum visitor walks through it.

In contrast, Boulanger's insistent violation of chronological order disrupted the smooth forward motion of the historical narrative—and its potential for evolutionary reading—by dismantling the correspondence between audible and inaudible time, and called attention to a normally unexamined set of assumptions that privileged historical sequence. At the same time, her programs avoided the sequestration of early and modern works into antiquarian early music programs or futurist avant-garde events. Instead, she attempted to negotiate the competing demands of progressivism and historicism by constructing a sphere where tradition and innovation could be reimagined and where the encounter between old and new could be simultaneously dramatized and controlled. Here the formal symmetry of her programs came into play, providing a temporal "frame"—the analogue to Valéry's architecture—for the counterpoint of new and old that was not straightforwardly teleological. Form becomes the domain in which this interaction occurs and provides the constraint necessary for the dynamic release of meaning.

An extreme material counterpart of Boulanger's approach can be seen in Albert Barnes's notorious installations at the Barnes Collection, which opened in 1925. The collection was designed to illustrate Barnes's formalist philosophy of art and his belief that the essential values of great painting were the same for all periods. His walls mixed old master and modern French paintings in installations where strong symmetries (both in the content of the artworks and in their arrangement on the wall) overrode the heterogeneity of the paintings' age and provenance.[31] Obviously there is nothing quite so extreme at Dumbarton Oaks. But, like the far more flamboyant Albert Barnes, the Blisses were both heterogeneous and Francophile in their collecting practices. Despite Royall Tyler's repeated urging to concentrate their resources on Byzantine art, they showed a similar disinclination to segregate their collecting, even in the most intensive phase of their work on Dumbarton Oaks prior to handing it over to Harvard University.[32]

The Music Room is a good example of their approach to display (fig. 4.9). It was the most extensive new addition to the house and occupied much of the Blisses' energies and budget between 1924 and 1929.[33] It incorporated a sixteenth-century French mantelpiece and two sixteenth-century Italian marble arches, as well as reproductions of a sixteenth-century ceiling and an eighteenth-century French parquet floor by Parisian designer Armand Albert Rateau and entryway wall murals by Allyn Cox. Among the artworks on display were fifteenth- and sixteenth-century Flemish tapestries, a fourteenth-century painting of the Madonna and Child with saints and angels by Bernardo Daddi, a fifteenth-century portrait attributed to the Maître de Flémalle, and a seventeenth-century painting of the Visitation by El Greco, as well as medieval French and German sculptures, ancient Chinese sculptures, and fine sixteenth- and seventeenth-century rugs. Before 1940, ancient and Byzantine sculptures, metalwork, and textiles also were displayed.

The Music Room organized these objects in ways that are not easily explained by straightforward opposition to public museum practices. There is no systematic chronological or geographical order to the installation. At the same time, the incorporation of a diverse group of artworks into the Music Room testifies to a historicizing desire to make the house a museum in which the new mode of exhibition has strong echoes of the past. And while the Blisses seem to have deliberately excluded the really new from the decor of the room, they repeatedly urged their architect to aim for "simplicity, broad lines, large space"—all catchwords of neoclassical aesthetics—and the disparate architectural and decorative elements were incorporated into an overall design of strong formal symmetry and balanced dimensions. Robert Bliss described the Music Room at Dumbarton Oaks as "a delightful

medley of Italian renaissance, French eighteenth century, Georgian and American!"[34] underlining the degree to which the room can be read as an experiment in the consolidation of European material culture in a new American context. The room was concieved as an architectural "frame" that would bring the historical treasures it displayed into new relationships with each other and with the present. Here Valéry's museum critique, which is often read as a simple and elitist call for the return of artworks to collectors' homes, takes on a larger resonance. Collectors like the Blisses were free to ignore the art-historical imperatives of the public museum (even when the collection was consciously designed to be or to become open to the public) and to employ architectural settings to construct formal and thematic links between artworks in the way Valéry imagined.

Nadia Boulanger seems to have been particularly sensitive to the potential resonance between the decoration of the Music Room, the compositional concerns of the *Dumbarton Oaks Concerto*, and her own experiments in concert program construction. The juxtaposition of Bach and Stravinsky brings their similarities—as well as their differences—into sharp relief, allowing the pieces to speak to each other across time in the same way that resemblances between material objects were emphasized by their juxtaposition within a single architectural frame. Boulanger was apparently successful in bringing Mildred Bliss to her way of seeing, so it seems fitting that this should be reflected in the new title Stravinsky's work acquired after the premiere. Originally titled simply Concerto in E♭, the work acquired the subtitle "Dumbarton Oaks–8-V-1938" at Mildred Bliss's request, thereby fixing the link

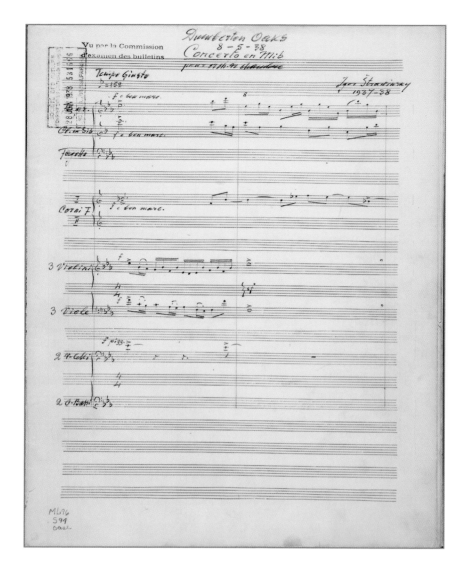

FIG. 4.10.

Title page of Igor Stravinsky, "Dumbarton Oaks 8-V-38 Concerto en Mi♭."

Rare Book Collection, ML.96.594, Dumbarton Oaks Research Library and Collection.

between the piece, the date, and the location of its first performance (fig. 4.10). The entire event, in Boulanger's hands, might be construed not just as a performance of the concerto, but as an enactment of a strain of modernist neoclassicism that, while appearing to emphasize history by setting up a dialogue with art of the past, in fact attempts the erasure of time.

Forty years later, when reminiscing about her relationship to Stravinsky and his music, Boulanger made explicit this goal, which she thought she had achieved in her concert programs. Explaining how she had put together the beginning of a Bach sonata with Stravinsky's *Dithyrambe*, she exclaimed: "They link together in such a marvellous way that time is abolished. It resituates memory in the present, the present

in memory and in the past."[35] As with her concerts for Mildred and Robert Bliss, these juxtapositions were as much about making history out of the new as making historic music modern. In that way, they worked as a musical analogue to the collecting practices of the Blisses and their generation in its mode of assigning value to art. That musical performances cannot be conserved at Dumbarton Oaks in the same way as the physical artifacts the Blisses acquired has meant that this aspect of their collection is more difficult to grasp today. The history of Stravinsky's concerto and its first performance, however, can help us to see the role that musical interactions of tradition and innovation could play in the Blisses' "home of the Humanities" at Dumbarton Oaks.

Notes

1 Igor Stravinsky, *Concerto en mi♭ pour orchestre de chambre: Dumbarton Oaks 8-V-38*, full score (Mainz, 1938).

2 It is unclear when the Blisses first met Stravinsky, though a signed photo of the composer from 1936 (fig. 4.1) in the Archives shows that they were acquainted before the commission was offered. Stravinsky's close working relationship with the violinist Samuel Dushkin (1891–1976), with whom he began collaborating in 1930 and for whom the Violin Concerto and Duo Concertant were written, provides one likely avenue for contact with the Blisses. Dushkin was the adopted son of Mildred Bliss's good friend Blair Fairchild (1877–1933), and Mildred Bliss was heavily involved in Fairchild's promotion of Dushkin's career. Correspondence with Fairchild and with Dushkin himself indicates that Dushkin regularly played in private concerts at the Blisses' Paris apartment between 1915 and 1919, and that Mildred Bliss retained an active interest in his subsequent activities. Papers of Robert Woods Bliss and Mildred Barnes Bliss, ca. 1860–1969, HUGFP 76.8, box 16, HUA.

3 Stravinsky had arrived in New York on Christmas Eve in 1936; his tour began in January 1937 in Toronto and continued with concerts in Boston, the Midwest, and Los Angeles before finishing in April with the premiere of *Jeu de cartes*. Stephen Walsh, *Stravinsky: The Second Exile; France and America, 1934–1971* (London, 2007), 56–66. Boulanger was in the United States from 5 April to 4 May 1937, mainly based in New York. Mildred Bliss's appointment book for 1937 notes that Boulanger came to Dumbarton Oaks between 30 April and 1 May. Papers of Robert Woods Bliss and Mildred Barnes Bliss, HUGFP 76.32, box 8, HUA. On the evening of 30 April, they had dinner with several other guests; the entry for the evening of 1 May is marked "(Stravinsky) X/Boulanger music," suggesting that Boulanger and the Blisses dined alone. The parentheses and "X" next to Stravinsky's name suggest that he had been invited but did not attend; an alternative explanation is that the evening was devoted to discussion of the commission with Boulanger. Boulanger's appointment books for spring 1937 are no longer extant, but she probably attended the *Jeu de cartes* premiere and certainly saw Stravinsky while they were both in New York. She and the composer traveled back to Paris together on the *Paris*, sailing 5 May. On her return, Boulanger telegrammed the Blisses confirming Stravinsky's acceptance, thereby supporting the hypothesis that Boulanger discussed the commission with Mildred Bliss and then communicated the idea to Stravinsky during the return trip. Walsh, *Stravinsky: The Second Exile*, 66. Letters from summer 1937 to Stravinsky from Samuel Dushkin, who would participate in the *Dumbarton Oaks Concerto* premiere, suggest that Stravinsky had not yet seen the house and Music Room. Box 30, III, nos. 821–823 and 825–826, Paul Sacher Stiftung, Basel. My thanks to Kimberly Francis for bringing these to my attention. Stravinsky's later confusion over the premiere seems to confirm this. Stephen Walsh, *Stravinsky: A Creative Spring; Russia and France, 1882–1934* (London, 2002), 76. Unfortunately, the correspondence to Mildred Bliss from Stravinsky, Boulanger, Dushkin, and other participants in the commission and premiere of the concerto is not found in the Bliss papers at Harvard University Archives, and does not appear to have been conserved at Dumbarton Oaks with the autograph manuscript of the piece. It seems clear that Mildred kept this memorabilia separate from her normal correspondence files (as she did for other materials related to the 1938 anniversary celebrations) and that it was subsequently misfiled or disposed of separately from the rest of her papers.

4 On Boulanger's wartime activities and the foundation of the Conservatoire, see Léonie Rosenstiel, *Nadia Boulanger: A Life in Music* (New York, 1982), 128–54. Correspondence from Boulanger to Mildred Bliss from 1923 onward can be found in the Papers of Robert Woods Bliss and Mildred Barnes Bliss, HUGFP 76.8, box 9, HUA. Letters from the 1920s concern Boulanger students that Mildred was supporting, including Melville Smith, Howard Hinners, and Israel Citkovitz. Boulanger's own papers (Musique, N.L.A 56, pièces 238–280, Bibliothèque Nationale de France, Paris) preserve Mildred Bliss's letters only from 1938 onward, but carbons of some of Mildred Bliss's responses are kept in the Boulanger file of the Bliss archive at Harvard University Archives.

5 Walsh, *Stravinsky: A Creative Spring*, 451. On Gardner, Coolidge, and other patrons, see Ralph P. Locke and Cyrilla Barr, eds., *Cultivating Music in America: Women Patrons and Activists Since 1860* (Berkeley, 1997). Coolidge was present for the *Dumbarton Oaks Concerto* premiere, according to correspondence (Musique, RÉS. VM DOS. 144, Bibliothèque Nationale de France, Paris), and she subsequently engaged Boulanger for concerts in the recently built Coolidge Auditorium at the Library of Congress.

6 See Sylvia Kahan, *Music's Modern Muse: A Life of Winnaretta Singer, Princesse de Polignac* (Rochester, N.Y., 2003); and Jeanice Brooks, "Nadia Boulanger and the Salon of the Princesse de Polignac," *Journal of the American Musicological Society* 46 (1993): 415–68. Mildred Bliss was an acquaintance of the princess, and Robert Bliss was involved with the Cercle Interallié, a Parisian diplomatic club also sponsored by the Polignac family, for whom Nadia Boulanger organized concerts from the mid-1930s.

7 More typical of this type of patronage were Mildred Bliss's activities in the year following the premiere of the *Dumbarton Oaks Concerto*, when she helped to organize support for Stravinsky's Symphony in C. Stravinsky had begun the piece without a commission, and Mildred Bliss worked with other influential American women to guarantee a commission from the Chicago Symphony Orchestra and the purchase of the autograph manuscript by the Library of Congress. See Walsh, *Stravinsky: The Second Exile*, 90–91. Boulanger was the source of this plan as well, according to Stravinsky's letter to her of 12 January 1939 (Musique, N.L.A. 108, pièce 134, Bibliothèque Nationale de France, Paris).

8 Mildred Bliss supported the organization from its foundation in 1921. Papers of Robert Woods Bliss and Mildred Barnes Bliss, HUGFP 76.12, box 6, HUA. Her friendship with Fairchild dates to the turn of the century, and they were clearly good friends already in 1902, the date of the first extant letter from Fairchild. Papers of Robert Woods Bliss and Mildred Barnes Bliss, HUGFP 76.8, box 16, HUA.

9 On the history of the Friends of Music, including programs for concerts held after 1940, see John Thacher, *Music at Dumbarton Oaks: A Record, 1940 to 1970* (Washington, D.C., 1977).

10 For details, see Jeanice Brooks, "Mildred Bliss Tells Nadia Boulanger to Think of Herself For Once," in *Cultivating Music in America*, 209–13.

11 Martha M. Hyde, "Stravinsky's Neoclassicism," in *The Cambridge Companion to Stravinsky*, ed. Jonathan Cross (Cambridge, 2003), 114–15.

12 For criticism of the concerto, see Walsh, *Stravinsky: The Second Exile*, 78–79. On the emergence of the values and vocabulary of neoclassicism and their application to Stravinsky (including in Boulanger's writing) in the 1920s, see Scott Messing, *Neoclassicism in Music: From the Genesis of the Concept through the Schoenberg/Stravinsky Polemic* (Ann Arbor, Mich., 1988), 87–149.

13 Mildred Barnes Bliss to Nadia Boulanger, 13 December 1937, Musique, RÉS. VM DOS. 143, Bibliothèque Nationale de France, Paris.

14 The concert took place at the Salle Gaveau on 8 June 1938; for the program, see Michel Duchesneau, *L'avant-garde musicale et ses sociétés à Paris de 1871 à 1939* (Liège, 1997), 330.

15 Nadia Boulanger, Section "Concerts" rubric "Concerts Colonne," *Le monde musical*, 32e année, nos. 5–6 (March 1921), 86–87: "Il ne s'agit évidemment pas de chercher un ordre chronologique qui aurait un caractère pédantesque et vain, mais bien de trouver, tant par la loi des contrastes que par les exigences de l'harmonie, l'idée d'ensemble qui permet les plus audacieux rapprochements sans rompre l'unité. . . . Il est facile de se représenter par la vision, l'erreur ainsi commise: certaines toiles ne peuvent être rapprochées sans se nuire, soit par un contraste trop grand, soit par une ressemblance trop marquée, soit par une supériorité écrasante. Tantôt l'une attire sur elle tout ce qu'on ne peut plus donner à celles qui l'entourent—tantôt elles s'affaiblissent réciproquement et deviennent monotones, tantôt elles se détruisent un peu. Chacune d'elles est pourtant une chose immobile et tangible dont la beauté semble immodifiable—or, non seulement leur mise en place aide à les voir, à les comprendre, à les ressentir, mais elle dégage une atmosphère dont chaque rayon semble répandre sur l'ensemble une harmonie favorable. La démonstration peut, hélas, être faite dans la plupart des musées. La profusion des oeuvres, le manque de place l'expliquent—mais ceci ne change pas plus le regret que cela ne diminue la fatigue et laisse au coeur la mélancolie d'une joie à laquelle a manqué un peu de silence, de respect et de solitude."

16 For details of the tour, see Rosenstiel, *Nadia Boulanger*, 178–79. Boulanger played the program with minor variations in Philadelphia, New York, and Cleveland.

17 For an overview of Boulanger's concert career, see Alexandra Laederich, "Au clavier et au pupitre: les concerts de Nadia Boulanger de 1901 à 1973," in *Nadia Boulanger et Lili Boulanger: Témoignages et Études*, ed. Alexandra Laederich (Lyon, 2007), 173–79.

18 Duchesneau, *L'avant-garde musicale*, 123–28.

19 Ibid., 330.

20 Hyde, "Stravinsky's Neoclassicism," 103–7.

21 Boulanger's review appeared in *Le monde musical*, 34e année, nos. 21–22 (November 1923), 365. Much

later, Stravinsky himself claimed that the piece was influenced by the taut clarity of Bach's two-part inventions.

22 Script for BBC radio broadcast, 16 November 1936, 6:40–6:55 pm, Nadia Boulanger Artist File I, BBC Written Archives Centre, Caversham, UK.

23 Christopher Butler, "Stravinsky as Modernist," in *The Cambridge Companion to Stravinsky*, 29–33.

24 On Tyler's introduction of the Blisses into the Parisian art world of the 1910s, see Robert S. Nelson, "Private Passions Made Public: The Beginnings of the Bliss Collection," in *Sacred Art, Secular Context: Objects of Art from the Byzantine Collection of Dumbarton Oaks, Washington, D.C., Accompanied by American Paintings from the Collection of Mildred and Robert Woods Bliss*, ed. Asen Kirin, 40–43 (Athens, Ga., 2005).

25 On the relationship between Boulanger and Valéry, see Robert Pickering, "A la recherche des rapports Nadia Boulanger–Paul Valéry: Les ressorts d'une affinité privilégiée"; and Brian Stimpson, "Nadia Boulanger et le monde littéraire," in *Nadia Boulanger et Lili Boulanger*, 157–70 and 139–56, respectively. On Valéry's involvement in the *Poétique*, first published in 1942, see Walsh, *Stravinsky: The Second Exile*, 96 and 102–3.

26 Paul Valéry, "Le problème des musées," in *Oeuvres*, 2nd ed., ed. Jean Hytier, *Bibliothèque de la Pléiade* (Paris, 1993), 2:1290–93: "Plus elles sont belles, plus elles sont des effets exceptionnels de l'ambition humaine, plus doivent-elles être distinctes. Elles sont des objets rares dont les auteurs auraient bien voulu qu'ils fussent uniques. *Ce tableau*, dit-on quelquefois, *TUE tous les autres autour de lui* . . . Je crois bien que l'Egypte, ni la Chine, ni la Grèce, qui furent sages et raffinées, n'ont connu ce système de juxtaposer des productions qui se dévorent l'une l'autre."

27 Ibid., 1293: "Peinture et Sculpture, me dit le démon de l'Explication, ce sont des enfants abandonnés.

Leur mère est morte, leur mère Architecture. Tant qu'elle vivait, elle leur donnait leur place, leur emploi, leurs contraintes. La liberté d'errer leur était refusée. Ils avaient leur espace, leur lumière bien définie, leurs sujets, leurs alliances. . . . Tant qu'elle vivait, ils savaient ce qu'ils voulaient."

28 Philip Fisher, *Making and Effacing Art: Modern American Art in a Culture of Museums* (New York, 1991), 8.

29 Further on this point, see Tony Bennett, *The Birth of the Museum: History, Theory, Politics* (London and New York, 1995), 44.

30 Pomian's position is set out in "Entre l'invisible et la visible: La collection," which was first published in the *Enciclopedia Einaudi*, ed. Ruggiero Romano (Turin, 1977–), 3:330–64 and reprinted in Krzysztof Pomian, *Collectionneurs, amateurs et curieux: Paris, Venise, XVIe–XVIIIe siècle* (Paris, 1987), 15–59. See also Bennett, *The Birth of the Museum*, 163–73.

31 For a summary of Barnes's theories and some photographs of early installations in the collection, see Richard J. Wattenmaker, "Dr. Albert C. Barnes and the Barnes Foundation," in *Great French Paintings from the Barnes Foundation: Impressionist, Post-Impressionist, and Early Modern* (New York, 1993), 3–27.

32 James N. Carder, "Mildred and Robert Woods Bliss and the Dumbarton Oaks Research Library and Collection," in *Sacred Art, Secular Context*, 33.

33 See ibid., 26–27, on the construction and decoration of the Music Room.

34 Ibid., 26.

35 Bruno Monsaingeon, *Mademoiselle: Entretiens avec Nadia Boulanger* (Paris, 1981), 86–87: "Cela s'enchaîne de manière si merveilleuse que le temps en est aboli. Cela replace la mémoire dans le présent, le présent dans la mémoire et dans le passé."

JAMES N. CARDER

5

The Architectural History of Dumbarton Oaks and the Contribution of Armand Albert Rateau

I n 1920, Mildred and Robert Woods Bliss purchased the Washington, D.C., house and property they would later name Dumbarton Oaks.[1] Although the five-bay core of "The Oaks," as the property was then known, dated to 1801 and to its first owner, William Hammond Dorsey (1764–1818), the house that the Blisses acquired comprised numerous additions and alterations, mostly in the nineteenth-century Italianate manner (see fig. 1.11). These alterations were largely due to the prosperous Georgetown hardware merchant, Edward Magruder Linthicum (1787–1869), who owned the property between 1846 and 1869. Linthicum's radical modernizing of the house undoubtedly stemmed as much from his desire to validate his prosperity as from the then-current fashion for mansard rooflines, bay windows, wrought-iron porches, and porte cocheres. His close friend, George A. Gordon, described the Linthicum house to the Columbia Historical Society thus:

> The house, which has been changed but not improved in appearance by the addition of a mansard roof and other alterations, was a large two-story brick, with hall from front to rear "wide enough for a hay wagon to pass through," on either side of which were great parlors beautifully proportioned covering with the hall the entire ground floor. . . . The east parlor opened into a bright, sunny dining room, which in turn looked out upon a well-filled greenhouse, with flower gardens on the east, wooded lawn in front, grove of forest trees on the west, and gently

sloping well-sodded hills in the rear, all of which were kept in perfect order. During the life of Mr. Linthicum, "The Oaks" was the show place of the District.[2]

Early in 1921, the Blisses embarked on a three-year renovation of what they saw as an old-fashioned house standing on rather neglected grounds that were encumbered with farm buildings. Although their initial intention was to raze all the buildings on the property,[3] they instead decided to retain the house and return it to an Anglo-American Georgian style—without, however, sacrificing the house's impressive size and grandeur. The Blisses wanted a symmetrical brick mansion with pedimented L-shaped end pavilions attached to the central block by hyphen extensions. They also approved such requisite Georgian revival details as alternating semicircular and triangular-pedimented dormer windows and an impressive frontispiece door and portico, which were reached by limestone steps protected by curved balustrades on either side (fig. 5.1). Similarly, the Blisses envisioned the creation of Georgian-style interiors with fielded wall paneling, ornamental plaster ceilings, modillioned cornices, and pedimented window heads, among other typical details (fig. 5.2). They searched for appropriate period interiors for this purpose, and employed, for example, a substantial amount of English seventeenth-century Jacobean oak paneling in their library— a decor conceit fairly typical of the American upper class in the late Edwardian period. For

FIG. 5.1.
Frederick H. Brooke,
Dumbarton Oaks as
renovated in 1923,
photographed ca. 1981.

Archives, AR.PH.MH.008,
Dumbarton Oaks Research
Library and Collection.

other rooms, they commissioned historically based reproductions. The Blisses chose the architect Frederick H. Brooke to undertake this renovation project. Brooke was a respected Colonial revival architect, who had recently completed the Georgian revival buildings of the Virginia Episcopal School and would later receive the commission for the Georgian revival interiors of the Lutyens-designed ambassador's residence at the British Embassy in Washington, D.C.[4]

The Blisses were not passive clients in the renovation of what Mildred Bliss amusingly referred to as "the box." Upon Brooke's appointment as architect, Mildred Bliss wrote her friend Frank Parsons, founder and director of what is now the Parsons School of Design, requesting that he recommend a young design student who

could facilitate her "cooperation with the architect's office." As she wrote: "It would be of great help if some one of your students could spend several weeks in Washington, expressing on paper the ideas of which my head is full, but which I cannot, unfortunately, draw."[5] Interestingly, she dispatched the chosen student almost immediately to Charleston, South Carolina, to make measured drawings of exterior and interior details that she wanted to employ at Dumbarton Oaks. Although the drawings do not survive, it is possible to speculate about Mildred Bliss's interest in the architecture of Charleston. Among the more notable and unusual features of the redesign of Dumbarton Oaks are the first floor elliptical wrought-iron balconies—sometimes connected between windows by

FIG. 5.2.
Frederick H. Brooke, first-floor gallery as renovated in 1923, photographed 1940.

Archives, AR.PH.HG.006, Dumbarton Oaks Research Library and Collection.

continuous "walkways"—that are enclosed by distinctive iron and bronze railings. The concept for these balconies, the final design and fabrication of which came from the Philadelphia foundry of Samuel Yellin, derives from the Nathaniel Russell House (1808) in Charleston, drawings of which were likely provided by the Parsons student.

Even though Robert Bliss's diplomatic career had prevented them from establishing a permanent residence, the Blisses acquired a large quantity of English antique furnishings during the first decade of their marriage. These included a large assembled set of Turkey-work upholstered Jacobean chairs and stools (acquired in 1912), a suite of walnut-veneered Queen Anne side chairs (acquired in 1914), and a number of carved mahogany Queen Anne and Chippendale chairs, tables, and torchères.[6] They owned important pieces representative of the full spectrum of English seventeenth-century through early nineteenth-century styles as well as English fireplace mantels. Their penchant for English antiques suggests an interest in eventually establishing a permanent residence in the English country house manner, and this interest was realized with the acquisition and renovation of Dumbarton Oaks, which Robert Bliss later described as their "country house in the city."[7]

With Robert Bliss's nomination as U.S. minister to Sweden in 1923, the Blisses decided to enter, in absentia, a second phase of architectural change at Dumbarton Oaks. They wanted a quadrangle of new service buildings, including

a duplex residence for the head gardener and butler, a greenhouse, an orangery, and a garage with dormitory accommodations for the chauffeur and other male staff. They entrusted this commission to Lawrence Grant White, son of the architect Stanford White and partner in the New York City architectural firm of McKim, Mead, and White. The service court buildings, which White designed partly in consultation with Beatrix Farrand, were again to be in the Georgian revival style. The garage (now the refectory) would ultimately be recognized as White's quintessential Georgian revival creation (fig. 5.3).

In 1924, the Blisses began contemplating the addition of a monumental music room, an undertaking that would involve the participation of the Parisian designer Armand Albert Rateau. The undertaking also signaled the beginning of a concerted departure from the Georgian revival style, as the Blisses envisioned a Renaissance interior for their Music Room. As the architect of record, White ensured a harmony between the addition and the surrounding architecture by employing a monumental Palladian window and decorative marble roundels—features equally expressive of the sixteenth-century Renaissance and the eighteenth-century Georgian styles (see fig. 1.14). In 1926, Robert Bliss imagined the character of the room in a letter to White: "We see marbré-stucco wainscot in music room; rough plaster walls; a very good polychromed ceiling (shall it be old or copied?); the best big mantel we can find, and we want a fine floor."[8] He later elaborated: "All things being equal, we do not want modern mechanical and structural details to intrude themselves on the impression of the whole, which we hope to make mellow and old-fashioned."[9] He seems to have appreciated that this addition would deviate from the established Anglo-American Georgian aesthetic at Dumbarton Oaks. As planning for the room advanced, he mused that the Music Room was "a delightful medley of Italian renaissance, French eighteenth century, Georgian and American!"[10]

The Blisses especially wanted a Renaissance ceiling and floor for the Music Room, and by October 1926, had engaged people "to hunt for old ceilings and floors."[11] Rateau may well have been one of these people, although this is not recorded. The preserved record of the Blisses' patronage of Rateau begins in late 1926 with a letter from Mildred Bliss's personal secretary, Thérèse Malye, in Paris. She informed her employer, who was then in Stockholm, that Rateau had telephoned in an agitated state because he had not received Mildred Bliss's response to his "various designs." Malye also stated that Rateau had fabricated a special frame for a medieval Islamic turban.[12] Rateau, in fact, was to later oversee the hanging of the textile in the Bliss apartment.[13] By 1927, the Blisses, through the offices of McKim, Mead, and White, had offered Rateau his first major commission at Dumbarton Oaks: the design and fabrication of a reproduction French Renaissance ceiling for the Music Room. Rateau confirmed the commission, specifying that: "The decoration of these beams will be executed after special studies of composition, painting and decoration with antique patina like the existing model selected in the guard room of the Château

of Cheverny.... The work will be executed in accordance with artistic standards and will be made like an antique ceiling with all irregularity of workmanship that would have existed in a ceiling of the period."[14] He estimated that the ceiling would cost $28,000.

Armand Albert Rateau[15] was born in Paris in 1882. Between 1894 and 1898, he studied drawing and woodcarving at the École Boulle, a prestigious technical school for cabinetmaking and related crafts in Paris. Beginning in 1904 and until early 1919, he was the artistic director of the Maison Alavoine, a respected interior design firm that specialized in traditional, period revival style. In 1920, Rateau established his own design firm and workshop in Paris, and by 1927, he was using the title "Architecte Décorateur" on his business card and letterhead. Importantly, he participated in the famous 1925 Paris exposition of modern decorative and industrial arts, where he collaborated with his patron, the couturier Jeanne Lanvin, on the installation of the Pavillion de l'Élégance.[16] For the pavilion's interior, Rateau designed display furniture for the haute couture of the fashion houses of Lanvin, Worth, Poiret, and Callot Soeurs. Rateau also decorated a number of spaces within the Grand Palais, and, at the antiques gallery of Jacques Seligmann and Co., he exhibited a celebrated bathroom—based on designs found in Persian miniatures—that he had created for the Duchess of Alba in Madrid (now in the Musée de Arts Decoratifs, Paris). Although it is unrecorded how the Blisses became acquainted with Rateau and his work, any of these exhibition venues might well have provided the occasion. Mildred Bliss was a great patron of Parisian couture—especially that of the house of Worth—and the Blisses acquired numerous artworks and furnishings from the Seligmann showroom.

The Blisses' association with Rateau initially might seem curious, given Rateau's reputation today as one of the more innovative advocates of the Parisian *style moderne* (now better known as the Art Deco style). His modernism would appear to conflict with their penchant for period historicism at Dumbarton Oaks. For example, it would be difficult to imagine them purchasing his famed bronze furniture, especially the idiosyncratic fish-and-cockleshell "curule" chairs that he designed in 1920 for the indoor swimming pool of his first American clients, George and Florence Blumenthal.[17] However, their artistic interests were highly sympathetic: the Blisses valued the modern, collected artworks by

Picasso and Matisse, and commissioned music by Stravinsky; Rateau sought inspiration in historical sources which he then imbued with a modernist aesthetic. Indeed, Rateau's work was categorized as "neoclassical modernist,"[18] and his biography was entitled *Un baroque chez les modernes*.[19] His designs were wide ranging; for example, his Renaissance-inspired bronze "curule" chairs were contemporaneous with his more traditional rococo-style boiseries for the ballroom of the Blumenthal's townhouse in New York City.[20] Rateau would continue to design historically inspired interiors for his conservative and very wealthy private clients, such as the Marquis d'Andigné in 1921.[21] His acknowledged interest in late Gothic and Renaissance interiors led directly to the commission for the Music Room ceiling at Dumbarton Oaks, as well as to the nearly simultaneous commission in 1927 from Mrs. Wilson-Filmer (Lady Baillie) to restore and augment the medieval interiors at Leeds Castle in Kent, England.[22]

By August 1927, Rateau increased the price for the Music Room ceiling to $35,000 "to enable him to create an absolutely perfect work from old wood painted in an old style as if for an antiquarian."[23] Members of his firm spent twelve days at the Château de Cheverny, taking exact measurements of the guard room ceiling and studying both its construction and its painted designs. Rateau completed a full-size mockup section, which was declared a great success when it arrived in the New York office of Lawrence White. White wrote to Robert Bliss in Buenos Aires: "Mrs. Farrand and Mr. Russell are here in the office as I am dictating this letter. We have just seen the full size sample of the ceiling which Rateau has sent over, and we are all delighted with it. The color and execution of the decoration are absolutely perfect, and it is hard to believe that it is not a genuine antique. Rateau has lived up to our expectations, and almost, I might say, to his price."[24]

In August 1928, the completed ceiling beams and parquet floorboards were shipped to Dumbarton Oaks. Rateau wrote to White: "I hope that the ensemble as it has been executed will give you entire satisfaction. It is the first time that an ensemble of such importance has been executed with so much regard for exactitude."[25] When Robert Bliss returned for a visit to Dumbarton Oaks in March 1929, he cabled White: "Just arrived and thoroughly delighted our music room."[26]

Rateau traveled to the United States in November 1928 in order to view his ceiling and floor installed in the Music Room. He met with Mildred Bliss, Lawrence White, and Beatrix Farrand for two days in mid-December; the summary minutes of these meetings record that he participated in discussions regarding the furnishing and decoration of the Music Room and that he was commissioned to "look around for various objects for the gardens."[27] The group also discussed the completion of the living room; Rateau suggested incorporating four canvases by Hubert Robert, which the Blisses had purchased in 1922, into the paneling of the end walls.[28] Mildred Bliss found this to be an "admirable suggestion."[29] She subsequently asked Rateau to consult on alterations to the oval salon; indeed, before his return to France at the end of December, he was sent "the plan of the living room, with corrected dimensions, and also the pattern of the walls of the oval salon, and the pattern of the curve of the oval wall." Photographs of the living room, oval salon, and gardens were to be sent to Rateau in Paris as soon as they were ready.[30]

Before leaving New York for Paris, however, Rateau made a discovery that would lead to one of the quintessential features of the Music Room at Dumbarton Oaks. At the showroom of Arnold Seligmann, Rey & Co. he saw photographs of an early sixteenth-century mantelpiece, which was originally from the Château de Théobon in France.[31] He immediately recommended that this monumental stone chimneypiece replace the smaller Italian Renaissance mantel that White had previously purchased and installed in the Music Room.[32]

Back in Paris, Rateau met frequently with Mildred Bliss to discuss new designs for the living room and the oval salon, both of which had been created by Frederick H. Brooke as part of the 1921–23 renovation. Mildred Bliss wrote to White, saying: Rateau "certainly does understand better than any one I have ever come across, how to reproduce old ébénisterie. My second visit from [him] was full of promise. . . . He is to submit a project for the oval room; instructions and plaster section for improving the library ceiling; information regarding the indirect lighting for the music room ceiling; [the same] regarding lighting for the Bosquet; and a formula for the aging of stone and wood. This man is a treasure, isn't he?"[33]

Although no extant photographs document Brooke's original living room design, the existing blueprints show a ceiling decorated with plaster

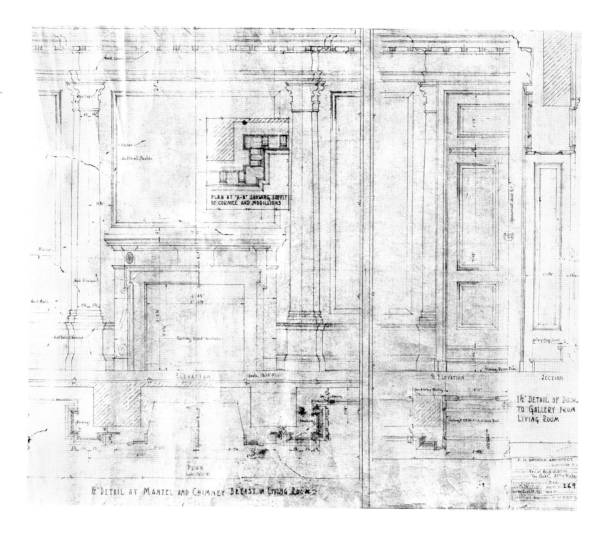

ornaments and walls articulated with fluted Corinthian wood pilasters and a modillioned cornice (fig. 5.4). For his design of the oval salon, Brooke superimposed an oval onto the rectangular plan of the east parlor in order to conceal an elevator in its northwest corner. He designed the oval walls to hide both the elevator shaft and a cloak room, and made the corresponding area on the southeast side of the room into a dressing room and toilet (fig. 5.5). He set arched niches into the four "corners," and designed gilt plaster-on-wood pediments for the windows and doors and gilt-plaster rinceau decorations for the ceiling (fig. 5.6), parts of which are still in place (although now hidden) above Rateau's later plaster cove. Mildred Bliss is known to have been generally displeased with Brooke's designs, and certain details—such as the disparity of the molding types that are all arranged at the same height—show that, indeed, he sometimes lacked

finesse. But her decision to redesign the oval salon was also prompted by her acquisition in Paris in 1926 of an eighteenth-century oval Savonnerie rug, which did not fit well into the Brooke salon.[34] Rateau's new design, however, would perfectly match the proportions of the walls to those of the oval rug (fig. 5.7).

Rateau's design for the living room (fig. 5.8) was based loosely on a French neoclassical scheme that involved carved and parcel gilt "palm tree" pilasters, a period French régence mantel, and mirrored sliding window and door shutters that, when engaged, would create something of the effect of a *gallerie des glaces*. He also cleverly covered the radiator boxes with simulated leather book spines. Above the paneling, however, was a lighted cove, and the joints of the textured paneling were concealed with gilt carved battens, both of these designs being more reminiscent of the Parisian style moderne than the neoclassical.[35]

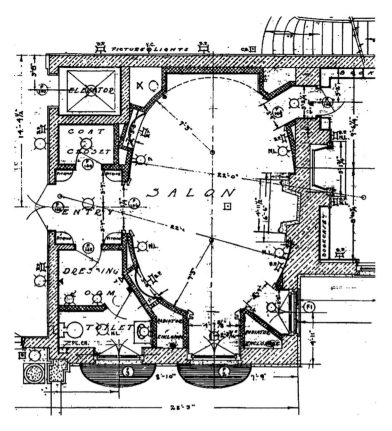

FIG. 5.5.
Frederick H. Brooke,
plan of the oval salon
(detail), 1925.

Archives, AR.AP.MH.PL.009,
Dumbarton Oaks Research
Library and Collection.

FIG. 5.6.
Frederick H. Brooke, oval
salon, completed 1923,
photographed ca. 1923.

Archives, AR.PH.OS.027,
Dumbarton Oaks Research
Library and Collection.

FIG. 5.9.

Armand Albert Rateau, oval salon as renovated in 1930, photographed 1940.

Archives, AR.PH.OS.003, Dumbarton Oaks Research Library and Collection.

Indeed, of all of Rateau's recorded designs for period room reproductions, the Dumbarton Oaks living room is the most innovative in its combined references to the moderne as well as the ancien régime. As Rateau's son would later reminisce, he was "respectful of classical tradition [and] searched for a delicate aesthetic interpretation in which [historic] influences were blended with his own highly personal modern style."[36] The living room design epitomizes this aesthetic.

For the oval salon, Rateau created a trompe l'oeil painted environment of Ionic pilasters, drapery swags, egg-and-dart cornices, and grisaille "sculptural" lunettes inhabited by playful putti—all based loosely on French neoclassical ideas (fig. 5.9). The interiors of the window

shutters were painted with a partial garden view. Doors leading to a window pocket at the south and to a passageway at the north were disguised as bookcases with applied book spines. As the design progressed, Mildred Bliss wrote that she awaited with great eagerness the sketches and suggestions from the "omniscient" Rateau, who was "an expensive but . . . indispensable luxury."[37]

On a trip to Paris in September 1929, White saw the plans for both rooms and wrote: "I . . . like the scheme for the living room very much indeed." He then continued: "As I was going to London, [Rateau] and his wife went with me and we stopped to inspect the simply amazing work he has been doing at Leeds Castle. I have never seen such incredible fakes: Medieval pavements worn almost through and simply extraordinary weathered oak shutters and ceilings. Incidentally, the floor of the dining room is exactly like your floor, and was made at the same time. It is amazingly successful. . . ."[38] When White saw the finished rooms after they were shipped to Washington, D.C., in November 1930, he wrote to the Blisses: "The color and finish of the living room woodwork is the best I have ever seen, and the detail of the carved vertical motives absolute perfection."[39]

Rateau's living room and oval salon, unlike the Music Room ceiling, follow no known models; instead, they are pastiches of late eighteenth-century formulas and contemporary innovations, which, of course, was his intention. Many style moderne rooms had silk-covered walls, and it is of interest to note that Lawrence White originally thought that the living room walls were to be hung with oyster gray satin, a design idea that must have been abandoned early on.[40] The trompe l'oeil painting in the oval salon is perhaps more evocative of eighteenth-century neoclassical decor, but the absence of moldings or other architectural articulations and the complete insistence on fakery—from the illusion of the shutters to the egg-and-dart "crown molding"—confirms Rateau's modernist penchant for linear surface detailing and playful but sumptuous interior spaces.

After deciding to renovate the living room and oval salon in a French neoclassical style, Mildred Bliss began to rethink the furnishings for these rooms. She removed most of the darker walnut and mahogany pieces that were listed in a 1924 inventory,[41] and kept the lighter wood and painted English neoclassical pieces that were acquired before or shortly after the purchase of Dumbarton Oaks in 1920. She augmented these furnishings with newly purchased French rococo and neoclassical pieces and with pieces taken from the Parisian apartment when the Blisses took up permanent residence at Dumbarton Oaks in 1933. All this signaled a significant change in Mildred Bliss's interior design interests at Dumbarton Oaks—a change from an English country house mode to a more sophisticated French eighteenth-century aesthetic. She continued to introduce a French aesthetic at Dumbarton Oaks, especially in its furnishings, gardens—most famously in the Pebble Garden of the early 1960s—and Rare Book Room, part of the Garden Library addition of 1963.

When Rateau visited Dumbarton Oaks in 1928, he also was commissioned to find suitable antique sculptures and ornaments for the gardens. The Blisses themselves had been searching for and acquiring garden objects prior to his visit, and the Parisian dealer Paul Gouvert assisted them in this endeavor. In 1927, he had written to Robert Bliss: "Your architect, Mr White, . . . has taken the photos of the two big stone statues and the marble and stone vasque that you have already seen, he likes them very much and thinks they would do very well in your garden."[42] This and similar correspondence reveals that the Blisses were considering figural sculpture for their gardens, and that Rateau was to help in the procurement of such works. However, as had happened with the redesign of the living room and oval salon, Rateau's role soon changed from advisor to designer.

An important group of previously unknown documents at Dumbarton Oaks gives an indication of the projects that the Blisses wanted Rateau to undertake for the gardens as well as the actual designs that Rateau submitted to the Blisses. These documents comprise an undated typescript list—probably prepared by Beatrix Farrand—of photographs to be taken and sent to Rateau; copies of the resultant photographs (some of which are dated to 1929 on the back); eight architectural drawings (each having, typically, a plan and elevation) that detail the physical settings for ten projects; Rateau's estimates dated 5 June 1929; thirty-eight undated photocopies of Rateau's drawings for garden projects; and an undated typescript—most likely from Beatrix Farrand's office and with pencil annotations by Mildred Bliss—with a critique of each of Rateau's proposed designs.[43] These documents also offer evidence that Rateau was prepared to execute the garden ornaments at his Paris workroom, in much the same way that he had undertaken the commissions for the three interior rooms at Dumbarton Oaks. However, these documents also indicate that Mildred Bliss and Beatrix Farrand wanted any acceptable designs to be made locally rather than in Paris. This latter condition may have been due to Farrand's interest in retaining control over the garden design projects. In September 1929, White saw the Rateau designs in Paris and reported to Robert Bliss: "The designs for the garden ornaments are, of course, entirely outside my province. I liked most of them but not all."[44]

Rateau's ornament and furniture designs for the gardens are of five types: finials, gates, vases and baskets, benches, and free-standing sculptures. These designs mostly conform to the project instructions, photographs, and drawings that

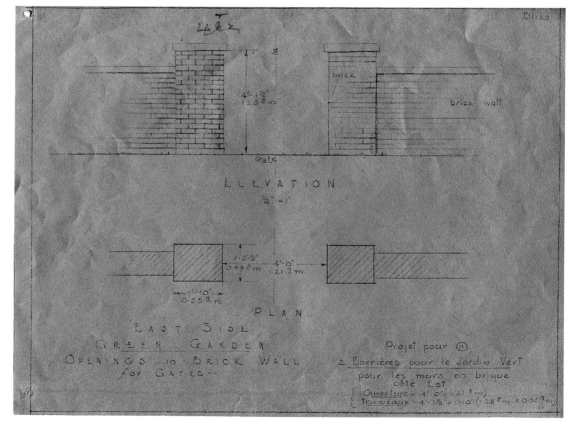

he received, although some are seemingly more fanciful than what was requested and a few are demonstrably reissues of preexisting workshop designs. His designs for gates and pier ornaments for the openings between the Green Garden and the Beech Terrace provide a typical example. Farrand's instructions to the photographer request two photographs of these openings, one at fairly close range and the other from under the living room window. The resultant photographs sent to Rateau show the location for the gates and ornaments and include meter sticks (fig. 5.10).[45] Similarly, Farrand's office prepared a drawing of the opening, including both a plan and elevation, with legends in both English and French and measurements in both inches and centimeters (fig. 5.11).[46] Rateau submitted both panoramic and detail drawings for the gates and ornaments (figs. 5.12 and 5.13).[47] He estimated the prices for making both the models and the finished pieces; in the margin of his estimate, Mildred Bliss questioned the acceptability of the gates, but marked the ornaments with a "W," thereby indicating her acceptance and possibly instructing Farrand's office to work on the proposed design. Indeed, Farrand's typescript critique advises: "To be suppressed" in reference to the gates, "but working on finials." The next year, her office produced a drawing for the Green Garden finials (fig. 5.14); the drawing was strongly influenced by Rateau's design and became the basis for the eventual production of the fruit basket ornaments.[48]

Perhaps the most interesting of Rateau's design submissions were those for three-dimensional sculptures, although only a few of these would be employed in the gardens. An example is a pair of sculptures intended for the North Vista, which were to be set against what was then a box hedge to either side of the box "tunnel" at the far north end. For these, Rateau again provided both panoramic and detail drawings. One group comprised a lascivious faun lifting the drapery from a sleeping nymph.[49] The other group showed a reclining Heracles—with the Nemean lion skin seen draped over the back of his head—and most likely a standing Athena (figs. 5.15 and 5.16).[50] Beatrix Farrand critiqued these as "most promising groups." She made two-dimensional mockups, or "dummies" as she called them, of the Rateau groups and photographed them at their intended locations (fig. 5.17).[51] However, neither of these designs was sculpted for the gardens.

Another interesting, but unused, design was for ornaments at the ends of the balustrade that

separated the North Court from the North Vista.[52] The project instructions inexplicably requested a sphinx, but Rateau's proposed design showed a triton supporting on his back a basket of fruit and flowers from which an infant surmounted on an adjacent pier took his pick (fig. 5.18). Farrand called this design "very interesting," and had a "dummy" made and photographed.[53] However, the eventual design was a cornucopia with an urn-shaped finial ornament inspired by an English neoclassical tureen model owned by the Blisses.[54] More successful in becoming part of the garden ornamentation was Rateau's design for a shell mounted on a fluted column fragment (fig. 5.19).[55] Its "dummy" was initially placed by the Lovers' Lane Pool, but the completed sculpture was ultimately employed as an engaged element at the back wall of the fountain on the horseshoe steps.[56]

Mildred Bliss and Beatrix Farrand mined Rateau's drawings for a considerable number of the hardscape and garden furniture designs that came out of Farrand's office in the 1930s and 1940s. Admittedly, Farrand often improved on his suggestions, as, for example, in her redesign of his fairly severe benches for the so-called "two friends seats."[57] Farrand's reworking of the grouping, however, employed without modification the design for a pedestal and urn as submitted by Rateau. Similarly, Mildred Bliss and Beatrix Farrand accepted Rateau's design for a vase for the west wall of the swimming pool loggia area (fig. 5.20),[58] but Farrand modified the design to include a pilaster-like pedestal which was included in the eventual fabrication of the design (fig. 5.21).[59] Even as late as the early 1960s, Mildred Bliss and her landscape architect, Ruth Havey, would revisit Rateau's drawings for what Mildred Bliss called her "bang-up finale"—the redesign of the tennis court as a water-covered Pebble Garden. Elements from his earlier design for the west wall of the swimming pool (fig. 5.22)[60]— especially the stalactite texture of its rocaille walls and piers and the Neptune sculptural group—would be employed on the north side of the Pebble Garden.[61] Even the waterspout masks of the Rateau drawing would find reinterpretation, albeit short-lived, in Don Turano's designs

for the masks that were installed at the Ellipse pool in 1960 and removed in 1966 (fig. 5.23).[62]

In 1938, having decided to give Dumbarton Oaks to Harvard University and establish the Dumbarton Oaks Research Library and Collection, the Blisses engaged the Washington, D.C., architect Thomas T. Waterman, who was then doing work for Colonial Williamsburg, to construct two pavilions for the library and collection to be located west of the Music Room (see fig. 1.17).[63] The design of these pavilions employed both Georgian revival and Renaissance revival elements in order to exist harmoniously within the complex. The pavilions originally flanked an open-air courtyard, but in 1987, the Washington, D.C., architect George Hartman roofed over this area to create a courtyard gallery. During the 2006–7 renovation, a sense of the original transparency between the pavilions and the courtyard was reestablished with the introduction of four see-through vitrines.

In 1941, Dumbarton Oaks, with the Blisses' approval and patronage, commissioned Waterman to retrofit the upstairs bedrooms and service rooms as library facilities. This rehabilitation project included the creation of an elegant Byzantine Studies Reading Room out of two guest bedrooms and employed the English eighteenth-century pine mantel and trim of one of the rooms as the design conceit for the larger reading room decoration. Also in 1941, Waterman retrofitted the garage and staff dormitory as a residence for the director and redesigned the superintendent's dwelling—designed by Beatrix Farrand in 1933—as the students quarters (or Fellows Building as it later came to be known, or Guest House as it is now known). With Waterman's construction in 1946 of a marble hallway between the Byzantine Collection office pavilion and the Main House, the Museum Wing became directly connected to the library and historic rooms. In the 2006–7 renovation, this hallway was redesigned as a special

FIG. 5.18.

Armand Albert Rateau, photocopy of a drawing for a sculpture intended for the balustrade of the North Vista, 1929.

House Collection, HC.MISC. RATEAU.06, Dumbarton Oaks Research Library and Collection.

FIG. 5.19.

Armand Albert Rateau, photocopy of a drawing for a sculpture for the horseshoe steps and fountain area, 1929.

House Collection, HC.MISC. RATEAU.31, Dumbarton Oaks Research Library and Collection.

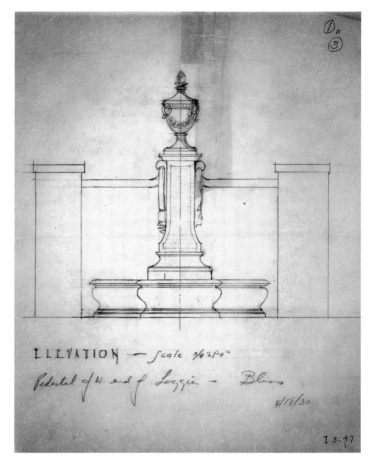

FIG. 5.20.
Armand Albert Rateau,
photocopy of a drawing
for a sculpted vase for
the horseshoe steps
and swimming pool
area, 1929.

House Collection, HC.MISC.
RATEAU.24, Dumbarton
Oaks Research Library
and Collection.

FIG. 5.21.
Office of Beatrix Farrand,
"Elevation, Pedestal of
W. end of Loggia–
Bliss," 1930.

Rare Book Collection,
LA.GD.I.3.47, Dumbarton
Oaks Research Library
and Collection.

exhibitions gallery, and provision was made for two elevators at either end.

After donating Dumbarton Oaks to Harvard University, the Blisses remained closely involved in the institution's activities. In 1959, they embarked on two final architectural projects to house their collections and enhance their research institute. They commissioned the New York City architect Philip Johnson to create a glass-walled, postmodern exhibition space for the Robert Woods Bliss Collection of Pre-Columbian Art (see figs. 3.1 and 3.2), which had been exhibited at the National Gallery since 1947.[64] In a 1992 interview about this important commission, Philip Johnson recalled the pavilion as one of his greatest triumphs: "It was a real collaboration and there was no budget, no money involved. It was just, 'If we like that better, we'll do it that way.' So I had total freedom and it was a simple project to build a little museum, and the owner and I worked together and it was

pure delight from beginning to end and it came out very well."[65] Just as Beatrix Farrand had collaborated with Mildred Bliss on the design of the gardens and the Blisses had collaborated with Thomas Waterman on the design of the Byzantine Collection gallery, Johnson insisted that the design of the Pre-Columbian pavilion be "Bliss and Johnson, architects." He claimed to have spent more time on the pavilion than he had spent on any comparable building since and credited its success to that fact.[66]

Johnson's building—with its eight domed circular galleries and unroofed central fountain area, all set within a perfect square—recalls Islamic architecture. Johnson later credited the design inspiration to his interest in the early sixteenth-century Turkish architect Mimar Sinan.[67] He built the pavilion in the Copse, one of the designed landscapes at Dumbarton Oaks, and employed curved glass walls to blend it into the surrounding landscape. Johnson later stated that

FIG. 5.22.

Armand Albert Rateau, photocopy of a drawing for a fountain for the west wall of the swimming pool area, 1929.

House Collection, HC.MISC.RATEAU.23.A, Dumbarton Oaks Research Library and Collection.

his idea was to fit a small pavilion into an existing treescape, and maintained that he wanted the garden to "march right up to the museum displays and become part of them," with the plantings brushing the glass walls with the sound of splashing water audible in the central fountain.[68]

The Blisses' choice of a modern design for the Pre-Columbian pavilion at first seems to be greatly at odds with the established architectural history of Dumbarton Oaks. Even Philip Johnson remarked: "It was curious that [Mildred Bliss] should have liked pineapple finials and still cared for what we were doing together."[69] However, the Blisses had always been selectively receptive to the modern, as was demonstrated by their commissions of musical compositions, their acquisition of artworks by living artists, including Picasso and Matisse, and their patronage of Armand Albert Rateau. Mildred Bliss even served as a trustee at the Museum of Modern Art in New York City.

And yet, it is perhaps also fair to say that the Blisses were little interested in modern art and design solely as an expression of the "avant-garde." They were more interested when they could perceive the modern as having an underpinning of

historicism or when they could appreciate the modern in light of the greater humanistic tradition that they valued. They were interested, as they themselves stated, that the everchanging present be informed and clarified by a knowledge of the continuity of the past.[70] For this reason, perhaps, their commission of Stravinsky's *Dumbarton Oaks Concerto* specified a work of Baroque *concerto grosso* dimensions and resulted in a modern piece in the manner of Johann Sebastian Bach's Brandenburg Concertos.[71] Similarly, their ink-and-wash drawing, *The Jester's Family* (1904), by Picasso was reminiscent of the commedia dell'arte subjects of eighteenth-century paintings, while their oil-on-canvas still life, *Buffet et Table* (1899), and pendant oil-on-canvas marinescapes (1906) by Matisse reflected those greater, long-lived iconographic traditions, even if painted in the fauvist and pointillist styles.[72] Certainly, as mentioned earlier, Rateau's modernist take on French neoclassical interior design epitomized the Blisses' appreciation of the contemporary melded with the historical. Therefore, their 1959 commission of Philip Johnson's glass pavilion—which is equally notable for its use of marble and bronze and its borrowing of a sixteenth-century domed prototype—is not

inexplicable when seen in this light. As Johnson himself has said: "Before Dumbarton Oaks, I had been a pure Miesian. [The Pre-Columbian pavilion] may have been my first postmodern building! It was the combination of daring design with the use of conventional, beautiful materials that made it all palatable to [Mildred Bliss]. I guess she didn't even think of the building as modern, just as materials and shapes."[73]

In 1959, at the same time as the Johnson commission, the Blisses commissioned Frederic Rhinelander King of the New York City architectural firm of Wyeth and King to create the Garden Library Rare Book Room for Mildred Bliss's collection of rare books and manuscripts on garden design, botanical illustration, and horticulture (see figs. 7.22 and 7.23). Although the exterior of the Garden Library imitated the existing Byzantine Collection pavilions, the interior reading room was of French eighteenth-century inspiration and is very reminiscent of the private library of the Blisses' good friends, Matilda and Walter Gay, at their château, Le Bréau, in France.[74] With these additions, both completed in 1963, Dumbarton Oaks now offered important museum collections, library holdings, and

research resources in Byzantine, Pre-Columbian, and Garden and Landscape studies. The financial stability of these additions—and particularly their collections and study programs—was eventually ensured by the Blisses' residual bequests.

The remarkable architectural legacy that Mildred and Robert Woods Bliss created at Dumbarton Oaks did not remain static after their deaths in 1962 and 1969, respectively. The 1987 George Hartman Byzantine courtyard gallery—which provided needed exhibition space as well as below-grade office and library space—has already been cited. In 1999, then director Edward Keenan addressed the critical need for increased library and research space at Dumbarton Oaks by finding a suitable building site away from the gardens and to the side of the service court. Keenan commissioned Robert Venturi of the Philadelphia architectural firm of Venturi, Scott Brown and Associates to design and build a 44,500 square foot, free-standing structure that would integrate the institution's diverse library holdings and become the centralized intellectual center of Dumbarton Oaks. This five-story structure was situated comfortably behind the McKim, Mead, and White–designed Gardener's

Cottage; its rear side offered four floors of panoramic views across the dell, while its front side presented itself as a two-story structure in scale with its Georgian revival neighbors. Its Venturi signature-style "decorated shed" façade incorporated darkened brick "graffiti"—bands of design that echoed motifs from the Byzantine, Pre-Columbian, and garden landscape worlds. Venturi also designed and built a gardeners' lodge behind the guest house; he renovated the original garage as a refectory and the original Gardener's Cottage as a facilities office.[75] In 2007, the firm completed their renovation of the Main House and Museum Wing.

The architectural history of Dumbarton Oaks is thus quite a remarkable one. The Main House retains the shells of an early nineteenth-century federal house and orangery now overlaid by a significant example of American Georgian revivalism. Also on the grounds are the important Renaissance revival Music Room by McKim, Mead, and White, a masterwork postmodern exhibition pavilion by Philip Johnson, and a postmodern library by Robert Venturi, to reiterate only the highlights. Inside are the less well-known but equally impressive interior rooms by Armand Albert Rateau, whose little-recognized role in the creation of Dumbarton Oaks is equally important in the hardscape designs of the gardens. The recent conservation and restoration of the Rateau rooms, along with the rehabilitation of all of the architecture at Dumbarton Oaks, has helped to ensure the continuation of the architectural heritage that the Blisses imagined and created for their home and institute. Their desire was for an architectural environment of beauty and sophistication within which one might engage in important conversation, perform or hear great music, and undertake scholarly research. For as Mildred Bliss wrote to the first director, John Thacher: Dumbarton Oaks was conceived in a new pattern. It was conceived as a "<u>House</u> of the Humanities and not merely a brick building holding books."[76]

Notes

1   Walter Muir Whitehill, *Dumbarton Oaks: The History of a Georgetown House and Garden, 1800–1966* (Cambridge, Mass., 1967); Maureen De Lay, Kay Fanning, and Mark Davidson, *Cultural Landscape Report: Dumbarton Oaks Park, Rock Creek Park*, pt. 1: *Site History, Existing Conditions, and Analysis and Evaluation* (Washington, D.C., 2000); Susan Tamulevich, *Dumbarton Oaks: Garden into Art* (New York, 2001); and Asen Kirin, ed., *Sacred Art, Secular Context: Objects of Art from the Byzantine Collection of Dumbarton Oaks, Washington, D.C., Accompanied by American Paintings from the Collection of Mildred and Robert Woods Bliss* (Athens, Ga., 2005).

2   Grace Dunlop Ecker, *A Portrait of Old George Town* (Richmond, Va., 1933), 303.

3   Grace Tytus McLennan to Mildred Barnes Bliss, 20 November 1921, Blissiana files, McLennan correspondence, Archives.

4   The Blisses had been acquaintances of Frederick H. Brooke since at least 1916. See the letter from Mildred Barnes Bliss to Anna and William Bliss, 8 December 1916, Blissiana Files, William H. Bliss correspondence, Archives.

5   Mildred Barnes Bliss to Frank Parsons, 18 April 1922, Blissiana files, Parsons correspondence, Archives.

6   Many of these pieces remain at Dumbarton Oaks in the House Collection: HC.F.1909.64, HC.F.1912.065–073, HC.F.1912.314, HC.F.1931.061.A and B, and HC.F.1914.014–019.

7   *Bulletin of the Fogg Art Museum* 9, no. 4 (March 1941): 63.

8   Robert Woods Bliss to Lawrence Grant White, 25 August 1926, Robert Woods Bliss House, Washington, D.C., call no. 396, McKim, Mead & White Archives, NYHS.

9   Robert Woods Bliss to Lawrence Grant White, 29 December 1926, Robert Woods Bliss House, call no. 396, McKim, Mead & White Archives, NYHS.

10 Robert Woods Bliss to Lawrence Grant White, 20 January 1927, Robert Woods Bliss House, call no. 396, McKim, Mead & White Archives, NYHS.

11 Robert Woods Bliss to Lawrence Grant White, 13 October 1926, Robert Woods Bliss House, call no. 396, McKim, Mead & White Archives, NYHS.

12 Thérèse Malye to Mildred Barnes Bliss, 10 January 1927, Blissiana files, Malye correspondence, Archives. The Blisses had acquired this Kufic-script inscribed turban from the Parisian dealer Paul Mallon in October 1926. Byzantine Collection, BZ.1926.2. See Harold W. Glidden and Deborah Thompson, "*Tiraz* in the Byzantine Collection, Dumbarton Oaks. Parts Two and Three: *Tiraz* from the Yemen, Iraq, Iran and an Unknown Place," *Bulletin of the Asia Institute* 3 (1989): 97–99 and fig. 16.

13 Thérèse Malye to Mildred Barnes Bliss, 24 February 1927, Blissiana files, Malye correspondence, Archives.

14 Armand Albert Rateau to McKim, Mead & White (office translation), undated, Robert Woods Bliss House, call no. 396, McKim, Mead & White Archives, NYHS.

15 Franck Olivier-Vial, *Armand Albert Rateau: Un baroque chez les modernes* (Paris, 1992).

16 Hélène Guéné, *Décoration et haute couture: Armand Albert Rateau pour Jeanne Lanvin, un autre art déco* (Paris, 2006).

17 Olivier-Vial, *Armand Albert Rateau*, 55–57.

18 Alastair Duncan, *A. A. Rateau* (New York, 1990), 37.

19 See note 15.

20 Olivier-Vial, *Armand Albert Rateau*, 86–87.

21 Ibid., 130–31.

22 *Leeds Castle* (London, 1989), 47.

23 Armand Albert Rateau to Lawrence Grant White, 10 August 1928: "Le prix de 35.000 $ a été très étudié pour obtenir un travail absolument parfait établi avec des vieux bois et peint à l'ancienne comme pour un antiquaire. Il est evident que l'on peut sur ce prix faire une economie mais j'ai tenu à vous donner un prix suffisant pour pouvoir realiser la perfection." Robert Woods Bliss House, call no. 396, McKim, Mead & White Archives, NYHS.

24 Lawrence Grant White to Robert Woods Bliss, 17 May 1928, Robert Woods Bliss House, call no. 396, McKim, Mead & White Archives, NYHS.

25 Armand Albert Rateau to Robert Woods Bliss (office translation), 6 August 1928, Robert Woods Bliss House, call no. 396, McKim, Mead & White Archives, NYHS.

26 Robert Woods Bliss to Lawrence Grant White, 1 March 1929, Robert Woods Bliss House, call no. 396, McKim, Mead & White Archives, NYHS. Unfortunately, the execution of the ceiling involved a critical flaw that brought about its early and continuous disintegration. This flaw, the nature of which was revealed in a 2007 laboratory analysis, was the absence of any protein binder—such as egg white—in the pigment medium used for the major beams. The paint—essentially a watercolor with sizing—was applied directly to a kaolin clay ground and then overvarnished. When subjected to climate changes, the pigment and varnish layers began to flake and fall off. Only the areas painted

in oil, principally the minor beams, had cohesion strong enough to adhere to the surface. This flaw resulted in no fewer than five recorded restorations, the penultimate attempt being undertaken in 1981 by an octogenarian decorative painter and having particularly disastrous results. During the 2006–7 restoration of Dumbarton Oaks, the ceiling was completely conserved to the original Rateau design. The analysis was completed by the Analytical Research Laboratory, Canadian Conservation Institute, Ottawa, in 2007. Kate Helwig and Philip Cook, "Analysis of Samples from the Music Room Ceiling of Dumbarton Oaks, Washington D.C.," in "Dumbarton Oaks Music Room, Ceiling: Paint Study, Mockup Report and Treatment Proposal," prepared by John Lippert for Evergreene Painting Studios, Inc., Oak Park, Ill., March 2007.

27 Minutes of meetings, 14–15 December 1928, House Collection files, Rateau correspondence, Archives.

28 House Collection, HC.P.1922.02–05.(O).

29 Mildred Barnes Bliss to Lawrence Grant White, 9 January 1929, Robert Woods Bliss House, call no. 396, McKim, Mead & White Archives, NYHS.

30 Lawrence Grant White to Armand Albert Rateau, 28 December 1928, Robert Woods Bliss House, call no. 396, McKim, Mead & White Archives, NYHS.

31 House Collection, HC.AE.29.002. Gudrun Bühl, ed., *Dumbarton Oaks: The Collections* (Washington, D.C., 2008), 320f.

32 Lawrence Grant White to Robert Woods Bliss, 13 May 1929, Robert Woods Bliss House, call no. 396, McKim, Mead & White Archives, NYHS.

33 Mildred Barnes Bliss to Lawrence Grant White, 9 January 1929, Robert Woods Bliss House, call no. 396, McKim, Mead & White Archives, NYHS.

34 House Collection, HC.T.1926.10.(R).

35 For the latter, see Émile Jacques Ruhlmann's design for a boudoir exhibited in his Hôtel du Collectionneur at the 1925 Paris Exposition. Léon Deshairs, *Intériors en couleurs, France* (Paris, 1926), plate 2.

36 François Rateau, foreword to *A. A. Rateau*, 7.

37 Mildred Barnes Bliss to Lawrence Grant White, 5 February 1929, Robert Woods Bliss House, call no. 396, McKim, Mead & White Archives, NYHS.

38 Lawrence Grant White to Robert Woods Bliss, 30 September 1929, Robert Woods Bliss House, call no. 396, McKim, Mead & White Archives, NYHS.

39 Lawrence Grant White to Robert Woods Bliss, 21 January 1931, Robert Woods Bliss House, call no. 396, McKim, Mead & White Archives, NYHS.

40 Lawrence Grant White to Robert Woods Bliss, 19 October 1931, Robert Woods Bliss House, call no. 396, McKim, Mead & White Archives, NYHS.

41 A.S. Vernay, *Appraised Inventory. Robert Woods Bliss, 'The Oaks,' Washington, D.C.,* 16 May 1924 (unpublished), 10–13. Archives.

42 Paul Gouvert to Robert Woods Bliss, 20 June 1927, House Collection, Gouvert correspondence, Archives.

43 These materials are in the Rateau Miscellaneous Documents, Archives and in the House Collection, HC.MISC.RATEAU.01 to HC.MISC.RATEAU.31.

44 Lawrence Grant White to Robert Woods Bliss, 30 September 1929, Robert Woods Bliss House, call no. 396, McKim, Mead & White Archives, NYHS.

45 Rare Book Collection, LA.GP.22.13.

46 Archives, AR.AP.GG.GG.001.

47 House Collection, HC.MISC.RATEAU.11.A and B.

48 Rare Book Collection, LA.GD.H.3.10.

49 House Collection, HC.MISC.RATEAU.03.A and B.

50 House Collection, HC.MISC.RATEAU.03BIS.A and B.

51 Rare Book Collection, LA.GP.20.60.

52 House Collection, HC.MISC.RATEAU.08.

53 Rare Book Collection, LA.GP.34.14.

54 House Collection, HC.F.1914.464.(BL).

55 House Collection, HC.MISC.RATEAU.31.

56 Rare Book Collection, LA.GP.29.01 and LA.GP.42.61. The Rateau design is not cited in his 5 June 1929 estimate, which lists only thirty of the thirty-two designs. It is cited, however, in Beatrix Farrand's undated, ca. 1929, typescript as: "No. 31 Horse shoe step fountain. Very promising possibility." Farrand's ca. 1935 employment of the design has an engaged column at the back of the fountain area supporting a shell that drips water into the basin. See note 43.

57 House Collection, HC.MISC.RATEAU.04.

58 House Collection, HC.MISC.RATEAU.24.

59 Rare Book Collection, LA.GD.I.3.47. This drawing by Beatrix Farrand's office is dated 18 April 1930.

60 House Collection, HC.MISC.RATEAU.23.A.

61 The eventual inclusion in the Pebble Garden of sculptures from the "Neptune group" that Rateau depicted in his drawing came about in a fairly complicated manner. This group—which included a Neptune figure, two amorini on hippocamps, and a triton—was first recommended to the Blisses in 1927 by Lawrence Grant White, who had seen them at the shop of the antiquarian Paul Gouvert

in Paris. Lawrence Grant White to Robert Woods Bliss, undated [ca. 15 June 1927], 20 June 1927, and 24 June 1927, Robert Woods Bliss House, call no. 396, McKim, Mead & White Archives, NYHS. Rateau had seen the group and, according to White, had made sketches of the sculptures. However, after learning that Irwin Laughlin had bought three additional pieces from this group— two amorini on hippocamps (House Collection, HC.GO.1959.01.A and B) and a triton (House Collection, HC.GO.1959.03)—for Meridian House, his home in Washington, D.C., the Blisses declined to acquire the recommended sculptures. Lawrence Grant White to Robert Woods Bliss, 26 and 28 June 1927: "I have learned that the Laughlins had bought three identical pieces: two tritons [on horses], and the small triton, from Gouvert. Gouvert's story is as follows. He bought the entire group (Neptune, six horses, and two little tritons) from the Porcelain Factory at Nevers. They had been given to it 'by a dauphin,' who had ordered them from Bouchardon." In 1959, having heard this narrative and knowing of the Blisses' interest in these sculptures, Irwin Laughlin's daughter, Mrs. S. W. Chanler, gave them to Dumbarton Oaks.

62   In 1957, the perimeter boxwood of the Ellipse was removed and replaced with hornbeam, according to a plan of Alden Hopkins, consulting landscape architect for Dumbarton Oaks. In 1960, Ralph Griswold, who succeeded Hopkins in the role now titled professional advisor, installed two elliptical walls between the central fountain and the hornbeam. These were ornamented with lead fountain masks—designed and cast by Don Turano—which emptied into interior moats. The Griswold additions were removed in 1966. See Elizabeth Jo Lampl, *Dumbarton Oaks Cultural Landscape Report*, pt. I: *History, Existing Conditions, Analysis* (unpublished, 2002), 1:VIII.7–8.

63   It is of interest that the numerous plans for the Byzantine Collection wing produced by Waterman's office cite Mildred and Robert Woods Bliss as the designers rather than Waterman as the architect.

64   See Jones, chapter 3.

65   "Interview Philip Johnson, Dean of Architects," Academy of Achievement, Washington, D.C., 28 February 1992, http://www.achievement.org/autodoc/printmember/johoint-1 (accessed 6 April 2009).

66   Philip Johnson, "Foreword: The Pavilion in the Garden," in Tamulevich, *Dumbarton Oaks*, 18.

67   Hilary Lewis and John O'Connor, *Philip Johnson: The Architect in His Own Words* (New York, 1994), 54.

68   Wolf Von Eckardt, "Dumbarton Pavilion's Scheme is Inside Out," *Washington Post,* 8 December 1963.

69   Johnson, "Foreword: The Pavilion in the Garden," 18.

70   The dedication plaque at the 32nd Street entrance of Dumbarton Oaks reads: "The Dumbarton Oaks Research Library and Collection has been assembled and conveyed to Harvard University by Mildred and Robert Woods Bliss that the continuity of scholarship in the Byzantine and mediaeval humanities may remain unbroken to clarify an everchanging present and to inform the future with wisdom."

71   See Brooks, chapter 4.

72   *The Jester's Family* and *Buffet et Table* are now in private collections, and the two Matisse marinescapes are in the San Francisco Museum of Modern Art (69.66-67), as a bequest of Mildred Bliss in 1969.

73   Johnson, "Foreword: The Pavilion in the Garden," 20.

74   William Rieder, *A Charmed Couple: The Art and Life of Walter and Matilda Gay* (New York, 2000), 62, plate 40.

75   See Martin Filler, "Concerto in Brick Major," *House & Garden*, January 2006, 50–52 and 116.

76   Mildred Barnes Bliss to John S. Thacher, 27 May 1941, Administration files, Thacher correspondence, Archives.

6

Beatrix Farrand's Design for the Garden of Dumbarton Oaks

When Beatrix Jones Farrand began her work at Dumbarton Oaks in 1921, she was one of the most highly regarded landscape architects, man or woman, in the United States (fig. 6.1). Among Farrand's commissions were several for nationally prominent individuals, including J. Pierpont Morgan and Ellen Axon Wilson, wife of President Woodrow Wilson, as well as several for family and friends, including Anna Dorinda Blaksley Barnes Bliss, mother of Mildred Bliss. Arguably, her most artistically significant project to date was her design for the campus of the new graduate college at Princeton University (1912), which led to her appointment as the university's consulting landscape architect, a post she retained for twenty-six years. Still, Farrand had never before encountered the richly collaborative potential that Dumbarton Oaks held in store for her. She would later describe the project as "the best and most deeply felt" of her career.[1]

As a young girl, Farrand summered at her family's large, seaside cottage in Bar Harbor, Maine. There she gardened alongside her mother, who preferred native plants to exotics. She also came to love the shadblow that grew in the island wilds near Reef Point and to know the feel of the soil and the ways of plants. In this regard, she resembled Ellen Shipman (1869–1950) and other young American women who would turn an early pastime into a professional career. Unlike Shipman, however, Farrand was close to several women who maintained professional lives, and these models, coupled with her own talent

and indomitable will, would lead to projects of remarkable ambition and scope. Only one other woman landscape architect of the country place era—Marian Cruger Coffin (1876–1955)—would produce such a distinguished body of work.[2]

Mary Cadwalader Jones (née Rawle), Beatrix Farrand's mother, was a social reformer who worked to improve conditions for nurses in New York City. As financial necessity grew, she became a literary agent for several authors, including her sister-in-law, Edith Wharton. Wharton wrote many highly esteemed novels, including *The Age of Innocence*, which won a Pulitzer Prize in 1921, the same year that Farrand began her work at Dumbarton Oaks—a convergence that must have given Farrand a strong sense of possibility. Wharton would remain an influential figure in Farrand's life until the writer's death in 1937. In one other important sense, Farrand's otherwise privileged childhood had been untraditional: her parents divorced when she was still very young. As has often been remarked, this circumstance was undoubtedly difficult for her, but it also offered a liberating alternative to the strictures of the typical Victorian family. She traveled frequently with her mother and often in the company of her aunt Edith Wharton, who was only ten years her senior.

Despite the presence of strong female role models in her life, the person Farrand was emotionally closest to was her mother's cousin John Lambert Cadwalader, a trustee of the Metropolitan Museum of Art and a founder of the New York Public Library. Cadwalader manifested

FIG. 6.1.

Beatrix Farrand, on the cover of *Reef Point Gardens Bulletin* 17 (1956). The volume was not published until after her death in 1959.

Dumbarton Oaks Research Library and Collection.

unusually staunch support for his young cousin's vocational aspirations, once remarking: "Let her be a gardener or, for that matter, anything she wants to be. What she wishes to do will be well done."[3] Author Mariana Van Rensselaer, a family friend who wrote often on the topic of American landscape design, apparently made the suggestion. Landscape gardening was one of the few professions open to women at the time, owing in large measure to its strong associations with the domestic sphere.

Farrand first forayed into landscape design about 1890 for her cousin Clement B. Newbold, who was developing a 190-acre estate, Cross-wicks, in Jenkintown, Pennsylvania. Newbold's house was designed by Guy Lowell, the son-in-law of Charles Sprague Sargent, with whom Farrand began a course of regular study in 1893 in preparation for a professional career. (The arrangement seems to have been facilitated by Sargent's wife, Mary, a talented painter and a friend of Mary Cadwalader Jones.) Sargent was one of the period's leading botanists and the founder of the Arnold Arboretum, where acres of plantings provided Farrand with a living classroom of outdoor study. Sargent's own estate, Holm Lea, was considered one of the most beautiful in America (fig. 6.2).

In her last piece of autobiographical writing—her obituary—Farrand recalled Sargent's influence, noting especially his advice to "make the plan fit the ground and not to twist the ground

to fit a plan."[4] She would heed her mentor's counsel, noting that "the artist must try to keep step with the great stride of Nature and copy as far as possible her breadth and simplicity."[5] But she would make important modifications to this principle by aligning herself almost equally with the formal approach promoted by Lowell and other architecturally oriented practitioners of the day, reflected in Charles A. Platt's admonition not to "be bound too closely by the natural conditions of the site, . . . [but] remold them nearer the heart's desire."[6] Farrand was one of the first American landscape architects to successfully fuse a deep response to nature with imaginative design and to confidently commingle passages of landscape that evoked a sense of wildness with passages of breathtaking artistic invention.

Farrand seems to have had little institutional training beyond one drafting class taught by William Ware at the School of Mines at Columbia University. In 1895, she embarked on a grand tour, accompanied by her mother and armed with letters of introduction from Charles Eliot and others, to finish her course of study.

Their itinerary began in Gibraltar and included Rome and several of the most important villas of Italy, the great gardens and parks of Germany, and the parks and botanical gardens of London. London also provided a base for excursions to the Surrey Hills, Sussex, Cumbria, and Scotland. The three-month tour concluded in Paris.

The lessons Farrand absorbed pacing out Italian villas—there were about twenty on her tour—left a particularly strong impression, and her travel notes presaged artistic concerns that would soon guide her work. Of the Villa Lante (fig. 6.3), for example, she wrote: "the grounds seemed the best combination I had seen of the landscape and the architectural styles." She thought it the most charming of those they visited—an assessment that her colleague Fletcher Steele would echo on his grand tour, taken nearly two decades later.[7]

Farrand's travel notes and an article she published in 1897, "The Garden in Relation to the House," reveal her close attention to a stylistic drama that was attracting attention in the professional press: the tension between proponents of naturalistic and formal landscape design. A

Fontana di Villa Lante a Bagnaia

debate over the merits of these two approaches had been the subject of several articles that argued passionately one side or the other. In 1896, Charles Eliot, writing in *Garden and Forest*, urged equanimity, encouraging, above all, adherence to the principle of fitness, from which he believed beauty would follow.[8] New methods of defining outdoor space were being explored by many practitioners of the day, including Platt, whose 1894 book, *Italian Gardens*, had helped launch the new fashion for the outdoor room. Farrand's design for Newbold marked her first experiment with classical lines in the landscape, but other examples from her early work reflected an interest in pursuing the judicious balance that Eliot recommended. For example, her incisive plan for

the Edward Whitney estate on Long Island (1912) vividly juxtaposed geometric formality and the organic lines of the wild garden (fig. 6.4).

Among the growing ranks of amateur designers laying out their own gardens was Edith Wharton, who purchased land in Lenox, Massachusetts, with her husband, Edward, in 1901 to develop a country estate, The Mount. Wharton's ambitious landscape scheme featured a formal garden with Italian lines and a large wild garden, where American plants were featured (fig. 6.5).[9] She commissioned her niece to lay out a winding approach that crisscrossed a small stream and to design a large kitchen garden. Wharton's book *Italian Villas and Their Gardens*, published in 1904, when her own landscape ambitions were

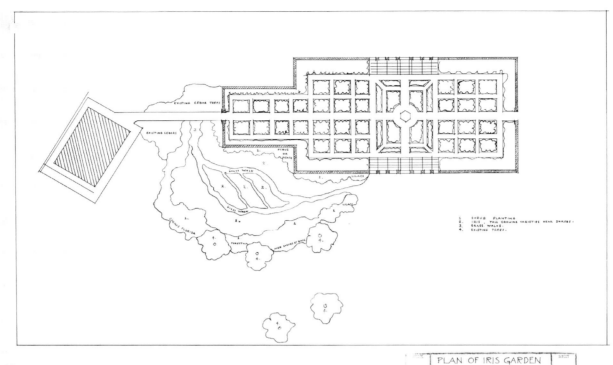

PLAN OF IRIS GARDEN

EDWARD F. WHITNEY, ESQ.
OYSTER BAY, L.I.

soaring, added fuel to the growing fervor for formal gardens in America.

Edith Wharton's country idyll ended in 1912, when she separated from her husband and relocated to Paris, where Mildred and Robert Bliss were soon to move. Wharton and Mildred Bliss saw one another frequently and shared many interests, tastes, and humanitarian causes—both were awarded the French Legion of Honor for their relief work during the war, as was Robert Bliss. But the relationship was not without its tensions. Mildred Bliss chafed at aspects of Wharton's personality and, one might imagine, her perspective on the newly arrived American elite—the subject of such novels as *The Custom of the Country,* published in 1913, the year after the Blisses landed in the city. Wharton wrote to one confidant that "I seem to poison [Mildred] after I've been with her for half an hour and she gets perfectly horrid."[10]

After the war, Robert and Mildred Bliss returned to the United States, determined to find a country house in the city. Somewhat to Mildred Bliss's dismay, they purchased a large and rather shabby federal-style mansion on six acres of sharply sloping property in Georgetown. (The Blisses would eventually enlarge this parcel to about sixty-five acres.) The site's major advantage was its trees—magnificent oaks and tulip poplars. There is little question that Mildred Bliss had already begun to imagine a layout for the grounds when she and Farrand met there in June 1921 to discuss a landscape plan. Key to her scheme would be the Italian device of the outdoor (or garden) room, a much-favored spatial vehicle during the period. A rather grand scope for the new design had also taken root in Mildred Bliss's imagination, undoubtedly stirred by knowledge of other expansive American estates, including The Mount and the opulent Casa Dorinda in Montecito, California, which was recently commissioned by Anna Dorinda Blaksley Barnes Bliss, Mildred's mother, and which she and Robert Bliss had visited immediately before settling in Washington, D.C.

Farrand was responsible for determining the size, location, and character of the new garden rooms, as well as the relationships among them, in consultation with her clients and their soon-to-be hired architect, Lawrence Grant White (the son of Stanford White). She returned for a second visit in August 1921 and met Frederick H. Brooke, the local architect who had been brought in to renovate the house. She also met Samuel Yellin, the renowned metalworker, who was creating fanciful ironwork for its interior staircases. Farrand and Mildred Bliss envisioned much of the garden's new layout on these visits, walking the steeply sloping land together and, in the process, discovering a strong aesthetic and emotional camaraderie.

The 1920s were a heady period for American women, who were increasingly given the authority to flex their artistic as well as political muscles. But the mutuality that characterized Farrand and Bliss's aesthetic endeavor characterized many other artist-patron relationships of the decade, regardless of gender. Most wealthy Americans of Mildred and Robert Bliss's generation were well traveled, and some were artistically sophisticated; the close, intensely collaborative relationships that such clients developed with their designers differed markedly from the tutorial ones that tended to characterize their parents' generation.[11]

Farrand's first letter to Mildred Bliss spelled out many remarkably specific suggestions that would eventually come to fruition at Dumbarton Oaks.[12] She turned her attention first to the south side of the property: "No planting should be countenanced which in any way would distract one's attention from the simple and beautiful lines of the grades and the magnificent oak trees which surround the house." She went on to sketch out many ideas for the development to the north, including a "green garden" off the library and heavy-textured planting on the looming house, "such as the large-leaved ivy or the evergreen magnolia pinned to the wall as it is often grown in England." She recommended that the groundcover be "very fine in leaf, as every effort should be made to exaggerate the already large scale of the oak." She listed specific plant palettes for both the north and the south sides of the Orangery and new plants to grow within.

Farrand also described a rose garden terrace that "must be practically flat in appearance," with a large stone retaining wall on its west side. A herbaceous garden just below the rose garden was to have a "very much less prim design . . . with considerable masses of perennials, none of them large in size, but giving a sort of general friendly mixture of color and form and entirely different in type from the upper level." Farrand enclosed a detailed list of suggested plants and groupings in her letter.

She went on to propose a pool below the herbaceous garden bordered by grassy seats and slopes, so "entirely romantic in type that all sorts of plants of the weeping-willowish variety will be appropriate." She envisioned a kitchen garden and adjacent cutting garden with "small fruit and large, planted on either side of the walks and also on the hillsides sloping down from the terraces to the garden," adding that it "would seem to tie the whole scheme of house, terrace and green garden, swimming pool and kitchen garden, into a unit."

Her letter also suggested a "large mass of forsythia planted on one of the hillsides." She continued: "In the writer's mind, the development of the north part of the place should be on the lines of a series of interesting plantations, each thought out for a certain season, and easily reached by a good walk and yet not conspicuously in view when it was not at its best." Finally, she envisioned a transformation of the acres at the north of the property into meadows and woods.

In sum, Farrand evoked a vision of terraces amid tall trees, paths and flights of stairs to connect them, cascades of yellow forsythia, curtains of weeping willow, cushions of boxwood, hillsides of flowering crabs and cherries, and a large, naturalistic park to the north that would provide views from the upper gardens—all part of a cohesive plan. Her suggestions were greeted with approval by her new client, who wrote: "Your letter and its enclosures have made us purr with contentment. You have got it exactly: in every respect, and I can't be patient until you get back here and start to realize your and our mutual dream."[13] The sense of the garden as a mutual dream is evident in many of the letters that flew back and forth between Farrand and her client over the years that Dumbarton Oaks was developed. The excitement of collaboration sparked both women's imaginations.

Although it has often been remarked that—in the tradition of eighteenth-century English landscape design—the gardens at Dumbarton Oaks become less formal as their distance from the house increases, this is not entirely accurate. Farrand's plan accommodated many great trees already growing on the site, some of them quite near the residence (fig. 6.6). She also set broad hillsides of informally massed plantings within the formal scheme and designed one area—the Copse—as "a distinct piece of forest."[14] Throughout the landscape, curving paths wind across and down sharply sloping hillsides in lines inspired by the rural tracings on the land, by Farrand's lyrical imagination, and, not least, by her response to the topography of the

site. These dynamic curves, soaring trees, forest-like plantings, and commanding views over billowing canopies bring nature into the gardens of Dumbarton Oaks. They are convincingly woven into the geometry of the Italian plan, a synthetic masterstroke.

Farrand's design was also a spatial tour de force. By screening views from one area to the next and using changes in level to create moments of surprise, she disguised the geometry of her plan (fig. 6.7). As the historian Michel Conan has observed, Farrand "plays with the crossing of the axes so you fail to see where they intersect."[15] "Rarely is the entire composition understood at once," wrote the garden historian Eleanor M. McPeck. "Often, when resolution is expected, a sudden turn in the walk leads to some unseen arbor, some unanticipated part."[16] Such moments make good garden theater also in the Italian tradition. Henry Wotton's 1624 playful account of the gardens he had seen in Venice captures the spirit of Farrand and Bliss's idea precisely: "I have seene a *Garden . . .* into which the first Accesse was a high walke like a *Tarrace,* from whence might bee taken a general view of the whole *Plott* below but rather in a delightfull confusion, then with any plaine distinction of the pieces. From this the *Beholder* descending many steps, was afterwards conveyed againe, by several *mountings* and *valings,* to various entertainements of his *sent,* and *sight:* which I shall not neede to describe (for that were poeticall) let me only note this, that every one of these diversities, was as if hee had beene *Magically* transported into a new Garden."[17]

By the mid-1920s, the terraces nearest the house were substantially complete and the plantings had been determined. Many of these were evergreen, such as the *Magnolia grandiflora,* which was trained against the house, and the *Hedera helix* (Baltic ivy) that covered the ground and also clothed the architectural forms. The Beech Terrace, named for the enormous *Fagus sylvatica* that once shaded it, is enlivened by views of the lower gardens and park beyond.

Already in place was a long, forced-perspective lawn known as the North Vista, which had been laid out, in the Beaux-Arts method, in relation to the architectural lines of the house.[18] This was the largest and most commanding of the spaces near the residence. Farrand planted it to terminate in a soft boxwood apse backed by lofty canopies of tulip trees that brought a sense of expansiveness to the landscape.[19] The character of this space and of the other terraces near the

FIG. 6.6.

Ernest Clegg, *Dumbarton Oaks, Topographical Map*, 1935 (digitally recolorized in 2007).

House Collection, HC.P.1935.01.(WC), Dumbarton Oaks Research Library and Collection.

FIG. 6.7.

Goat Trail, 1999.

Photograph by Carol Betsch.

FIG. 6.8.

View to the house from the North Vista, 1999.

Photograph by Carol Betsch.

house was more restrained than that of the outlying gardens. From the start, these areas were intended to provide settings for the "semipublic" gatherings that were an anticipated part of the Blisses' lives as members of the diplomatic corps. Farrand's treatment of them recalls aspects of her work at Princeton University and other campuses, particularly her use of large trees and massive wall plantings and her avoidance of strong color effects (fig. 6.8).[20]

In Farrand's original layout, the North Vista was bordered to the west by a densely planted woodland known as the Copse, whose "poetic and delicate" appearance made it, as she later wrote, "the sort of place in which thrushes sing and in which dreams are dreamt." She regarded this intimate area as "a distinct piece of forest" and specified that visitors seated in the Music Room at the west end of the house should "feel themselves in an open woodland."[21] Farrand's several allusions to forest and woodland in describing this area indicate her desire to bring

an experience of wildness into the design. But the woodland also had more pragmatic functions, as it served as a dense visual screen between the garden and 32nd Street.

The stylistic and metaphorical opposite of the Copse was the sunny, open Fountain Terrace, located east of the Rose Garden and reached by a double flight of stairs. The diminutive setting comprises a lawn, a pair of pools (antique fountains were later added), herbaceous borders, and a framework of tall trees, including a magnificent English beech. Farrand recommended that the borders here be filled with a "revolving series of flowers" in a scheme guided by color rather than exact species (fig. 6.9).

One of the first areas to be planted was the Rose Garden, a large (123 x 88 ft.) terrace reached by a long flight of steps descending east from the Orangery. By virtue of its position and scale, this was the most important of the new gardens at Dumbarton Oaks. Nowhere else is space so forcibly wrought or its impact so sublime. The

exquisitely proportioned room seems to hover—suspended, almost—over the landscape below (figs. 6.10 and 6.11). The garden room is defined on the west by a looming stone wall planted with climbing roses, jasmine, and "a wispy veil of *Forsythia suspensa*."[22] The north and east sides open to views across the orchards, to the trim fields of the kitchen garden, and, below, to the treetops of Dumbarton Oaks Park. The geometric layout of the beds is enlivened by large boxwood specimens, which provide an evergreen foil for the roses. The architectural components were completed by 1922, and photographs show that planting was under way within a year.

Farrand specified that the northern third of the beds was to be filled with yellow roses; the center third, with salmon and yellow-pink ones; and the southern third, with pink, salmon, and a few red varieties. She described these as "a wash of color . . . deepening in hue from north to south."[23] As the landscape architect Diane Kostial McGuire has observed, in June the garden becomes a "grand ballroom," and the roses appear as "figures in bright costume gracefully moving in the late afternoon breeze."[24] McGuire also noted that the blossoms were secondary to the general design of the garden and its form and mass. Because it was expected that the garden would be often seen in winter, it was designed, in Farrand's words, with regard to "enduring outlines and form."[25]

The layout of the Rose Garden had been determined, as so many others at Dumbarton Oaks would be, through a series of detailed exchanges between the landscape architect and her client. In a letter to Mildred Bliss dated 11 September 1922, for example, Farrand carefully explained a problem: if the steps leading down to the Rose Garden from the Box Terrace above[26] were built to the tread dimension she considered necessary, about fifteen inches, they would reach beyond the Rose Garden's west retaining wall. Farrand enclosed blueprints and described various solutions to resolve this awkwardness. Bliss wrote back to approve Farrand's preferred solution of changing the dimensions of the terrace. But it is clear from the correspondence that the choice was Bliss's to make.

In the same package, Farrand sent three different patterns for brick walks and four alternative plans for the beds in the Rose Garden. She included a descriptive paragraph on each of the four layouts, citing a range of design sources from Italy, eighteenth-century England, and, playfully,

Babylon. Any of these would work, she explained to Bliss, and any could be adapted to any other. "The whole thing is fluid," she wrote. "And I want your help arranging it." She concluded with even more direct encouragement: "Do tear up the designs as much as you will—mark them up and return them to me with your comments. I eagerly await your sharp criticism."[27]

That the design process at Dumbarton Oaks involved Mildred Bliss in such a primary role did not hinder Farrand. Neither does it, from a current vantage point, call into question Farrand's authorship of the design. The two women inspired each other, and the design of Dumbarton Oaks benefited as a result. The collaboration evident in the design of the Rose Garden occurred throughout the landscape, and when the general spatial framework of the gardens had been settled, it was applied again as plantings were refined, and again as the decorative arts program was addressed. Attention to these various layers of design overlapped and intermingled over many years.

Below and to the east of the Fountain Terrace is Lovers' Lane Pool, one of the most transporting landscapes at Dumbarton Oaks. Farrand cited the open-air theater at the Accademia degli Arcadi Bosco Parrasio in Rome as her inspiration for the seats and the shape of the small theater. The secluded, shady retreat is surrounded by cast-stone columns of Italian Baroque design, which are connected with wood lattice laced with honeysuckle, ivy, and jasmine. A large silver maple and large walnut once arched over the quiet surface of a shallow pool edged with curving walks of brick. A weeping willow was planted at the north. A thick stand of bamboo and privet screened the area from the east (fig. 6.12).

Lovers' Lane provides a passage to Mélisande's Allée, a wide lane bordered by silver maples underplanted with swaths of naturalized daffodils, squill, grape hyacinth, and other spring bulbs in the manner recommended by Gertrude Jekyll and William Robinson, both of whom Farrand knew and admired. The lane traces the route of an old cow path and eventually leads to a grape arbor at the eastern edge of the kitchen garden (fig. 6.13). Below the arbor is the Lilac Circle, whose original shrubs were later replaced with mock orange. Intimate and unexpected, the circle extends the geometry of the plan into the outmost corner of the gardens, a surprising counterpoint to the wildness of the Copse, sited close to the house.

Unlike the layers of historical reference embedded in these garden rooms, Farrand's planting of informal areas was characterized by simplicity of intention. The most remarkable of these informal areas is the Forsythia Dell, where one acre of *F. intermedia* 'Spectabilis' bursts into color each spring, a golden tangle that covers the hillside and reaches to the creek in the park below. Farrand instructed that the planting be kept to one variety and the shrubs be pruned to reveal the modeling of the hill (fig. 6.14).

She created two other such massed plantings. Crabapple Hill is located above and to the south of the Forsythia Dell, between the North Vista and the tennis court. Farrand suggested that it be planted with a limited number of varieties (including *Malus spectabilis, M. floribunda, M. ioensis* 'Plena,' *M. hupehensis,* and *M. toringoides*). "The attractiveness of this part of the design," she wrote, "should consist of the mass of flowering trees in the early season—each one having at least room enough to develop adequately, if not completely—and the hanging fruit in the autumn."[28] The other informal planting is

Cherry Hill, located north of the kitchen garden. Farrand noted: "It is purposely isolated from the rest of the plantations, so that the area may be devoted to a display beautiful at one specific time of year and not a conspicuous part of the design in constant view."[29] Even when the trees are not in bloom, their curving trunks trace intricate patterns against the strong slope (fig. 6.15).

By contrast, the Ellipse was designed as a secluded oval, "constructed out of a series of curves," a room originally bordered by a rumpled wall of box twenty feet tall. Farrand considered it "one of the quietest and most peaceful parts of the garden." Historic photographs capture the repose of this area, which is enlivened by a single jet in an ivy-bordered pool that brought, in Farrand's words, "a spot of light" to the end of the walk.[30] In 1958, the Ellipse was redesigned by the architect Alden Hopkins, who replaced the box with a clipped hornbeam hedge, altering the oval from a softly enclosing bower to a crisp, architecturally defined space (fig. 6.16).

Farrand developed the acres north of the garden rooms into a park (now Dumbarton Oaks

Park) that stretches along either side of a small tributary to Rock Creek. The woodland and accompanying meadows were meant as a counterpart to the formal gardens, although Farrand intended that their "wild" appearance be carefully managed. She laid a system of paths through the park, and connected it with the home grounds so that a tour of the gardens could include both. The woodland is integral to the formal gardens in one other important regard: it provides billowing views from almost every vantage point in the garden rooms. More than any other element at Dumbarton Oaks, the park gives the gardens a feeling of breadth, expanse, and vitality. In later years, this heavily planted area also came to provide a critical buffer to encroaching development.

Farrand's methods in designing the park recalled those of her somewhat older colleague Warren H. Manning (once an apprentice of Frederick Law Olmsted), who utilized nature-based design principles throughout his long career. As Farrand wrote to Mildred Bliss in June 1922: "The whole scheme should properly be studied from the ground itself rather than from any plan, as the contours and expressions of the ground will control the plantations more strongly than any other feature."[31] Like Manning and Olmsted, Farrand relied on a water feature (in this case, the stream) as the organizing spatial element in her layout. To increase the drama of the feature, she added a series of eighteen dams, waterfalls, and pools (fig. 6.17).

FIG. 6.15.
Cherry Hill, 1999.
Photograph by Carol Betsch.

FIG. 6.16.
Ellipse, 1999.
Photograph by Carol Betsch.

Although she lived abroad during the years that the garden was created, Mildred Bliss stayed in close touch with the project through her correspondence with Farrand. Their letters often included sketches, and, in some cases, photographs of mock-ups of ornaments and other architectural elements. Mildred Bliss was not unsophisticated about plants, but her passion was more sharply focused on ornament, and this aspect of the garden's design assumed more prominence as the years passed. In time, Lawrence White introduced her to the work of the French designer Armand Albert Rateau, whom she asked to scout for interesting ornaments and furniture in Paris. The relationship expanded, and in 1928, Rateau traveled to

Dumbarton Oaks to view the installation of his design for a ceiling for the Blisses' new Music Room. The results so pleased Mildred that she asked Rateau to submit drawings for ornaments throughout the gardens (fig. 6.18). Farrand and her staff adapted some of his designs—with more or sometimes less enthusiasm—but also continued to work from their own. As the years wore on, Mildred Bliss's tastes became increasingly rococo, and one senses a rising tension in her correspondence with Farrand, whose preference was for the more robust styles, particularly the Arts and Crafts, that had guided her earlier design decisions (fig. 6.19).

In 1939, Mildred and Robert Bliss invited the public into the gardens for the first time. Opening

FIG. 6.17.

Dumbarton Oaks Park, ca. 1931.

Rare Book Collection, LA.GP.13.13, Dumbarton Oaks Research Library and Collection.

FIG. 6.18.

Armand Albert Rateau, photocopy of "Pineapple Ornaments for the Piers of the North and South Gates of Terrace C," 1929.

House Collection, HC.MISC. RATEAU.02, Dumbarton Oaks Research Library and Collection.

FIG. 6.19.

Herbaceous Border looking north through the original gates, summer 1932.

Rare Book Collection, LA.GP.24.08, Dumbarton Oaks Research Library and Collection.

the gardens and collections for cultural and educational purposes had been the Blisses' plan for years, but the date of the transfer was quickly moved forward as war in Europe became a certainty. In 1940, Harvard University accepted the 16¼-acre core of the property for use as a library, museum, and research center. John S. Thacher was appointed the first director and was charged with overseeing the grounds as well as administering the new institution's scholarly affairs. An additional twenty-seven acres of the estate were turned over to the National Park Service and became a public park. The Blisses moved into a smaller house in the neighborhood nearby, having lived at Dumbarton Oaks for only seven of the twenty years they had owned it.[32]

The decision to split the estate between the home grounds and the park made bureaucratic sense, but it did violence to the design by permanently altering not just the circulation patterns but important aspects of the experience of Farrand's work. She had always intended the

gardens and the park to be visually and physically connected, in the same manner as many other country estate layouts of the time. The division had the effect of orphaning the meadows and woodland, whose designs were not well understood—and subsequently not well maintained—by the National Park Service. But even in its most unkempt state, Dumbarton Oaks Park continued

to provide a heavily treed canopy, a viewshed for the gardens above.

During the Depression, Farrand's practice was sharply reduced and her health also began to decline. Nevertheless, in 1940, she took on the task of writing a plant book for Dumbarton Oaks to guide the garden's future upkeep, addressing the complexities of its planting design and

FIG. 6.20.
"Terrior" Column, 1999.
Photograph by Carol Betsch.

offering advice about its long-term care. She included forty-two plant lists of the species represented in the gardens. This remarkable book continues to provide crucial insight to the garden's
stewards even today.[33]

Despite their differing aesthetic perspectives,
which had emerged over the decades, Mildred

Bliss and Beatrix Farrand remained good friends.
Their collaborative ardor was reawakened in 1940,
when Bliss began assembling a garden library with
Farrand's guidance. Even so, Farrand resigned her
post as landscape adviser to the garden that year.
The decision was "a good deal like tearing off an
arm or a leg or cutting out one's heart," but, she

continued, "the change has got to come some day and Dumbarton develop on lines that I might not be able to approve or follow."[34] At this juncture, Farrand's assistant, Ruth Havey, was overseeing the development of several new features at Dumbarton Oaks that more explicitly reflected Mildred Bliss's French tastes.

Each of the gardens Beatrix Farrand designed for Dumbarton Oaks possesses its own unique character, and the experience of each is affected by what precedes and follows. The garden unfolds sequentially in time as well as space. As Eleanor M. McPeck observed, "It is the chambered nautilus of gardens, suggesting at every turn deeper levels of meaning and experience."[35] In laying out these gardens, Farrand was guided both by a firm grasp of Italian and English landscape principles and by an emphatic American regard for place, as she articulated in one undated essay with a musical metaphor: "A garden should be a series of variations on an air, through which one feels the lilt of the original melody and throbs of the original rhythm."[36] At Dumbarton Oaks, and elsewhere in the landscape architect's work, the underlying rhythm was provided by nature, the spirit of the place (fig. 6.20).

ACKNOWLEDGMENTS

This paper is based on research and analysis previously published in *A Genius for Place: American Landscapes of the Country Place Era* (Amherst, Mass., 2007). I am grateful to the authors who reviewed portions of the earlier manuscript and offered invaluable help with it. For this version, Mary Bellino, Carol Betsch, and Sara Taylor offered many helpful editing suggestions, and Carol graciously loaned beautiful images to illustrate it. I am also grateful to the various archives that granted permission to reproduce historical photographs and quotes, and to Kevin Sprague, for use of his photographs of The Mount. MacKenzie Greer generously presented an early version of this paper at the symposium that gave rise to this book.

Notes

1   Susan Tamulevich, *Dumbarton Oaks: Garden into Art* (New York, 2001), 30.

2   Marian Coffin's architectural and engineering training at MIT greatly enhanced her capacity for designing in three dimensions. This background also gave her the authority to supervise male construction crews, a requirement for most public work. For more on Coffin, see Valencia Libby, "Marian Coffin," in *Pioneers of American Landscape Design*, eds. Charles A. Birnbaum and Robin Karson (New York, 2000). For more on Shipman, see Judith B. Tankard, *The Gardens of Ellen Biddle Shipman* (Sagaponack, N.Y., 1996).

3   Mildred Bliss, "An Attempted Evocation of a Personality," in *Beatrix Farrand's Plant Book for Dumbarton Oaks*, ed. Diane Kostial McGuire (Washington, D.C., 1980), xxi.

4   "Beatrix Jones Farrand," *Reef Point Gardens Bulletin* 1, no. 17 (n.d.): 112.

5   Beatrix Jones, "The Garden as a Picture," *Scribner's Magazine*, July 1907, 5.

6   Charles Downing Lay, "An Interview with Charles A. Platt," *Landscape Architecture* 2, no. 3 (April 1912): 127–31.

7   Tamulevich, *Dumbarton Oaks*, 94.

8   Beatrix Jones, "The Garden in Relation to the House," *Garden and Forest* 10 (7 April 1897): 132–33; and Charles Eliot, "What Would Be Fair Must First Be Fit," *Garden and Forest* 9 (1 April 1896): 131–32.

9   Between 1902 and 1907, Edith Wharton and George Bucknam Dorr (1853–1944), founder of Acadia National Park, corresponded about wild garden plantings at The Mount. The extent of the wild gardens at The Mount has not yet been determined, but it is clear that such a garden or gardens existed. See Ronald H. Epp, "Wild Gardens and Pathways at the Mount: George B. Dorr and the Mount Desert Island Influence," in *Edith Wharton and the American Garden* (Lenox, Mass., 2009).

10 R. W. B. Lewis, *Edith Wharton: A Biography* (New York, 1985), 373.

11 One illuminating comparison is that between Fair Lane, the ca. 1911 estate that Jens Jensen designed for Henry Ford, and the Edsel and Eleanor Ford estate, commissioned by Henry's son in 1926. For more on these projects, see my chapters on Jensen and the Edsel and Eleanor Ford estate in *A Genius for Place: American Landscapes of the Country Place Era* (Amherst, Mass., 2007).

12 Beatrix Jones Farrand to Mildred Barnes Bliss, 24 and 25 June 1922, Rare Book Collection.

13 Mildred Barnes Bliss to Beatrix Jones Farrand, 13 July 1922, Rare Book Collection.

14 *Beatrix Farrand's Plant Book for Dumbarton Oaks*, 128.

15 Michel Conan, quoted in Tamulevich, *Dumbarton Oaks*, 96.

16 Diana Balmori, Diane Kostial McGuire, and Eleanor M. McPeck, *Beatrix Farrand's American Landscapes: Her Gardens and Campuses* (Sagaponack, N.Y., 1985), 57–58.

17 Henry Wotton, *Elements of Architecture* (London, 1624), quoted in *The Genius of the Place: The English Landscape Garden, 1620–1820*, eds. John Dixon Hunt and Peter Willis (Cambridge, Mass., 1988), 48.

18 The plan was by George Burnap, who worked as a landscape architect for the Office of Public Buildings and Grounds in Washington, D.C., between 1912 and 1917.

19 The North Vista posed a difficult challenge for Farrand, who felt it was "one of the most important pieces of planting to be done, requiring both delicacy and solidity of treatment." *Beatrix Farrand's Plant Book for Dumbarton Oaks*, 41.

20 This suggestion is based on Diana Balmori, "Dumbarton Oaks: The Design Process of a Garden," in *Beatrix Jones Farrand (1872–1959): Fifty Years of American Landscape Architecture*, eds. Diane Kostial McGuire and Lois Fern (Washington, D.C., 1982), 101. She argues that the Blisses envisioned semipublic functions for these outdoor rooms from the earliest stages of the design.

21 *Beatrix Farrand's Plant Book for Dumbarton Oaks*, 128–29.

22 Ibid., 63. An early letter to Bliss also reflects Farrand's wish to avoid any appearance of artifice—not a simple task in a garden of this size and scope: "The wall and steps, while not in any way ambitious or pretentious in scheme, could be a vital part of the plan and if made of fairly large rough stone, perhaps buttressed as many of the old stone walls are and simple in parapet, whether of iron, or stone, or hedged, would hardly give the dressed-up appearance so repellent in many modern gardens." Beatrix Jones Farrand to Mildred Barnes Bliss, 24 and 25 June 1922, Rare Book Collection.

23 *Beatrix Farrand's Plant Book for Dumbarton Oaks*, 63.

24 Diane Kostial McGuire, "The Gardens," *Apollo* 119 (April 1984): 43. McGuire points out that the vibrant hues of the roses were intensified by the limited color schemes of the adjacent gardens. Bliss, according to McGuire, considered "the many hues of white to be the essential colour of the garden."

25 *Beatrix Farrand's Plant Book for Dumbarton Oaks*, 63.

26 Farrand wrote that the Box (later Urn) Terrace was intended as "an introduction to the Rose Garden, rather than a garden of importance on its own account." Ibid., 59. This narrow terrace was later redesigned by Ruth Havey to feature an ornate pebble mosaic. The simple, low hedges of box were replaced by arabesques of English ivy.

27 Beatrix Jones Farrand to Mildred Barnes Bliss, 11 September 1922, Rare Book Collection.

28 *Beatrix Farrand's Plant Book for Dumbarton Oaks*, 83.

29 Ibid., 93.

30 Ibid., 78.

31 Beatrix Jones Farrand to Mildred Barnes Bliss, 24 and 25 June 1922, Rare Book Collection.

32 Farrand also worked for the Blisses on a redesign of the garden at their new residence at 1537 28th Street, NW. The garden's original design was by Rose Greeley.

33 Diane Kostial McGuire edited Farrand's manuscript and oversaw its publication in 1980.

34 Beatrix Jones Farrand to Mildred Barnes Bliss, 28 February 1947, Rare Book Collection.

35 Tamulevich, *Dumbarton Oaks*, 96.

36 Beatrix Jones Farrand, undated manuscript 12, Farrand Collection, Environmental Design Archives, University of California, Berkeley.

7

Mildred Barnes Bliss's Garden Library at Dumbarton Oaks

It is difficult to identify a single moment when Mildred Bliss's collection of garden books started. In her history of the garden library at Dumbarton Oaks, art historian Agnes Mongan wrote that the first book acquired for the library was recorded in 1948: Charles Stevens and John Liebault's *Maison rustique, or The Countrie Farme*, published in 1600 (fig. 7.1).[1] Elisabeth Blair MacDougall, the first director of studies in the History of Landscape Architecture at Dumbarton Oaks, identified an earlier entry of 1944 as the first garden book in the collection: Nikolaus Joseph Jacquin's *Icones plantarum rariorum* (fig. 7.2).[2] Mildred Bliss, however, already had a large private library with many relevant books and works of art.

The idea for the Garden Library is generally dated to the spring of 1947, seven years after the announcement of the gift of Dumbarton Oaks to Harvard University. Its oft-repeated purpose was the preservation of countless illustrated volumes that were threatened in the postwar period by the aggressive book and art market.[3] While this was no doubt true, I would like to suggest that the evolution of the Garden Library dated from an earlier point in the building of Dumbarton Oaks as a research institute, having emerged from myriad activities, discussions, and associations.

In this brief history, I will first discuss the origins of the idea of a garden library and the models for it, then consider the intended and actual users of the collection and the changing definitions of its purpose, and finally show how the collection was built through extensive communication with dealers, friends, and advisors as recorded in the deep archives of Dumbarton Oaks. The essay is illustrated with treasures of Mildred Bliss's original collection that I can only briefly identify here. Each one warrants its own bibliographic and acquisition history, for, as others have written, the acquisition of an old book is its rebirth.[4]

Scholars on the history and culture of collecting agree that a great collection is more than the sum of its parts. Leah Dilworth has written that the histories of the book and of collecting have always been intertwined, and that books brought together signify collectivity as well as individuality: "they have the potential to construct a narrative or narratives, juxtaposed, they alter each other's meanings."[5] Susan M. Pearce has described collecting as the act of lifting discrete materials from their immediate surroundings and moving them somewhere else.[6] In this sense, a garden is a collection of natural specimens and man-made elements, which are lifted, moved, and reconstructed into a new cultural whole. A library is the same. I would like to suggest that at Dumbarton Oaks, the Garden Library and the gardens are collections that are parallel creations, yet intertwined so that to understand one, we must consider both.

For nearly forty years, Mildred Bliss's most influential advisor was her correspondent, confidant, and "Garden Twin" Beatrix Farrand (1872–1959) (figs. 7.3 and 7.4). Much has been written about their creative relationship.[7] Elisabeth Blair MacDougall has pointed out that Farrand articulated the desire to build "as scholarly a garden

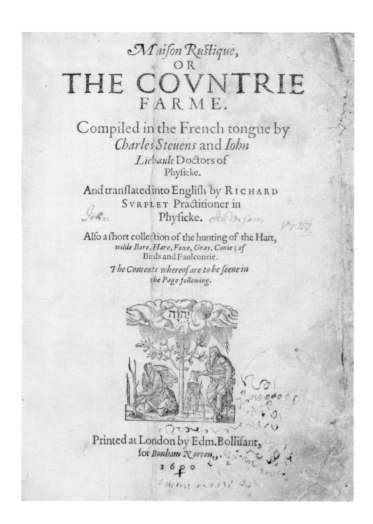

Pafsiflora incarnata.
Jacq. Miac. vol. 3.

library as that you have for Byzantium and the middle ages ..." but "the rare botany books (Loudon, the great Iris book, etc.) should be part of both collections."[8]

There is one architectural feature of the Dumbarton Oaks Garden, the Catalogue House, that aids our understanding of the interconnection of, as Bliss and Farrand called them, the "out of door and indoor collections." In a letter from 26 May 1947, Beatrix Farrand wrote to Mildred Bliss in her capacity as a consultant to the garden: "You see where your Catalogue House has led me: to a series of garden rooms, for books, for casual reference and more profound study" (fig. 7.5).[9]

The Catalogue House is emblematic of the collections that were underway, in which both living and bibliographic material were gathered, united by their purpose of study. It is one of the humbler elements in the garden, and often

escapes the attention of scholars. Deriving from the public park or community garden tradition, it contains reproductions of prints and drawings that illustrate the plants and birds found in the garden at Dumbarton Oaks. These displays were not intended to simply identify the garden specimens—as Farrand noted in her 1937 instructions for the garden house, they also gave an in-depth "botanical biography" of the garden and offered cultivation advice. (Today it is still appropriately decorated with reproductions from the Garden Library collection.)[10]

Built around 1935, there are no extant working drawings of the Catalogue House. But it is recorded in a sketch reproduced in a book published in 1939 on the occasion of the death of the Blisses' friend Vernon Kellogg (fig. 7.6).[11] Its inscription explains that the building was intended "for the study of the birds and plants of this region in their seasons." The dedication of

garden features to friends was part of a tradition of the Blisses. The Arbor Terrace, for example, was given to Gelasio Caetani, a scholar of Dante.[12]

In a 26 May 1947 letter to Bliss, Farrand elaborated on the dual aims of the library and garden collections:

> The physical gardens should, as we agree, be kept up well, tended and continued in beauty, but alongside them and a part of them the cultural and intellectual basis on which they have been developed should be at hand for gardeners of various ranks of ability and also for students of the art. Dumbarton has an opportunity to serve its community and visitors as no other place has. It combines the human and artistic side with the possibility of lifting the level of outdoor art in its whole neighborhood.
>
> This implies more than the actual gardens—it means a reading room where current and useful magazines, catalogues and books may be freely consulted, a small but well chosen collection of really first rate books on the development of the art of gardening. This second group would

FIG. 7.5.

Catalogue House.

Archives, AR.PH.GP.09.056, Dumbarton Oaks Research Library and Collection.

FIG. 7.6.

Sketch of the Catalogue House, ca. 1937.

Reprinted from *Vernon Kellogg, 1867–1937* (Washington, D.C., 1939), 110.

appeal to the student rather than to the casual visitor or the exclusively delphinium-minded Garden Club member. The current literature and the older source books should be supported by prints, monographs, and plans of well designed gardens. Record files of the Dumbarton plantations should be at hand telling of individual plants, their planting, care and development. The student could consult not only books covering local and present conditions, but the foundation books and prints underlying garden philosophy and design.[13]

Farrand was describing what, in the transition from a private estate to a public institution, were the guiding principles of the library and garden collections: "casual reference and profound study."

REEF POINT GARDENS

Beatrix Farrand had been engaged in a similar project since the 1920s, when she and her husband, Max Farrand, planned a reference library and collection at Reef Point, her family summer home in Bar Harbor, Maine. The Reef Point Corporation, founded in 1939, had an extensive horticultural library, archive (with a very important collection of Gertrude Jekyll papers), and herbarium. It was a public garden and, as she wrote to her aunt, Edith Wharton, in 1936, "a little horticultural institute."[14] In 1946, Farrand began to publish the *Reef Point Gardens Bulletin*, a periodical that continued for the next ten years until the Corporation was dissolved. In her history of the *Reef Point Gardens Bulletins*, Paula Deitz claimed that the idea originated with Max Farrand, who became the first director of the Huntington Botanical Garden Library and Art Gallery in San Marino, California, in 1927.[15] Both Farrands believed that the "permanent value of the Reef Point Gardens scheme lay in the library" and that "publication was an essential part of the garden's work."[16]

Beatrix Farrand wrote that "as a further part of the educational side it was hoped to establish [at Reef Point Gardens] a few scholarships for students . . . to broaden the outlook and increase the knowledge of a small group of hand-picked students who are in training to become landscape architects."[17] Reef Point Gardens received fifty thousand visitors in its brief history, and as Deitz wrote, despite the Depression and World War II, it "survived in a mode that combined the most advanced thinking in scientific and educational techniques with a kind of gracious Edwardian summer life."[18]

A garden, library, art collection, and fellowship program, then, were the key components of both the Huntington Library and Reef Point enterprises, which (albeit at different scales) presaged the program at Dumbarton Oaks. Another feature of Reef Point that was emulated at Dumbarton Oaks was its collection of garden views. In an essay on the print collection at Reef Point that appeared in the *Reef Point Gardens Bulletin*, Farrand explained that garden views (in addition to books) were critical for teaching exemplary garden models. Because she lived in a period before there were academic programs in landscape architecture, she relied on these images to learn her craft.[19]

In 1956, the final *Bulletin* reported that "the library at Reef Point had been manifestly the keystone of the plan but its use problematical in a place distant from other educational surroundings of like calibre. Therefore she [Beatrix Farrand] felt her duty led her to make the material a part of a teaching institution where it would be used and cared for in a manner fitting its educational value. Thus, the library and related collections were given to the University of California at Berkeley for the Department of Landscape Architecture . . ."[20]

Reef Point has been called a "mini-Dumbarton Oaks."[21] But it is more correct to think of the Garden Library as an expanded Reef Point, particularly as it emphasized the training of landscape architects and served as a community garden center. In both cases, the gardens were to be laboratories as well as exemplars of the art of landscape gardening. Farrand makes the point that for her laboratory and classroom, she was not limited by the six acres of Reef Point. Mount Desert Island also offered for extensive study Acadia National Park and more than fifty private gardens that she had designed.[22]

We must also recall that it was during these same years that Beatrix Farrand was designing for Mildred's mother (Anna Dorinda Blaksley Barnes Bliss) the Blaksley Botanic Garden (now the Santa Barbara Botanic Garden), a public garden with a mission to study and preserve the regional landscape of Southern California (fig. 7.7). Reef Point was similarly focused on regional horticulture and gardening in Maine. Was Farrand hoping that Dumbarton Oaks might take on this responsibility for the Mid-Atlantic region, in addition to

FIG. 7.7.

Catalogue House at the Blaksley Botanic Garden (now the Santa Barbara Botanic Garden), 1938.

Archives, AR.PH.MISC.147, Dumbarton Oaks Research Library and Collection.

its service to the history and practice of the art of landscape design?

To place Farrand's efforts in a broader context, we should note that since the beginning of the twentieth century, the movements for social and environmental improvement were bases of support for the emergence of landscape architecture as a profession. The Progressive Era was marked by a growing interest in the conservation of natural resources; this interest had an influence on the development of the profession. The beginnings of a new ecological awareness can be related to Farrand's desire to promote regional plant and bird life and to educate amateurs and professionals in "out of door beauty" at the community and regional levels.[23]

In 1947, Farrand continued to encourage Mildred Bliss to establish a community garden center for public and professional audiences: "The community is ready for such a centre; it might give a fuller mental diet than the successful and well administered popular Garden Centre at Cleveland. It might be as useful as the Arnold Arboretum and appeal to lovers of garden flowers as well as those interested in trees and shrubs."[24] Farrand continued:

As I see Dumbarton Oaks and the future it will not only be an institution to foster learning in the history of past days, but its lovely frame must be as much a part of it as it has been from the start. Those who cannot be fed by the library and collections will gain from the gardens: some, the pleasant casual joy of the passerby, and others will glean from the gardens, the records and the accompanying books a little deeper realization of what a lovely growing picture can mean, as a part of learning and the appreciation of the value of beauty. It means so much in the way not only of plants and planting, but of principles of design and the fitness of a design to its surroundings that it seems as important to me as it does to you to carry it forward in step and cadence with the indoor collections.[25]

This foundation, following in the Reef Point tradition, explains the acquisition of botanical and horticultural books alongside the practical gardening, natural history, and ornithological portions of the collections which grew in support of a garden center and a research library. Mildred Bliss was clearly well along in this direction by the late 1940s, when she sought advice from sister institutions, such as the Morton Arboretum Library in Chicago, to whom her librarian wrote: "we are trying to build up a practical garden reference library for the pleasure of garden visitors."[26]

CONTEMPORARY COLLECTORS AND COLLECTIONS

The Blisses' plan to transform Dumbarton Oaks from private home to public institution was not very different from what their contemporaries were doing abroad: Bernard Berenson at the Villa I Tatti, Sir Harold Acton at Villa La Pietra, and Lawrence Johnston at Hidcote Manor.[27] Closer to home, the great American country estate of the DuPont family, Winterthur, with gardens designed by Marian Cruger Coffin, was in the process of becoming a research center, library, and museum based on Henry Francis DuPont's vast collection of Americana. DuPont served on Dumbarton Oaks's first Garden Advisory Committee, which was established in 1953.[28] In addition to their elaborate gardens, the relevant comparison is with their great art collections, libraries, and, in several cases, their founders' commitments to give them to academic institutions or government trusts. Each of these distinguished museums or research institutes have complex histories that warrant scholarly attention, at minimum, to understand their roles in the development of garden and landscape history through their support of advanced research.

Two important American women collectors —Rachel McMasters Miller Hunt and Rachel Lambert Mellon—should be mentioned for having interests parallel to those of Mildred Bliss. They built rich libraries of books and manuscripts on agriculture, horticulture, medical botany, gardening, and landscape design; these collections were supplemented by portraits of botanists, autograph letters and manuscripts, botanic prints, drawings, and fine bindings.

FIG. 7.8.

Elizabeth Shoumatoff and Audrey Avinoff, *Portrait of Rachel McMasters Miller Hunt*, undated.

Photograph courtesy of the Hunt Institute for Botanical Documentation, Carnegie Mellon University, Pittsburgh, Pa.

Rachel McMasters Miller Hunt (1882–1963), a bookbinder herself, was an exact contemporary of Mildred Bliss (1879–1969) (fig. 7.8). In 1913, she began to amass a great collection of incunabula, herbals, medicine texts, and color plate books of the sixteenth to nineteenth centuries. By mid-century, she had one of the finest private libraries of its kind. It was transferred to the Carnegie Institute of Technology in Pittsburgh in 1960. Thus, at the same time that Mildred Bliss's new library building was close to completion, the Rachel McMasters Miller Hunt Botanical Library opened in an International-style building. In contrast to the exterior, the Rare Book Room was a walnut paneled room in the French Regency mode, very similar to Dumbarton Oaks's new Garden Library.[29]

While I have not come across evidence that Mildred Bliss had a personal acquaintance with Hunt, she did have a long relationship with Rachel Lambert Mellon (b. 1910), Paul Mellon's second wife, from as early as 1949, when they seemed to be in Paris together book buying.[30] Mellon's Oak Spring Library in Upperville, Virginia, is a celebrated collection of rare books, manuscripts, works of art, and related artifacts concerning gardens, gardening, landscape design, horticulture, and botany. We know the two expanding libraries kept abreast of acquisitions through correspondence between assistants at Oak Spring Library and the Founders' Room at Dumbarton Oaks. For example, Willis Van Devanter at Oak Spring Library described a 1963 acquisition in a letter to the secretary in the Founders' Room: "Mr[s?] Mellon has purchased the copy of Kerner's *Hortus sempervirens* (71 voluminia bound in 12,851 tabulae or plates in British Museum copy) not as complete as your set, only 15 vols containing 76 watercolors but original decorated boards" (fig. 7.9).[31] In 1967, Mildred Bliss brought Margaret Mee, the botanical artist, to Washington, D.C., to lecture and then took her to Oak Spring Library to meet Mellon. Both collectors bought paintings (fig. 7.10). In 1970, Rachel

Lambert Mellon was the first woman (other than Mildred Bliss) to serve on the Garden Advisory Committee at Dumbarton Oaks.[32]

Other celebrated libraries were making the same transition from private to public or institutional ownership in the same period. Also in Washington, D.C., Henry Clay Folger and Emily Jordan Folger's (of Standard Oil) collection of Shakespeareana and library (built by Paul Philippe Cret) were donated to the nation in 1932. The Folgers' primary dealer was A. S. W. Rosenbach, who was also selling to the Huntington Library and to Lessing Rosenwald, who, in 1943, deeded his collection of rare books and prints to the National Gallery of Art and the Library of Congress.

Southern California, where the Blisses had another home, had in the 1920s and 1930s evolved toward world-class stature as a library and research area. Collectors—such as Estelle Doheny and the book dealer Alice Millard, who commissioned Frank Lloyd Wright to build the famous house La Miniatura in 1922—were everywhere.[33] The Huntington Library, whose founding director was Max Farrand and which had extensive botanical gardens and rare book, manuscript, and art collections, must have served as an important model for the Blisses. One of the earliest books purchased after the decision to build the Garden Library at Dumbarton Oaks—*The Huntington Botanical Gardens, 1905–1949: Personal Recollections of William Hertrich, Curator Emeritus*—was ordered from the Huntington Library.[34]

LANDSCAPE ARCHITECTURE IN AMERICA

In the 1950s, there was a decreasing interest in certain collecting areas as well as the rejection and even sale of books, as the landscape studies program at Dumbarton Oaks shifted its focus from practical gardening and garden design to art, architectural, and landscape architectural history. It is useful to consider the state of the field of landscape architecture in this period for some context for this trend. Harvard University always had held a leading role in the development of the field because it established the first degree program in 1901. In his history of the Harvard architecture and landscape architecture schools, Anthony Alofsin wrote that the "post-war period surged with enthusiasm for the reconstruction of a devastated Europe as well as of an America that had finally shaken off the

misery of the Great Depression."[35] This had an effect on the direction of landscape architectural training and, consequently, the profession. For example, Norman Newton, professor of landscape architecture at Harvard University, said that "the day when landscape architects were trained for the gardens of great houses was over." The profession was undergoing a radicalization and a push to concentrate on large-scale public works.[36] Until the 1950s, a tension persisted between the historically-based Beaux-Arts tradition and the new modernist approach to landscape design, which was influenced by Bauhaus educational methods. As the Department of Landscape Architecture began to lose autonomy and status, it shrank in size. In contrast, the architecture and planning departments were greatly expanded to meet the modernist demand for new buildings and rebuilt cities. Landscape architecture underwent an identity crisis, but one thing was clear: the separation of history from practice was well entrenched in modern design.

As the profession moved away from the historically-based approach to landscape design, Dumbarton Oaks underwent parallel shifts in focus. Farrand, a proponent of the traditionalist approach to landscape design, had proudly used historic books and prints as resources for her work and depended on having this material at her fingertips at Reef Point, the Huntington Library, or Dumbarton Oaks. One example of her reliance on historical design features at Dumbarton Oaks is the Arbor Terrace.[37] Farrand identified its source in her plant book, which she made for the future maintenance and preservation of the gardens: "This arbor was modified from a design of Du Cerceau (from his drawing of the garden of the Château Montargis)." She is referring to Jacques Androuet du Cerceau's *Le premier volume des plus excellents bastiments de France*, published in Paris in 1576–79 (figs. 7.11 and 7.12).[38]

For the first twelve years, the Garden Advisory Committee at Dumbarton Oaks was made up of some of the era's leading landscape architects, who worked very much in the Beaux-Arts tradition of Beatrix Farrand—that is, they were not among the pioneering avant-garde modernists concentrated at Harvard University who were beginning to revolutionize the field (fig. 7.13). This committee included the last of the country house–era landscape architects and the leading Colonial revival practitioners of the century: Arthur Shurcliff and Alden Hopkins of

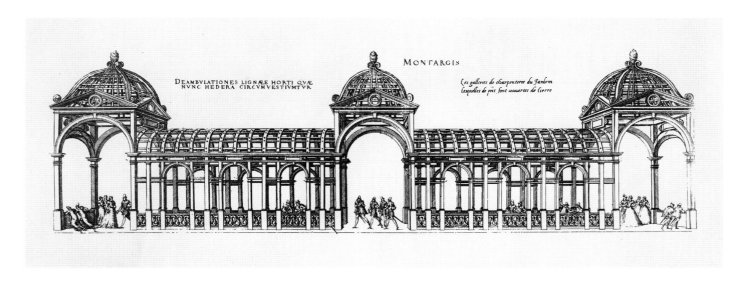

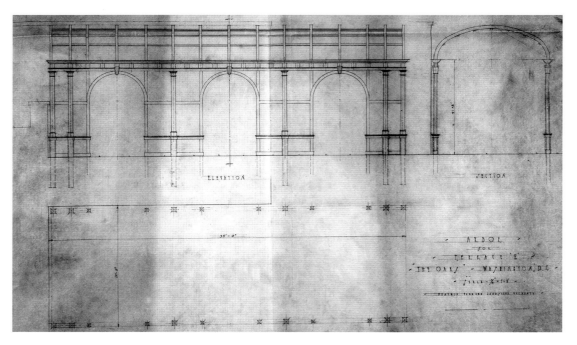

Colonial Williamsburg, Michael Rapuano, president of the American Academy in Rome, and Perry Wheeler, who would work with Rachel Lambert Mellon in designing the White House Rose Garden, among others.[39] The presence of these people must have had some influence on the direction of the library and the research program in the early years.

Like the early committee members, the early fellows followed the historicizing approach of Farrand. Ralph E. Griswold became the first Landscape Architecture Studies fellow at Dumbarton Oaks in 1956.[40] He wrote a 1959 article in the professional journal *Landscape Architecture* that promoted the program. It described the scholarly atmosphere of Dumbarton Oaks, its dedication to creative research in the arts and humanities, and its collection, which was of unique importance to garden design and landscape architecture. He exclaimed: "Imagine the satisfaction of reading from the same manuscript that was used by Claude Mollet in his instruction of André Le Nôtre!" referring to the French seventeenth-century designer of Versailles (fig. 7.14).[41]

FIG. 7.13.

Mildred Barnes Bliss
and the Garden
Advisory Committee,
ca. 1965.

Rare Book Collection,
LA.GP.06.14, Dumbarton Oaks
Research Library
and Collection.

Although the ahistoricism of modernist land-scape and garden design was a marked contrast to the approach of Beatrix Farrand and her cohort, the contemporary movement was immediately included in the library collection, as is attested by the receipt of books by Christopher Tunnard, Geoffrey Jellicoe, and other pioneers of modern design.

In 1951, the Blisses established the Dumbarton Oaks Garden Endowment Fund at Harvard University. It provided for garden maintenance and development, fellowships, publications, maintenance and enlargement of the Garden Library, support of a Garden Information Center, and other related educational purposes. Although the fellows during the early years of the garden program were predominantly landscape architects, there was, as Joachim Wolschke-Bulmahn

has written, a movement away from a praxis-oriented focus toward a scholarly or historical interest in garden and landscape architecture.[42] This is corroborated by the trends in collecting for the expanding library. Four eminent historians, whose work is considered foundational in the emerging field of landscape history, were fellows in residence during those early years: Albert Fein (1965–67), Georgina Masson (1966–67), Charles McLaughlin (1967–68), and George B. Tatum (1967–68).[43]

BUILDING THE COLLECTION

Through the records of purchases and sales, it is possible to trace the efforts to define and build the collection from the early years, when practical gardening as well as "The Gentle Art of

Landscape Gardening," as Mildred Bliss called it, were both pursued. Agnes Mongan wrote that Mildred Bliss "called on three different sources for advice: her friend and designer of the gardens, Beatrix Farrand; the Houghton Library (the rare book library at Harvard); and the librarian at the Harvard School of Architecture." In fact, she sought advice much more broadly from various friends, professional acquaintances, and institutions. At the same time that she ordered the Massachusetts Horticultural Library's list of four hundred books for an amateur garden library, she also requested a bibliography from Harvard's Department of Landscape Architecture and Regional Planning. She and her assistants also closely studied the Reef Point book list and inventories.[44]

Mildred Bliss constructed a *desiderata* (wish list) on the basis of several sources. Sent out to dealers routinely, it was compiled and edited in many versions, usually undated, that exist in the Archives. In one undated note, Farrand instructed Mildred Bliss to follow a bibliography from *Garden and Forest*.[45] I believe this referred to a bibliography that had been published as "A List of Works on the Art of Landscape-Gardening" on 12 March 1890 in the short-lived journal *Garden and Forest*, founded by Charles Sprague Sargent, Beatrix Farrand's mentor and director of the Arnold Arboretum. This bibliography was compiled by Henry Sargent Codman, landscape architect, who trained in France and worked in the firm of Frederick Law Olmsted. It is a remarkably comprehensive list of works in English, French, German, and Italian from 1625 to what was then contemporary design, the work of Olmsted.[46] Many of these books form the basis of the library today; they reflect

the breadth and broad interdisciplinary framework of a profession that included a wide range of outdoor forms and spaces, including (but not limited to) parks, urban open spaces, cemeteries, monument sites, estates, and gardens of all sizes and types. Adhering to the bibliography so closely laid a very solid foundation upon which the library could (and would) expand in the future.

The effort to find their desiderata was international, utilizing professional and personal links in their search. For example, in a 1964 letter, the Dumbarton Oaks librarian wrote to the Embassy of Canada on Mildred Bliss's behalf to enlist its help in finding Jacques Le Moyne watercolors (fig. 7.15).[47] William M. McCarthy Jr., a dealer at the Rosenbach Company and agent for Mildred Bliss at the Biddle sale at Parke-Bernet, wrote following a 1952 visit to her Garden Library: "The beauty of the place I always find breath-taking and, this time, there was the added excitement of the process of creation. The collection, as you plan it, will certainly become a center for the design and creation of beauty in your uniquely selected field." He was successful in acquiring Johann Simon Kerner's multivolume *Hortus sempervirens* (1795–1830) for Mildred Bliss, despite the fact, McCarthy wrote, that flower books had become very popular among collectors in the 1950s.[48] Their popularity was probably in no small way linked to Mildred Bliss, Rachel McMasters Miller Hunt, and Rachel Lambert Mellon, who actively scooped up every flower book on the market.

"This book is of very great rarity."
BOOK DEALERS AND MILDRED BLISS

The heart of the Garden Library was the Founders' Room in the early years of the program. Separate from the Dumbarton Oaks Research Library, it was presided over by Mildred Bliss, referred to by one dealer as The Foundress, who worked with a long succession of assistants or keepers.[49] It dealt with the most prominent booksellers of the twentieth century, such as A. S. W. Rosenbach.

PIERO CRESCENTIO DE AGRICVLTVRA.

Hans P. Kraus, the most famous of the émigré booksellers in New York, was the most successful and dominant rare book dealer in the world in this period.[50] He sold Mildred Bliss the Francesco Melzi copy of Pietro de' Crescenzi's *Il libro della agricultura* (Venice, 1495) (fig. 7.16). John Fleming sold her George Washington's copy of John Abercrombie and Thomas Mawe's *The Universal Gardener and Botanist* (London, 1778), a work the first president often referred to in his garden book (fig. 7.17).[51] Bernard Quatrich and Son sold her the earliest book in the collection, the *Hortus sanitatis* (Mainz, 1491), by the Hausbuchmeister (fig. 7.18). That London book company was another giant of the antiquarian book world in the period after World War II, when important book auctions attracted many prominent American book buyers.[52]

That Mildred Bliss considered herself a builder of an institutional library (and no longer a private one) is made very clear in her dealings with booksellers. Many times she, or her librarian on her behalf, insisted on the conventional ten percent discount afforded educational institutions.[53] This could be a deal breaker. Nonetheless, the dealers flooded her with offers, which she reviewed and on which she neatly penciled her instructions, "no" or "keep." On some occasions, she made more extended comments, such as "should like the history of these volumes" in regard to Pierre Joseph Redouté's *Les liliacées* (Paris, 1802–16) (fig. 7.19).[54]

An increasingly frequent response to an eager dealer was "Mrs. Bliss already has a better one." In a 1961 letter to a German publisher, who was promoting a facsimile of Leonhart Fuchs's *De historia*

THE
UNIVERSAL GARDENER
And BOTANIST;
OR, A
GENERAL DICTIONARY
OF
GARDENING and BOTANY.

Exhibiting in Botanical Arrangement, according to the Linnæan System,

Every TREE, SHRUB, and Herbaceous PLANT, that merit Culture,
either for Use, Ornament, or Curiosity, in every Department of GARDENING.

Comprising accurate Directions, according to real Practice, for the Management of the

KITCHEN-GARDEN,	NURSERY,	HOT-BEDS,
FRUIT-GARDEN,	PLANTATIONS,	FORCING-FRAMES,
PLEASURE-GROUND,	GREEN-HOUSE,	HOT-WALLS, and
FLOWER-GARDEN,	HOT-HOUSE, or STOVE,	FORCING in general.

Describing the proper Situations, Exposures, Soils, Manures, and every Material
and Utensil requisite in the different Garden Departments ;

Together with

PRACTICAL DIRECTIONS

FOR

Performing the various Mechanical Operations of GARDENING in general.

By THOMAS MAWE,
Gardener to his Grace the Duke of Leeds.

And JOHN ABERCROMBIE,
Authors of Every Man his Own Gardener, &c.

LONDON,
Printed for G. Robinson, in Pater-noster Row ; and T. Cadell, in the Strand.
MDCCLXXVIII.

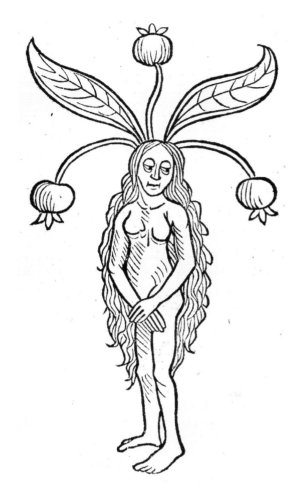

stirpium commentarii insignes (fig. 7.20), her librarian wrote: "Mrs. Robert Woods Bliss wishes me to inform you that she has in her Dumbarton Oaks collection FUCH'S Kräuterbuch (herbal book), three editions: first edition in Latin, 1542; first edition in German, 1543; first edition in German in colour, 1545. Therefore, she does not believe she would be interested in subscribing to the reproduction. However, Mrs. Bliss believes it would be a most interesting and worthwhile project and that there is probably much demand for such a reproduction or facsimile."[55] Somewhere else, perhaps, but not at Dumbarton Oaks. Statements such as "Mrs. Bliss is not interested in works of the latter part of the 19th century," made in 1963, leave one confused and wondering if this was a new collecting policy or a mere ploy to fend off a dealer's offer.

She obviously got great pleasure from comparing copies of works in the collection to new offers. She already had the 1763 edition of Nikolaus Joseph Jacquin's *Selectarum stirpium americanarum historia*, but took a 1780 copy for review just so she could compare the two (fig. 7.21).[56] In 1956, an exasperated bookseller complained of her approval requests, saying that most books would be returned with the excuse of already having it in the collection.[57] This proved difficult for smaller dealers, especially those, like Elizabeth Woodburn, who specialized in a narrow area. Major dealers, such as John Fleming and William H. McCarthy Jr., could afford the inconvenience and effort. They visited Dumbarton Oaks with their wives and friends and made special arrangements to meet any of her demands. For example, McCarthy sent a letter to Mildred

Lilium Penduliflorum   *Lis à fleurs pendantes*

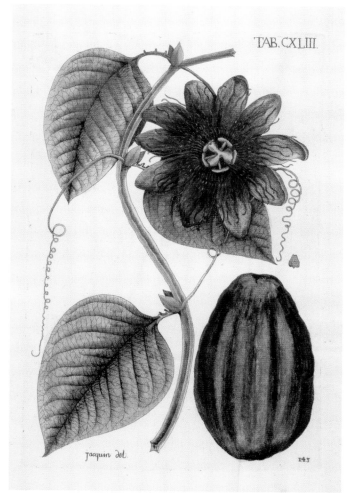

Bliss's librarian on 2 July 1952: "the Garcilaso de la Vega is at hand and will await Mrs. Bliss in her cabin on the Mauretania."[58]

NEW GARDEN LIBRARY BUILDING

As the collection expanded, so did plans for the garden study program, and exhibition, storage, and study space became a problem. The Garden Library History file in the Rare Book Collection has notes for a new library building that would accommodate fifty to fifty-five researchers.[59] The ambitious plan was obviously scaled back to about one-tenth the size. The Garden Library was designed by Frederic Rhinelander King of Wyeth and King, Architects in New York ca. 1960–64 (fig. 7.22). Decorated in a French Regency style, it stood in stark contrast to Philip Johnson's post-modernist Pre-Columbian pavilion that opened

the same year. It was a two-story structure, with a foyer with an exhibition case, reference room, and adjacent staff offices upstairs, and two studies, stack room, and restoration room downstairs. King's library had one striking feature in common with Johnson's museum wing—its full-length bowed windows brought the garden and light into the interior space (fig. 7.23).

Word spread quickly among booksellers about the Garden Library and Mildred Bliss's interest in acquiring manuscripts and rare books in the fields of garden landscape architecture and design. Mildred Bliss's librarian wrote, "we have assembled the Garden Collection in this new Library Building. Another matter which has come to mind is the offer you made to Mrs. Bliss quite some time ago, of a number of volumes of Buffon. At that time Mrs. Bliss decided not to acquire them, as we had very limited space in which to

FIG. 7.24.

Frontispiece to
Carl Linnaeus,
Hortus Cliffortianus
(Amsterdam, 1737).

Rare Book Collection,
RBR K-3-4 LIN, Dumbarton
Oaks Research Library
and Collection.

house the collection. However, Mrs. Bliss is now very anxious to acquire Buffon's ornithology collection."[60] This is a reference to the Comte de Buffon's *Histoire naturelle*, a monumental thirty-five-volume publication of 1749–88.

By 1966, Mildred Bliss wanted it known that the "Garden Library has a sufficient number of volumes on natural history . . . and there is not as great need for this type of work for scholarly research, as there is for garden landscape architecture and design material."[61] However, in the same

year, she purchased the botanist Carl Linnaeus' *Hortus Cliffortianus* (Amsterdam, 1737), with drawings by Georg Dionysius Ehret (fig. 7.24). It fit well with the subcollection of Linnaean materials she had previously amassed. This collection, which cuts across the various media areas of the library, includes four letters signed by Linnaeus, which are in the large holographic letters collection at Dumbarton Oaks. Among the portraits of eminent botanists and landscape gardeners that Mildred Bliss collected is one of Linnaeus.[62]

Mildred Bliss also acquired a large number of books, drawings, and manuscripts by and about women naturalist-artists.[63] I will mention just two unique items: the first is the red and black chalk portrait of Giovanna Garzoni in the portfolio volume entitled *Piante varie* that once belonged to the Strozzi family of Florence (fig. 7.25). The second is an almost unknown handwritten manuscript entitled *A British Flora after the Sexual System of Linnaeus* by the famous Mary Granville Delany (1700–88), an artist renowned for her silk embroidery and paper cut botanicals. This five-hundred-page manuscript was made at Bulstrode, where Delany spent a great deal of her time with the Duchess of Portland (fig. 7.26).[64]

This collection is rich in association volumes, where the interest and value of the book lies in the intersection of text and owner. For example, the botanist Jan Commelin's (1629–98) name is inscribed with that of the important naturalist Thomas Pennant (1726–98) on the title page of Carolus Clusius's *Rariorum plantarum historia* (Antwerp, 1601). Commelin annotated most of the 1,100 woodcuts with Latin names in his own hand (fig. 7.27). The associative and scientific value of this important botanist's own notation is evident. These are just a few of the treasures in the library, which are here noted to give a sense of the depth and range of Mildred Bliss's collecting.

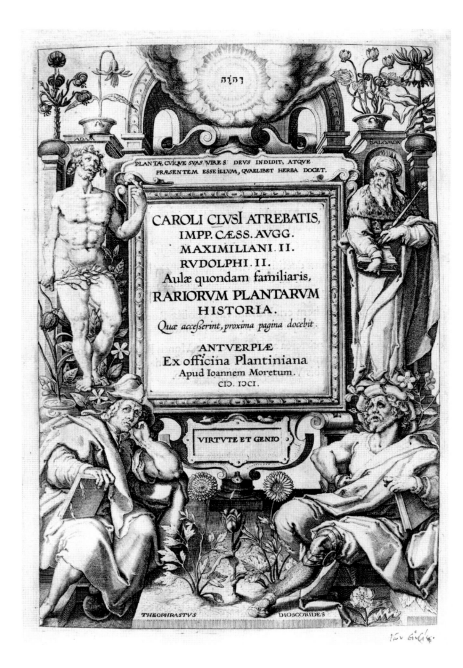

In his famous essay "Unpacking My Library," Walter Benjamin identified four ways of acquiring books that are relevant to the history of the Garden Library at Dumbarton Oaks. Writing them, he claimed, is the most praiseworthy. Borrowing, with its attendant non-returning, is a second, though less praiseworthy, technique. Purchasing books is the most common approach, but inheriting them is the soundest way.[65] To these, I would add a fifth way of acquiring books: receiving them as gifts. Elsewhere I have written that the garden, historically a setting of gentility and diplomacy, has been a site for gift giving and exchange—an idea which pertains very much to Dumbarton Oaks.[66] Mildred Bliss's Record Book of Accessions to the Garden Library lists the many books and artworks presented to her by friends and colleagues. I will highlight three gifts she received and one gift she made. *Nützliches Khünstbüech der Gartnereij* was given to her in 1956 by her close friend, the pianist and composer Ernest Schelling (fig. 7.28).

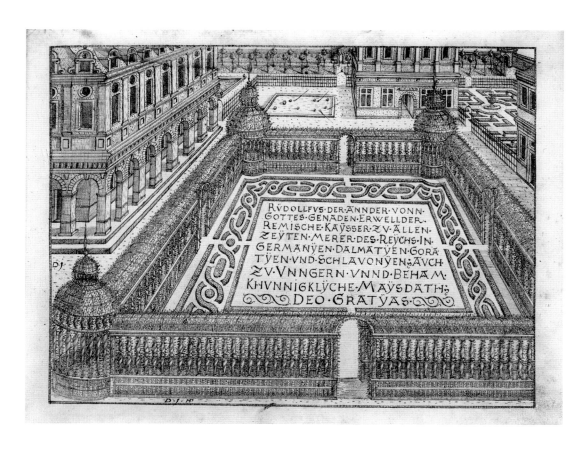

It was for forty years catalogued as "follower of Vredeman de Vries" until Erik de Jong attributed it to Hans Puechfeldner, gardener to Rudolph II, to whom it is dedicated, and linked it to two other albums in Vienna.[67] Another gift, a set of embroidered table linens based on the Badianus manuscript (a sixteenth-century Aztec herbal in the Vatican Library), was a gift from a Baltimore couple after they saw that the Garden Library had the complete set of watercolors also based on the manuscript (fig. 7.29).[68] A painting of a vase of flowers by Odilon Redon (fig. 7.30) was given by Beatrix Farrand, who intended it specifically for the Garden Library. It had hung in Edith Wharton's library in France.[69] Finally, Mildred Bliss made gifts to other collections from her Garden Library. For example, when Mount Vernon was collecting materials related to the first president's home, Mildred Bliss donated an aquatint showing the west front and bowling green of Mount Vernon, which was made by the British artist George Isham Parkyns ca. 1797.

In 1968, Mildred Bliss became seriously ill, and curtailed her acquisitions. Upon her death in early 1969, book orders were cancelled and a period of review and planning commenced. As John Thacher wrote in 1971, Harvard University had been awarded the garden endowment in 1951, but the Garden Library had remained the property of Mildred Bliss until her death, and its character reflected the strong personal concern she had for its development.[70] Benjamin has written: "the most distinguished trait of a collection will always be its transmissibility."[71] The real test of that distinction for the Garden Library began after Mildred Bliss's death.

When she died, the Garden Library had 2,400 rare books, 5,000 reference books, 1,000 holograph items, and an unknown number of unpublished manuscripts, prints, and drawings. The list of highly significant publications that have originated in the Garden Library in the sixty years of its existence and the roster of world-renowned scholars who have been readers and fellows testify to the important position it occupies in the evolution of the field of garden and landscape studies. Mildred Bliss's wish that the interest of scholarship at Dumbarton Oaks be extended to the field of garden design, giving full recognition to its place in Western culture, has been realized to an extent she and Beatrix Farrand could not have imagined. Using receipts, invoices, letters, catalogs, and book lists from the Archives and Rare Book Collection, we can follow how Mildred Bliss, through her librarians, bought and sold, was given, and exchanged books, prints and drawings, and various visual materials to build the library. Through a vast correspondence from the 1920s to 1960s with advisors, book sellers, and other collectors, it has been possible to trace the evolving goals and purpose of the Garden Library at Dumbarton Oaks. The value of this collection was expressed most poignantly by Beatrix Farrand, who wrote that the garden "library, like the garden, is intended to contribute its mite [sic] to the art of living as expressed in gardening."[72]

ACKNOWLEDGMENTS

I would like to thank James Carder, Linda Lott, and Joe Mills of Dumbarton Oaks, and from the Center for Advanced Study in the Visual Arts in Washington, D.C., Anne Nellis, Sara Taylor, and Jessica Ruse, for their help in preparing this paper.

Notes

1   Agnes Mongan, "A Fête of Flowers: Women Artists' Contribution to Botanical Illustration," reprint of *Apollo* 119 (April 1984): 59. See also Ethel B. Clark, "The Founders' Room Library at Dumbarton Oaks," *Harvard Library Bulletin* 4, no. 2 (Spring 1950): 141–71.

2   Elisabeth Blair MacDougall, "Prelude: Landscape Studies, 1952–1972," in *Perspectives on Garden Histories*, ed. Michel Conan (Washington, D.C., 1999), 18.

3   John S. Thacher, "The Garden Library," *Harvard Library Bulletin* 19, no. 2 (April 1971): 211–13. "The Collection was begun by Mrs. Robert Woods Bliss at the end of World War II and reflects her desire that the interests of scholarship at Dumbarton Oaks be extended to the field of garden design, giving full recognition of its place in the development of western culture. While garden design, as the gardens of Dumbarton Oaks so clearly demonstrate, was a life-long interest of Mrs. Bliss, her purpose in establishing the Garden Library reflects a somewhat broader concern. The upheavals of the wartime and postwar years threatened the existence not only of a large majority of the great historical examples of garden design, but many of the long-established private libraries as well. As these libraries were broken up, dealers often found it more profitable to sell the plates from volumes on architecture and gardens individually rather than to find purchasers for the complete books. Thus, in establishing the Garden Library, Mrs. Bliss assured that many rare books which would otherwise have been lost were preserved intact."

4   Walter Benjamin, "Unpacking My Library," in *Illuminations*, ed. Hannah Arendt, trans. Harry Zohn (New York, 1969), 61.

5   Leah Dilworth, introduction to *Acts of Possession: Collecting in America* (New Brunswick, N.J., 2003), 8.

6   Susan M. Pearce, *On Collecting: An Investigation into Collecting in the European Tradition* (London and New York, 2000), 14.

7   Diane Kostial McGuire and Lois Fern, eds., *Beatrix Jones Farrand (1872–1959): Fifty Years of American Landscape Architecture* (Washington, D.C., 1982). See also Jane Brown, *Beatrix: The Gardening Life of Beatrix Jones Farrand, 1872–1959* (New York, 1995); and Diana Balmori, Diane Kostial McGuire, and Eleanor M. McPeck, *Beatrix Farrand's American Landscapes: Her Gardens and Campuses* (Sagaponack, N.Y., 1985).

8   Beatrix Jones Farrand to Mildred Barnes Bliss, 17 June 1947, Beatrix Farrand file, Rare Book Collection. Cited in MacDougall, "Prelude," 18.

9   Beatrix Jones Farrand to Mildred Barnes Bliss, 26 May 1947, Beatrix Farrand file, Rare Book Collection.

10 Beatrix Jones Farrand to Anne Sweeney, 27 January 1937, Beatrix Farrand file, Rare Book Collection. "It seems to me quite desirable from the point of view of information to include the accent of pronunciation on the cards and to also add the approximate native habitat. Of course each card may later be made to include the family to which the plant belongs, the quality of the soil it needs and its height and spread, but it seems to me that these brief cards will at least serve as an identification and later they may be expanded to the full biography of the plant if this be thought advisable."

11 I would like to thank my colleague Helen Tangires, who brought this drawing to my attention. *Vernon Kellogg, 1867–1937* (Washington, D.C., 1939). Kellogg was a Stanford professor of entomology, expert in insect taxonomy, and director of the American Commission for Relief in Belgium under Hoover.

12 Caetani was the Italian ambassador to the United States in 1920–25, and owner of Ninfa, a garden south of Rome. Linda Lott, "The Arbor Terrace at Dumbarton Oaks, History and Design," *Garden History* 31, no. 2 (Winter 2003): 209–10.

13 Beatrix Jones Farrand to Mildred Barnes Bliss, 26 May 1947, Beatrix Farrand file, Rare Book Collection.

14 Susan Tamulevich, *Dumbarton Oaks: Garden into Art* (New York, 2001), 146.

15 Paula Deitz, introduction to *The Bulletins of Reef Point Gardens* (Bar Harbor, Maine, 1997), xv.

16 *Reef Point Gardens Bulletin* 1, no. 17 (1956): 113–14.

17 Beatrix Farrand, quoted in Deitz, introduction to *The Bulletins of Reef Point Gardens*, xv.

18 Deitz, introduction to *The Bulletins of Reef Point Gardens*, xix.

19 *Reef Point Gardens Bulletin* 1, no. 14 (August 1955): 88.

20 *Reef Point Gardens Bulletin* 1, no. 17 (1956): 113. See also Michael M. Laurie, "The Reef Point Collection at the University of California," in *Beatrix Jones Farrand (1872–1959)*, 9–20.

21 Tamulevich, *Dumbarton Oaks*, 146.

22 Deitz, introduction to *The Bulletins of Reef Point Gardens*, xv.

23 Melanie L. Simo, *Forest and Garden: Traces of Wilderness in a Modernizing Land, 1897–1949* (Charlottesville, Va., 2003), 121–22 and 140.

24 Beatrix Jones Farrand to Mildred Barnes Bliss, 26 May 1947, Beatrix Farrand file, Rare Book Collection.

25 Beatrix Jones Farrand to Mildred Barnes Bliss, 7 April 1947, Beatrix Farrand file, Rare Book Collection.

26 To Morton Arboretum Library, February 1947, Rare Books and Material Acquisition file, Archives.

27 Tamulevich, *Dumbarton Oaks*, 39.

28 Joachim Wolschke-Bulmahn, *Twenty-Five Years of Studies in Landscape Architecture at Dumbarton Oaks: From Italian Gardens to Theme Parks* (Washington, D.C., 1996), 33.

29 *The Rachel McMasters Miller Hunt Botanical Library, Carnegie Institute of Technology: Its Collections, Program, and Staff* (Pittsburgh, Pa., 1961), v–vi and 1–4.

30 Rachel Lambert Mellon to Rose Wildgoose, librarian at Dumbarton Oaks, 2 September 1949, Rare Books and Material Acquisition file, Archives. The Mellons also established the Center for Hellenic Studies, another research institute of Harvard University, on land formerly abutting Dumbarton Oaks in 1961.

31 Willis Van Devanter, Oak Spring Library, to Miss Mink, secretary in the Founders' Room, 17 September 1963, Rare Books and Material Acquisition file, Archives. Van Devanter later served on the Garden Advisory Committee (1973–74). Wolschke-Bulmahn, *Twenty-Five Years of Studies*, 33.

32 Wolschke-Bulmahn, *Twenty-Five Years of Studies*, 33.

33 Nicholas A. Basbanes, *A Gentle Madness: Bibliophiles, Bibliomanes, and the Eternal Passion for Books* (New York, 1995), 217–18, 228, and 410–64.

34 Letter to Huntington Library, March 1949, Huntington Library file, Rare Book Collection.

35 Anthony Alofsin, *The Struggle for Modernism: Architecture, Landscape, and City Planning at Harvard* (New York, 2002), 196.

36 David Jacques and Jan Woudstra, *Landscape Modernism Renounced: The Career of Christopher Tunnard (1910–1979)* (London and New York, 2009), 48–50.

37 Rare book librarian Linda Lott examined the specific reference identified by Farrand to a source for the arbor. Lott, "The Arbor Terrace at Dumbarton Oaks," 209–11. See also Linda Lott with James Carder, *Garden Ornament at Dumbarton Oaks* (Washington, D.C., 2001), 16–19.

38 Diane Kostial McGuire, ed., *Beatrix Farrand's Plant Book for Dumbarton Oaks* (Washington, D.C., 1980), 171.

39 Wolschke-Bulmahn, *Twenty-Five Years of Studies*, 33 and 46.

40 Ibid., 20.

41 Ralph E. Griswold, "Landscape Architecture at Dumbarton Oaks," *Landscape Architecture* 50, no. 1 (Autumn 1959): 44.

42 Wolschke-Bulmahn, *Twenty-Five Years of Studies*, 22.

43 Ibid., 35–36.

44 Mongan, "A Fête of Flowers," 59. See also Elisabeth Blair MacDougall, introduction to *Hortus Librorum: Early Botanical Books at Dumbarton Oaks* (Washington, D.C., 1983), iii.

45 Beatrix Jones Farrand to Mildred Barnes Bliss, undated, Beatrix Farrand file, Rare Book Collection.

46 "The following list of works treating of landscape-gardening which have been published in English, French, German and Italian since 1625, the date of Bacon's classical essay, has been prepared in the library of the British Museum, in the Bibliothèque Nationale and in other public and private libraries, and is as complete as I have been able to make it. I have endeavored to include all books, pamphlets, articles and reviews except those, which have appeared in horticultural and agricultural papers. Such a work is necessarily liable to error, and I shall be glad of any suggestions or corrections, which will help to make the list more complete and correct." *Garden and Forest* 3 (12 March 1890): 131–35.

47 Letter to the Embassy of Canada, 1964, Rare Books and Material Acquisition file, Archives.

48 William H. McCarthy Jr. to Mildred Barnes Bliss, 3 June 1952, Rare Books and Material Acquisition file, Archives.

49 William H. McCarthy Jr. to Mildred Barnes Bliss, 2 July 1952, Rare Books and Material Acquisition file, Archives.

50 Nicholas A. Basbanes, *Patience and Fortitude: A Roving Chronicle of Book People, Book Places, and Book Culture* (New York, 2001), 279.

51 Hans P. Kraus, 23 June 1961, and John Fleming, 2 December 1963, Rare Books and Material Acquisition file, Archives.

52 Basbanes, *Patience and Fortitude*, 262.

53 Letter to Harvard University Library, 18 April 1950, Rare Books and Material Acquisition file, Archives. "Will you kindly send Mrs. Bliss at Founders Room a copy of your publication *The Place of the Library in a University* which she is presenting to Harvard University The Dumbarton Oaks Research Library and Collection. Mrs. Bliss would like also to have the bill with the usual inter-library discount."

54 Notations by Mildred Bliss on a letter from Hamil and Barker, Rare Books and Material Acquisition file, Archives.

55 Librarian Mary L. Wilkens (?) to Karl F. Haug, Verlag, 31 July 1961, Rare Books and Material Acquisition file, Archives.

56 Librarian (?) to Lathrop C. Harper, 11 February 1966, Rare Books and Material Acquisition file, Archives.

57 Letter from book dealer Katherine Gregory, 1956, Rare Books and Material Acquisition file, Archives. See also Emil Offenbacher to Mrs. C. I. Dennison, keeper of the Founders' Room, 15 January 1959, Rare Books and Material Acquisition file, Archives.

58 William H. McCarthy Jr. to Elsa A. Needham, 2 July 1952, Rare Books and Material Acquisition file, Archives.

59 Garden Library History file, Rare Book Collection.

60 Librarian Mary L. Wilkens to Miss Francis Hamil of Hamil and Barker, 8 April 1964, Rare Books and Material Acquisition file, Archives.

61 Librarian Mary L. Wilkens to Verena Taumann of Erasmushaus Book Dealers, 15 March 1965, Rare Books and Material Acquisition file, Archives.

62 "We do have a fine portrait of Carl Von Linnaeus by Alexander Roslin, as well as one of J. J. Rousseau, both in aquatint. These are the types of portraits we are looking for, and we would appreciate your continued search for important portraits of old botanists and of well known landscape architects." Librarian Mary L. Wilkens to Verena Taumann, 7 April 1965, Rare Books and Material Acquisition file, Archives.

63 Mongan, "A Fête of Flowers," 59–67. See Lucia Tongiorgi Tomasi, "'La femminil pazienza': Women Painters and Natural History in the Seventeenth and Early Eighteenth Centuries," in *The Art of Natural History: Illustrated Treatises and Botanical Paintings, 1400–1850*, eds. Therese

O'Malley and Amy R. W. Meyers (Washington, D.C., 2008), 166–69.

64 Mark Laird in correspondence with this author has tentatively identified the work to be a copy of William Hudson's *Flora Anglica* (1762?), the first English flora arranged according to the Linnean system. See *Mrs. Delany and her Circle*, eds. Mark Laird and Alicia Weisberg-Roberts (New Haven, 2009), 10.

65 Benjamin, "Unpacking My Library," 61–63.

66 Therese O'Malley, "Cultivated Lives, Cultivated Spaces: The Scientific Garden in Philadelphia, 1740–1840," in *The Culture of Nature: Art and Science in Philadelphia, 1740 to 1840*, ed. Amy R. W. Meyers (New Haven, forthcoming).

67 Erik A. de Jong, "A Garden Book Made for Emperor Rudolf II in 1593: Hans Puechfeldner's *Nützliches Khünstbüech der Gartnereij*," in *The Art of Natural History*, 187–204.

68 Gilman D'Arcy Paul to Mildred Barnes Bliss, 1 April 1958. The De la Cruz-Badiano Aztec herbal, translation and commentary directed by William Gates, published by the Maya Society, in Baltimore, 1939. Cardinal Tisseraut's niece was commissioned by the Smithsonian to make aquarelles for publication produced by the Maya Society, Baltimore. Following a visit to Mildred Bliss in 1958, Gilman D'Arcy Paul or Julian and Anne Greene sent to Mildred Bliss the embroidered linens based on the Aztec herbal.

69 Beatrix Jones Farrand to Mildred Barnes Bliss, 28 September 1937 and 31 May 1938, Beatrix Farrand file, Rare Book Collection.

70 Thacher, "The Garden Library," 211. Librarian Laura Byers to the editor of the Washington Irving edition, 17 December 1975: "the Garden Library, the depository of Mrs. Bliss's original rarebook collection in Horticulture and Botany, has now taken a slightly different direction, to become the Center for Studies of Landscape Architecture. Our efforts have been concentrated entirely on reorganizing our library and developing it as a research center in this discipline." Garden Library History file, Rare Book Collection.

71 Benjamin, "Unpacking My Library," 66.

72 *Reef Point Gardens Bulletin* 1, no. 15 (July 1950): 27.

Contributors

JEANICE BROOKS is professor of music at the University of Southampton. Her research interests include music and French culture of the Renaissance, British music ca. 1800, and twentieth-century French music. She is currently finishing a study of Nadia Boulanger's performing career, focusing particularly on the period between World War I and World War II.

GUDRUN BÜHL is curator and director of the Dumbarton Oaks Museum in Washington, D.C. As a graduate student, she specialized in early Byzantine art, with a focus on the representation and meaning of personifications of cities, especially Roma and Constantinopolis. After teaching Byzantine art and archaeology at the University of Göttingen, she was assistant curator of the Byzantine Collection at the Bodemuseum in Berlin and lectured on Byzantine art at the Berlin Freie Universität. As an archaeologist, she has participated in surveys of Byzantine rural settlements in Turkey. Her significant contributions to the field of Byzantine ivory carvings have been published in articles, exhibition catalogues, and books.

JAMES N. CARDER is archivist and manager of the House Collection at the Dumbarton Oaks Research Library and Collection in Washington, D.C., where he curates the museum's collections of historic architecture, interiors, and Asian, European, and American paintings, sculptures, and decorative arts. He has published and lectured widely on varied decorative arts topics, architectural history, and collecting and patronage. In collaboration with Robert S. Nelson, he is currently preparing a publication of the annotated correspondence between Mildred and Robert Woods Bliss and Elisina and Royall Tyler.

JULIE JONES is curator of Pre-Columbian art and Andrall E. Pearson Curator in Charge of the Department of the Arts of Africa, Oceania, and the Americas at the Metropolitan Museum of Art. She has organized many exhibitions for that institution, both small and large, on specialized Pre-Columbian topics. Her museum career began in the Museum of Primitive Art in New York, the first of its kind in the United States, which showcased the art of Pre-Columbian America, the Islands of the Pacific, and Africa south of the Sahara.

ROBIN KARSON is founder and executive director of the Library of American Landscape History (LALH) in Amherst, Massachusetts, and author of more than one hundred articles about American landscape history. She has also written several books, including *Fletcher Steele: Landscape Architect; The Muses of Gwinn: Art and Nature in a Garden Designed by Warren H. Manning, Charles A. Platt, and Ellen Biddle Shipman; Pioneers of American Landscape Design* (as coeditor); and *A Genius for Place: American Landscapes of the Country Place Era,* which recently received a J. B. Jackson Prize from the Foundation for Landscape Studies. In 2009, her work for LALH was recognized by an Arthur Ross Award in history and publishing from the Institute of Classical Architecture and Classical America. In 1992, Karson founded the Library of American Landscape History to develop scholarly books about American landscape history. LALH has since published twenty-five titles.

THERESE O'MALLEY is associate dean at the Center for Advanced Study in the Visual Arts at the National Gallery of Art in Washington, D.C. Her publications have focused on the history of landscape architecture and garden design, primarily in the eighteenth and nineteenth centuries, concentrating on the transatlantic exchange of plants, ideas, and people. Her recent books include *Keywords in American Landscape Design* (Yale University Press) and *The Art of Natural History*, coedited with Amy R. W. Meyers. She is a former president of the Society of Architectural Historians, a board member of the Foundation for Landscape Study and the Mount Vernon Place Conservancy, and a technical advisor for the U.S. Ambassadors Fund. O'Malley lectures internationally and has taught at Harvard, Princeton, Pennsylvania, and Temple universities.

ROBERT S. NELSON is professor of the history of art at Yale University and chair of its Medieval and Renaissance Studies programs. He studies the art of Byzantium and its reception in the culture of its making and afterward. A continuing concern has been the Italian engagement with Byzantium in the Middle Ages and the Renaissance and the collecting of Byzantine art in Europe and America during the nineteenth and twentieth centuries.

JAN M. ZIOLKOWSKI is Arthur Kingsley Porter Professor of Medieval Latin at Harvard University and director of the Dumbarton Oaks Research Library and Collection in Washington, D.C. He has published books on fairy tales, Abelard's letters, musical notation of the classics in the early Middle Ages, Solomon and Marcolf, and, collaboratively, a twelfth-century anthology and a guide to the Virgilian tradition. Most recently he has edited a special issue of *Dante Studies* on "Dante and Islam."

Index

Photographs and illustrations are indicated by numbers in **bold** type.

Guérin, Jacques, 39
Guilmant, Alexandre, 79–80
Gustaf Adolf (Prince of Sweden), 22n24

Hacha (Veracruz), 57, **57**
Handbook of the Robert Woods Bliss Collection of Pre-Columbian Art (Benson and Coe), 69
Hartman, George, 108, 111
Harvard University: Robert Woods Bliss attends, 1, 59; Robert Woods Bliss awarded honorary doctorate by, 18; Blisses' personal library passed to, 47n26; Blisses' residual estates given to, 18, 20, 69; Center for Hellenic Studies established with, 164n30; Dumbarton Oaks administered by, 18–20, 43; Dumbarton Oaks Garden Endowment Fund entrusted to, 18, 20, 149, 162; Dumbarton Oaks inaugurated under, 16, 37, 64; Dumbarton Oaks transferred to, 1, 13, 15–16, 20, 61, 132; Garden Library left to, 162; Harvard Club, xvi, 28; Harvard University Archives, 27, 89nn3–4; landscape architecture program at, 147; libraries at, 150; people affiliated with, 10, 53, 64, 65, 69; Pre-Columbian Collection transferred to, 67; Trustees for, 18; Villa I Tatti given to, 33
Hausbuchmeister, 152
haute couture, 97
Havey, Ruth, 107, 135, 137n26
Head of a Pratyeka Buddha (Chinese), 31, **34**
Heliconia psittacorum (Mee), **146**
Hessen, Philipp von, 42
Hidcote Manor, 145
Hinners, Howard, 89n4
Histoire naturelle (Buffon), 155–57, **157**
Hofer, Evelyn, 20, 25n95, **138**
Holland, Jean (Mrs.), 59
Holm Lea (estate), 118, **119**
Honegger, Arthur, 81
Hoover, Herbert, 10, 163n11
Hopkins, Alden, 115n62, 129, 147
Hortus Cliffortianus (Linnaeus), 157, **157**
Hortus sanitatis (Meydenbach), 152, **153**
Hortus sempervirens (Kerner), 146, **146**, 151
Houghton Library, 150
House Collection, xv–xvii. *See also* Music Room; *individual objects*
Hudson, William, 165n64
Human figure (Muisca), **59**
Hume, Martin Andrew Sharp, 46n4
Huntington Botanical Gardens, 1905–1949: Personal Recollections of William Hertrich, Curator Emeritus, The, 147
Huntington Library, 143, 147
Hunt, Rachel McMasters Miller, 145–46, **145**, 151

Hunt, William H., 1, 59
Hyde, Martha, 77

Icones plantarum rariorum (Jacquin), 139, **140**
Icon of the Incredulity of Thomas (Byzantine), 28, **29**, 42
Incidents of Travel in Central America, Chiapas, and Yucatan (Stephens), 63, 71n40
Indigenous Art of the Americas: Collection of Robert Woods Bliss (exhibition and catalogue), 65
Islamic architecture, 109
Islamic art, 31–33, **33**, 38, 43, **44**, 97
Italian Gardens (Platt), 120
Italian Villas and Their Gardens (Wharton), 120

Jacques Seligmann and Co. (art dealers), 97
Jacquin, Nikolaus Joseph, 139, **140**, 153, **155**
James, Henry, 6
Jekyll, Gertrude, 128, 143
Jellicoe, Geoffrey, 149
Jensen, Jens, 136n11
Jeu de cartes (Stravinsky), 75, 89n3
Johnson, Philip, xvii, 53, 109–11, 155
Johnston, Lawrence, 145
Jones, Mary Cadwalader, 117, 118
Joyce, T. A., 59

Kaiser Friedrich Museum, 42
Kalebdjian Frères (art dealers), 37
Keenan, Edward, xix, 111
Kellogg, Vernon, 140, **142**, 163n11
Kerner, Johann Simon, 146, **146**, 151
King, Frederic Rhinelander, 18, 111, 155
Kleinkunst, 28
Koechlin, Raymond, 22n21, 31, 33, 37, 47n26
Kraus, Hans D., 152

Laird, Mark, 165n64
landscape architecture: English, 123; the garden room, 120, 122; Italian, 119, 120, 122, 123, 128; and modernism, 147, 149; naturalistic vs. formal design, debate over, 119–22; in the 1950s, 147; and women, 117, 118; styles: Arts and Crafts, 131; Beaux-Arts, 123
Landscape Architecture (journal), 148
Laughlin, Irwin, 115n61
League of Nations, 22n23, 27, 37, 41, 43
Le Moyne, Jacques, 151, **151**
Le Nôtre, André, 148
Leopold of Prussia, 42
Library of Congress, 8, 18, 76, 89n5, 90n7, 147
libro della agricultura, Il (Crescenzi), 152, **152**
Liebault, John, 139, **140**